THE
MIGHTY
SIERRA

El Capitan, its granite summit lighted by a winter sun, rises sheer from the bank of the Merced River to dominate the entrance to Yosemite Valley.

These pages: Crescent Meadow in Sequoia National Park becomes a little smaller each year as young trees crowd in along its edge. Bright aspens stand out against the more somber pines, firs, and sequoias.

Following pages: Mount Muir, at 14,025 feet, is only one of many imposing peaks in the region around Mount Whitney, east of Sequoia National Park.

THE MIGHTY SIERRA

Portrait of a Mountain World

BY PAUL WEBSTER
and the Editors of
The American West

With a Foreword by
Francis P. Farquhar

The Great West Series

American West Publishing Company

Palo Alto, California

Golden-mantled ground squirrel feeding on a red fir cone.

Library of Congress Card Number 74-184068

ISBN 0-910118-23-X

CONTENTS

FOREWORD

By Francis P. Farquhar

In this book on the Sierra Nevada, Paul Webster has set forth the subject in great detail in its various parts, as well as giving us a comprehensive view of the whole. The Sierra Nevada is an entity in itself. It is a unit. It is also a barrier, as was shown in the early days when it prevented further exploration of the Spaniards, and when it presented an obstacle to the Americans coming from the East.

When the Spaniards came north from Mexico, they eventually reached the San Francisco Bay region, and there, from a hill overlooking the interior valley, they beheld in the distance what they called *una gran sierra nevada* ("a great snow-covered range"). This was at first merely a general description, but in the course of time, after repetition on various maps, Sierra Nevada became an established place name. The Sierra is now crossed by highways and railroads, and the upper passes by well-graded trails. In the summertime it is occupied by thousands of people seeking recreation.

Paul Webster describes the features of the country in a way that offers a luring invitation to those who will come for the first time and provides nostalgic reminiscences for those who have been there before. As a background for his detailed description, he gives an account of the geologic changes that have gone on throughout the ages—the uplifts and denudations and scouring by water and glacial ice that have produced the present Sierra Nevada.

He describes the various sections of the terrain, from the high granite plateaus near Mount Whitney in the south to the devastated mining country of the Yuba in the north, even going so far as the volcanic overlay from Mount Lassen still farther north. He makes us familiar with the trees, from the small whitebark pine of the Sierra crest, to the foxtail pine, the juniper, and lodgepole pine of the middle country, down to the great red and white firs and the sugar and ponderosa pines of the great forest belt. And he introduces us to the flowers: from the high mountain blossoms that crouch under the lee of rocks above timberline, to the lush growth of the meadows and river banks, down to the lilies of the pine belt.

Mountain lions and wolverines are now very scarce, and the great grizzly bear is extinct; but there are still plenty of deer and smaller folk such as the rabbits, the squirrels, the conies, and the wood-rats. The birds are always with us—the black and white Clark nutcracker of the highlands, even the golden eagle, and the plentiful smaller birds of woodland and meadows, especially the grouse, the water ouzel, and the hummingbird. Then there are the trout—the native rainbow, the exotic golden trout of the uplands, and the more recently introduced varieties, such as the Eastern brook.

All in all, the Sierra Nevada provides a rich setting for the recruitment of body and spirit under the blue skies of summer, leaving behind the worries and cares of the city.

Paul Webster's text is complemented by a wealth of beautiful photographs. The volume is large—too big to carry in a knapsack on the trails but a treasure to be turned to in preparation for a Sierra trip or to be returned to at home. On opening the book, one literally enters the High Sierra; one camps beside the high mountain meadow or on the shore of a lake and thanks Paul Webster and the publishers for a job well done.

After a day on the trail—the warmth of campfire, coffee, and good conversation.

PROLOGUE

T HIS IS THE SIERRA NEVADA, the snowy and sawtooth range, high on the east, low on the west, born of the convulsions of earth, roughly molded by fire and ice, finely molded by time and wind and the flowing of water. The lush and productive Great Valley, the gold-giving old foothills, the middle mountains with vesture of forest, and the peaks and crests and summits—all are part of a tilt to the westward, a trend like the trend of the nation. Snow-covered much of the year, the high passes closed and deep-drifted, the range seems remote and untouchable, yet this is the playground for thousands every week in the winter—and in the summer, it is a playground for millions.

To the slopes and meadows and mountains of the Sierra Nevada come an endless variety of people—the skier, seeking a measure of himself in speed and skill and danger; the mountain-climber, meeting the austere challenge of naked rock; the hiker, pack on back, with feet in the dust of the trail and eyes on some distant objective; the naturalist, counting the stamens and pistils, scanning the sky for its bird life, often finding a new subspecies growing among the familiar; the fisherman and the hunter, seeking the vestigial pleasures of taking from the wild the food they eat; the thinker, in search of no more than quiet, the strength of space and solitude.

Everyone who knows the Sierra has his own version of it. Like the packrats of the mountains, each gathers glittering baubles, bright jewels, little tools, bits of this and that from his own experience and the experiences of others, combining these with the scientific facts of books and lectures. The writer of this book has gathered his own special pile of treasure from many sources and has attempted to give it life. But nothing can really take the place of being in the Sierra Nevada in person and seeing and feeling all that goes on there; the farther back and the higher up you go, the better it all becomes. Words are no substitute for the real experiences of hand and foot and eye as you probe into the recesses of this range, but let me try to give an account of such an expedition; it will serve perhaps as well as anything else to introduce the wonders and delights of this mountain world.

It makes no practical sense. On the one hand is a comfortable place to sit or lie, plenty of good things to eat, a cold drink nearby, complete protection against the elements, a minimum of physical exertion, carefully rehearsed sounds and sights to hear or witness: *home*. On the other hand is hard rock to sit on, an inevitable pebble or pinecone under an inadequately padded sleeping bag, rationed food of dubious gourmet quality, tepid water in a tin bottle, wind, rain, thunder, lightning, the most penetrating of all suns—and one's own muscles.

What drives people to leave their padded homes with all those expensive appurtenances and propel themselves into the wilderness? Atavism? Masochism? Curiosity? Discontent? Competitive instinct or whatever its opposite is? Scientific interest? For each person the reasons are different and usually are never fully stated; for each it is enough that the urge is there and can be satisfied.

The main problems are elemental ones: food, water, shelter, mobility and survival. Thoreau, widely quoted by conservationists and wilderness advocates, might never have made it in the high country; he could not have built a cabin for twenty-eight dollars, nor could he have grown vegetables, taken odd jobs, gone for rambling and contemplative walks in the woods. For Thoreau in California, the foothills would have been the place, or a cabin in the coastal hills. Effort is required to live in the high country.

JOHN MUIR, ON THE CONTRARY, was the epitome of harmonious adaptation to the High Sierra; he has not yet been matched. For food, he took a crust of bread and sometimes some tea; for a bed, he took a constitution that let him sleep without blankets, getting up from time to time to restoke a fire or jump around and wave his arms; for water, he drank from the streams, or sucked some snow, or went without; for shelter, he

crawled under the lower branches of a whitebark pine. Mobility was built in, for without a pack and with great endurance and agility, he went where he pleased; survival seemed no problem. During his Sierra years, Muir could have lived all summer on the cash now laid out for a packframe and down sleeping bag, and all winter on the cost of dehydrated food and color film for a two-week trip.

YOU CAN WALK ACROSS THE SIERRA from east to west in a few days, finding each day some of the experiences which make such a trip more than just exercise. A week is better; two weeks, fine, although carrying food for that long may be a chore. Let's take a week-long hike, which can be done without consuming an entire vacation.

You have figured it out during the winter, when the discomforts of last year's trip were forgotten in the afterglow and only the glorious parts remained in your memory. You don't want to walk more than a few miles a day, because you want some time for fishing and picture taking and just loafing; you think forty miles in a week is about right. You want to be off the paths of heaviest travel, but you wouldn't mind seeing other humans once in a while; you don't want to get lost—after all, you have only a week—but you're willing to try a little cross-country bit.

For a couple of dollars you have bought topographic maps of the Mount Morrison, Mount Abbot and Kaiser Peak quadrangles and a trail-guide book—not only to help stay on the trail in case of confusion, but to identify the peaks as you see them from the valleys, and the lakes as you see them from the peaks, and there is always the chance a bear has demolished a trail sign at just the junction you are haziest about. You may also have sent for a map or two from the Forest Service; in this case the recreation map of the Mammoth–High Sierra area. You winnow your equipment down to manageable weights and carefully work out the food; you make a checklist so you won't forget dark glasses and something to cover blisters, or you use a list from the Sierra Club. You read all about the area of the trip and then find someone who will drive you to the end of the road on the east side and pick you up the next weekend at trail's end on the west side.

The trail starts near Buzztail Springs at the end of the McGee Creek road off U.S. 395 west of Lake Crowley. It's going to be a climb today (all trips which start on the east side go steeply uphill the first day, that being the nature of the place), so you start at daybreak. Starting at about 8,000 feet, you'll climb to Big McGee Lake at about 10,500 in six miles—not too severe, but a good breaking-in of pack and hiker. The trail moves upward beside a creek, and you fight off a temptation to unfurl the fishing gear and have a go at it, especially when you move down from the open trail to rest in the streamside shade. Past a beaver dam, the path (which has been an old mining road) gets steeper, and the brushy slopes give way to lodgepole pine; soon the lodgepole thins to hemlock, and then to rock at the lake. During the afternoon, loafing; for an hour or two before dark, fishing, while the sun goes down and the mountains are lighted in a brief twilight with the special Sierra glow. In a few hours you have gone from civilization to the high country, and this first day was just barely enough to get used to it; you get into the sleeping bag early, for there isn't much wood for a campfire and somehow bed is appealing—even a bed with a thin ribbon of plastic foam for a mattress and beneath that the hard granite.

You will awaken every few hours this first night, and that is good, for overhead sweep the stars, never before so bright; you pick out one group and in half-awake moments check its progress against the sky as Saturday changes to Sunday. In wakeful moments you recall yesterday's climb and the compensations—views eastward over Mono Valley and westward toward the heights . . . the stream and its wildflowers . . . should have tried for a trout . . . that leg muscle aches a little . . . and sure enough, there is a small pinecone under the sleeping bag.

In the morning it is cold. Today is an exploring day, not a hiking day, so it feels good to stay in the sleeping bag an hour or so longer, especially when that leg muscle twinges. A day here at McGee Lake will help lungs get used to the thin air, will use up some food to lighten the packs, and may even provide a fish dinner. There are pictures to take and mountain peaks to look at; but mindful of the need not to run out of film in a frenzy of photography the first day or two, you restrain yourself—you're not even over the pass yet. Firewood is scarce, but you have all day to rustle up enough for a small campfire at dark, bringing in a piece or two from each exploring walk.

A few clouds that appeared late in the afternoon are gone, but as you pull the sleeping bag up around your ears, you think about the sunset light that suffused this rocky basin, and the loveliness that was added by the glow on those dwindling clouds. The stars wheel; you awaken less often to see them and to shift in your hard bed; there is only a rustle or two to accentuate the silence. In the morning your ballpoint pen is gone, and you recall the rustle of the rustler, a pack rat. He didn't even leave you the legendary lump of solid gold in exchange. You'll hear more about gold, though, later today and will wish the rat had been more considerate.

There is an early riser on every expedition; yours is up before five and has coffee and bacon ready. It is still dark, but the plan calls for a climb of a mile and a half to see the sunrise from McGee Pass at just under 12,000 feet. Munching the bacon and trying to keep from scalding a lip on the tin cup, you realize you don't know anything about this McGee person who left his name on all your trail signs.

The rocky climb takes longer than expected; you were delayed hunting for your pen, and the sun hasn't waited because it never does—but the sight is superb anyway. Nearby to the north and a thousand feet higher is Red Slate Mountain; to the east is a ridge almost level with this saddle, on the far side of which is the stream along which you hiked in on Saturday. Southward is Red and White Mountain, which you will flank day after tomorrow after a roundabout trip. Westward is the meadow at the head of Fish Creek—"Horse Heaven"—and to the southwest is the Silver Divide, one of the lateral ranges that are common in the Sierra and keep it from being a series of parallel troughs.

The early light adds to the ruddy glow of the iron oxides on the granites and in the slates, and intensifies the buff and light browns of layers of rocks more ancient than the granite. It is long into summer, but there are still patches of snow near the trail and in sheltered spots along the ridges as far as one can see. While you let the warming sun soak in, the talk turns to glaciers, for the basic sculpture everywhere visible was done by the ice machine, with the finishing touches made by snow, frost, and gravity. Would the glaciers come back if the average temperature went down ten or fifteen degrees?

This speculation gives way to a more fascinating one as up the switchback trail from the west comes a group of hikers leading pack burros, a reminder of an old tale. It seems, the story goes, that some sheepherders were moving along here with their packs on mules in the early days, and to balance one of the packs, they added a heavy rock on one side. The rock was heavy, it turned out, because it was full of gold—but neither the sheepherders nor those who backtracked them could ever find where the rock came from—another "lost lode" in the Sierra.

Today's hike is only about five miles down those switchbacks along Fish Creek through a grassy meadow, and then a hairpin turn back along a small creek to Tully Lake, ten pleasant acres of water in the granite at about 10,400 feet, said to have golden and brook trout in it. The fish don't cooperate at midday, however, and there are a few other people camping there; maybe you should go on a mile or so to Red and White Lake through that little saddle a few hundred feet higher. So you do—and find you are paralleling the morning's trail about a half mile distant on the map. Your early riser, who is also your "let's take a shortcut" hiker (something to do with the thyroid, no doubt), points out on the "topo" map that you could have saved two or three miles by coming around on the 10,800-foot contour. But he will have his cross-country exercise soon, and sufficient to this Monday are the trails thereof. The lake with the bicolored name is soon reached, and a camping place found on the east cove; the sun goes off the water, the trout rise to the fly, the dehydrated supper is thus reinforced with some delicious protein—and today's more abundant afternoon cumulus clouds light up in glory as the sun goes down behind a shoulder of Mount Izaak Walton.

It never rains at night at this time of the year in the High Sierra, so you have no tent—and when it starts raining about four in the morning, you are out in the open. You do have a sheet of light plastic, though, and by scrunching all your worldly goods around you and by twisting and squirming without leaving the sleeping bag, you get the plastic between you and the elements, more or less. Less, it turns out, for you begin to feel the wet long before bright daylight. The clouds are right down on the ground as you shiver your breakfast together; but they are soon burned away by the sun, and for a few hours your world of rock steams in the radiation.

You have only a few miles to go today (you gained a little yesterday), but it is all cross-country, so you pick up your pack and start, hoping to arrive at Grinnell Lake in time to dry out your sleeping bag before nightfall. The route is rocky from the start, but the objective is clear: a saddle to the right of Red and White Mountain, the spectacular 12,850-foot top of which is only about two-thirds of mile from last night's camp as the eagle flies. There are patches of snow again, with little rosy finches picking up insects along the edges of them. In the rock piles, conies give their nasal bleat as they disappear into the maze. The footing is loose rock, and each person picks what seems to be the easiest way, stepping carefully; a twisted ankle or broken arm or leg here would be inconvenient. These tricky stepping stones up to the saddle are chips from an ancient sea bed and may be two hundred million years old; by the time you reach the top, you feel a certain kinship to their age.

In the saddle, you look back; it really isn't far, and down there a thousand feet lower is the Fourth of July —Red and White Lake with its bright blue water—and beyond it the green of the Fish Creek meadows in a setting of buff and ochre. In the distance are the Minarets and the sawtooth Ritter Range east of Yosemite; the Mammoth Crest is a little to the right and closer. The mountain whose flank you are on is part of the main crest, and you are looking northwestward along the top of the Sierra Nevada, one of nature's grandest sights.

Turning to pick your way down another steep and shaly slope, you look across a chain of rocky lakes, across the green slopes of the Mono Creek Canyon, across knobs and cliffs and creeks and gorges to the Mono Divide, which cuts across the John Muir Wilderness—almost all granite.

The rock-hopping continues past Little Grinnell Lake, and then the route opens out into a grassy swale above Grinnell Lake. You haven't come far today, but the going was rough; halfway down this mile-long lake you call its quits and make camp. No clouds today, and somehow your nose has become sunburned in spite of the lotion you nearly forgot to put on it this morning. From your camp on a little ledge above the water, you can see all along the lake, admire the 800-foot cliffs across the way, and look back at the saddle you came through a while before. You're south of the Silver Divide now, and from this point to trail's end is almost all downhill.

Here your party is the only one on the lake; here you feel more intensely the satisfaction of remoteness; here is the hard earth, the shimmer on the water, the sweep upward to the heights, the absolutely clear sky above; here you sense the beauty of simplicity, the stripping away of the gadgets of the city and the possessions that encumber your life. Tonight you will sleep without waking at all, one with your lofty world, and the stars will have to make their sweep without your attention. And while you sleep, a pack rat will take away your spoon.

You were going to lay over a day, but you've heard the fishing is better at smaller Laurel Lake a mile farther along the route. With customary Sierran disregard for the hike plan, you go there, and you find plenty of firewood and all the brook trout you can eat, and for the rest of this Wednesday you take it easy at 10,300 feet. You try to analyze your feelings—the release on Saturday when you looked back and no longer could see an automobile; the first day's fatigue and anticipation; the mood of exhilaration and exuberance on crossing the pass through the crest; the relaxed, rhythmic feeling of the easy going along Fish Creek; the keen awareness of feet, muscles, balance, breathing, self, and the tingle of surmountable danger in the rocky cross-country passage, followed by relief and a sort of pride when it was over. Now you just feel good, one with time and the mountains; if you could just see a bighorn sheep, your life would be climaxed. This is the complete life, and you are the complete mountain person. You're out of coffee, but there is tea at supper, and it has a flavor and aroma to savor; in the quiet talk around the ample evening fire, someone remarks that for two days or more there has not been a sight of a beer can, and this seems somehow a personal victory for you, if not for civilization.

On Thursday morning, you find the down trail through lodgepoles, then through manzanita and past aspen. The trail is not too good, but you step and slip down seven or eight hundred feet of canyon bank to Mono Creek, and down that stream about a half mile to Fish Camp. You are still pretty high, at 8,500 feet,

but after the high country where you've been this seems a little like foothills, even though the views across the creek and up through Second Recess to the cliffs of Mount Gabb and Mount Hilgard remind you that you are still in the Sierra. You are down in a canyon now, and the spacious feeling is gone; you note too, that most of your food is gone, and so for the last time you bring in some trout—rainbow this time—and know that you are living, at least partly, off the land.

MONO CREEK DRAINS A LARGE AREA, but at 7,600 feet it is captured in Lake Thomas A. Edison. You sense this impending doom for a fine stream as you hike down beside it on Friday. For the first three miles or so it is a free stream, aspen-edged since it is about 8,000 feet; then you leave it for a while, climbing up over rocky switchbacks to meet the John Muir Trail, here a long way from the crest. (Next winter, when the Trail is mentioned, you can casually murmur, "Oh, yes . . . we were on it for a time last summer," even though today you're only going to be on it while it switchbacks down to the creek a mile or so downstream.)

The Muir Trail fords the creek and starts upward and southwestward to Mount Whitney; for a moment you stand there at the junction and wish you had another ten days to try it, for you are on your way home, and it is on its way to the freedom of the high country. But instead you walk through the forest at the edge of Quail Meadows and find your friends who were to meet you at the other end of the lake tomorrow; they have come this far with steaks and a bottle of wine and fresh sourdough French bread—the kind with the gorgeous crust—and yesterday's newspaper. The dinner is wonderful, and the unread paper will do to wrap the trash.

There is another surprise: a boat will meet you on the lake, and instead of a six-mile hike to the road, you'll ride in style. You grumble at this easy end to your trip, but not much, for the trail along the lake would be more of a chore than an adventure; adventure is in the high places, not here. Having tasted the majesty of the high country, you rationalize, it is only fitting that you forego pedestrian problems and, like the pharaohs of old, ride the royal barge to a triumphant ending at Vermilion Camp.

How soon would you go again? Tomorrow.

PART ONE

SIERRAN PROFILE

Looking down this tributary of Lundy Canyon (right foreground), one can see how it has been scooped into a broad U by glaciers, which once filled the canyon to the tops of the talus slopes that now line each side. Burro Lake is at the far end.

Chapter 1

THE IRRESISTIBLE SCULPTORS

*Ceaseless forces, deep in the earth and high in the
clouds, that change the unchanging mountains*

YOU CAN DEFINE AND DESCRIBE the physical Sierra
Nevada in dozens of ways—and be right each
time. There is even a certain amount of uncertainty about where the boundaries lie, depending on
one's viewpoint.

People who live in the small towns along the foot-hills and (especially their chambers of commerce) refer to their vicinity as "the heart of the Sierra," or at
least "the gateway to the Sierra," and when driven to
poetry, as "the jewel of the Sierra." Sometimes they
even commit the heinous crime of saying "Sierras" with
an *s* on the end, which arouses the same reaction as
calling San Francisco "Frisco" to the face of an old-timer.

Some diehard backpackers will not consider anything
below timberline as the real Sierra; some others will
start lower down the slope, perhaps where the sugar
pines grow. Many dedicated hikers feel the Sierra extends no farther north than, say, Sonora Pass, although
most will include the vicinity of Lake Tahoe; and
almost all high-country people believe the Sierra (and
perhaps the world) ends about the bend of the Kern
River on the south.

Botanically-minded visitors slice the range neatly
into horizontal bands in which certain things grow, and
use the change of vegetation and other life forms as a
sort of altimeter to gauge how high they are at any
given time. These zones tend to overlap in places, are
more compressed in the north than in the south, and
act very peculiarly on the eastern escarpment. Even
the north side of a hill joggles the edges of the botanist's
slices somewhat.

Highway builders think in terms of the passes from
Fredonyer on the north to Walker or Tehachapi on the
south; highway maintainers think of two layers, above
and below the normal snow line, although they know
from years of experience, sometimes bitter, that there
is no "normal" snow line any more than there really is
a normal depth of snow—or a normal winter, for that
matter.

Loggers are concerned with areas where trees grow
which can be cut and hauled economically, and they
look on the Sierra as a sort of vegetable garden that
needs weeding and harvesting, with some parts consisting of rocks and gorges which can reasonably be
assigned to bird watchers and nature lovers; the logger's
Sierra is the part with trees, preferably big and preferably where the original growth still stands and where
there are good grades to build roads to speed the time
when the original growth will no longer be standing.

Skiers cluster around machinery complexes, concentrating more on the slope they are about to plunge
down than on the Sierra Nevada as a mountain range;
for them, the Sierra is fresh powder on a good base.
Skis, which made cross-country travel in the winter
possible, are now so highly developed they can only
be used when pointed downhill (except for a few touring skis); now only a few of the hardier skiers can be
found on cross-country trips.

To the sheep man and cattle rancher, the Sierra is a
vast summer pasture where grass grows on upland meadows especially for meat animals. There are restless

*The rolling uplands north of Yosemite Valley end abruptly in a great granite
precipice, magnificently sculpted by the slow chisel of glaciers.*

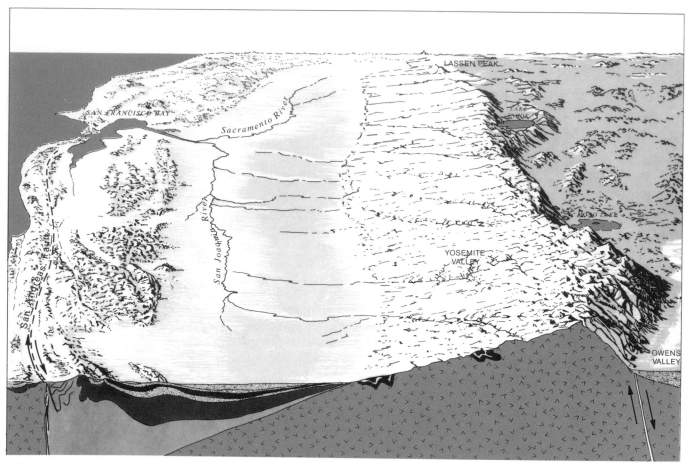

The Sierra is a "fault block" range, rising out of the desert to the east in a steep escarpment, then sloping gently into the Central Valley on the west. Its granite, however, is part of a much older batholith, as can be seen in this diagram. Pacific moisture waters the mountains, then returns by Sierra rivers to the sea.

growls when controls are applied on public lands which the grazers have been using and in which they feel a vested interest acquired by many years of use.

Bird watchers skirt the fringes, staying usually within an easy walk of their cars, and a lesser number of animal watchers seem to do the same. The off-the-highway hiker and camper usually combines an interest in botany, birds, animals, and geology with his interest in just being out there in the mountains, and he mixes these with photography, meteorology, and sometimes joyous yodeling.

All of which is to say that the Sierra Nevada is many things to many people. At the same time, it is a recognizable geographic unit—no matter what individual interpretations may be applied to it—one of great complexity and enormous scope. To understand it properly, we must gain some sense of its broadest outlines.

THE NORTHERLY PART OF THE SIERRA, from Donner Pass north (see map, page 59), is the tamest, for the elevations are lower, the passes easier, the weather more temperate, the life zones more closely compressed, and there is almost no extensive area above timberline. There are some outstanding mountains and a great deal of snow in the winter, but much of the area is threaded by roads, and there are numerous year-round communities.

The basic outlines of the northern range were set more by volcanoes than glaciers, and many of the present stream canyons once were filled with volcanic debris; many of the ridges and outcrops are old volcanic mudflows now hardened to rock. Much of the lumber is produced here, and extensive mining was done before the value of gold became less than the value of the labor needed to extract it. Great amounts of energy are generated by the force of falling water, and the rivers have become electricity producers but there is still one wild stream, the Middle Feather, untouched and untamed for miles.

The *central* part of the Sierra, from Donner Pass to Sonora Pass (see map, page 60) , is higher and rougher, part volcanic and part glacial, but still with a network of roads—some open all year, many closed by snow by November. The Sierra contrasts and paradoxes are here in abundance: highly developed Lake Tahoe, and beside it the wilderness of Desolation Valley; elaborate winter resorts with every possible comfort, and just over the hill two sets of tracks marking the passage of ski-tourists out for a camping trip on a weekend; the glitter of neon to draw pilgrims into casinos, and beside other smaller lakes only the glint of the stars. In the central area, the life zones are spread out a little more, the glacial cirques are higher and deeper, some of the canyons plainly show the U-shape caused by grinding of ice more than the V-shape caused by cutting of creeks or rivers.

The *southern* part of the Sierra, from Sonora Pass to Tehachapi Pass (see map, page 61) , is the highest. Some of the peaks were never covered by ice, so the rocks date back to the ocean bed; with so little moisture there is no stream erosion, but on the highest peaks the leverage of frost continues to break up the rocks and cliffs. There are many square miles above timberline in the southern part, sometimes called "the highest of deserts," but the austere high country is not devoid of life, and has a spell of its own which captures the imagination. Through roads are few, and other roads reach back toward the heights only a short way; from there all traffic is by foot—human feet, or the feet of horses, mules or burros. All through the moister parts of the Sierra, great pines and firs grow. The higher elevations have tougher trees less valuable for lumber, but only the southern area is the home of the giant sequoia, for north of Yosemite there are only a few scattered groves.

The east side of the southern Sierra is a world of its own. The great escarpment caused by a subsidence of huge blocks of land rears up majestically two miles above the inhabited valley, so that the sun sets earlier in Lone Pine than in Los Angeles or San Francisco. Many species of plants and animals are different, although (because there are few absolutes in the Sierra) some are the same. The sagebrush of the desert country reaches far up into the mountains, and the other east-slope plants are also adapted to aridity; the height and shape of the Sierra wrings most of the moisture out of the clouds driven against the mountains by the Pacific winds, so that the east side is not only shadowed from the setting sun, but is in a rain-shadow, too.

The airplane passenger has the most comprehensive view of this immense mountain world. Even from the highest-flying jet, the Sierra Nevada presents an absorbing sight when the air is clear and the movie boring. From a small plane at a lower altitude, both the broad sweep and the special details can be examined easily in spite of occasional stomach-suspending drops and bumps caused by ever-moving air. The panorama is surprising at first, because this collection of mountains which seems a jagged pile of rock and a maze of deep canyons from the ground turns out to be, from an altitude of a few thousand feet, a gently sloping, humpy plain for the most part, cut by narrow parallel east-west canyons every twenty miles or so, and in many places appearing nearly flat.

As one looks straight down, some of the ruggedness shows up; but in the broad view through the window of a light aircraft, what is visible is a rolling plain tilted two or three degrees and covered with a soft-looking verdure of trees and brush through which knobs of granite sometimes protrude, while off in the distance some jagged edges show a little above the rest.

Even a great gorge like Yosemite is lost in the immensity, and except for the eastern escarpment and the peaks in the vicinity of the Kings-Kern headwaters, the appearance from a distance is almost gentle. Even in the highest High Sierra there are broad, mildly modeled plateaus and mountain tops. Mount Whitney, the highest of them all, presents rugged, sculptured cliffs to the east; but from the summit westward for almost half a mile, it is a broad, gently sloping platform.

As mountain ranges go, the Sierra Nevada is a new-

GEOLOGICAL TIME CHART

YEARS AGO (Approximate)	ERA	PERIOD	EPOCH	IMPORTANT EVENTS (Italic type indicates events in Sierra Nevada)
10,000—	Cenozoic	Quaternary	Recent	*Period of relative stability in Sierra Nevada. Climate warms; old glaciers vanish, and present smaller glaciers replace them. Land sinks to form Lake Tahoe.*
3,000,000—			Pleistocene	*Great Basin area sinks, forming sharp eastern escarpment of Sierra Nevada.* *Glaciers cover most of Sierra in four successive Ice Ages, carving Yosemite Valley and Kings Canyon.* First evidence of man.
				———— *Final uplift of Sierra Nevada.* ————
		Tertiary	Pliocene	*Volcanic cone of Lassen Peak begins forming.* Series of uplifts; valleys are formed.
11,000,000—				——Alps and Himalayas rise.——
			Miocene	*More uplifts in Sierra, resulting in some faulting.* Extensive erosion on Appalachians and Rockies. *Volcanic activity in northern Sierra.*
25,000,000—			Oligocene	*Sierra lifted to moderate height.*
40,000,000—			Eocene	*Period of uplift, tilting, faulting, volcanic activity.*
60,000,000—			Paleocene	Development of basins between ranges of Rocky Mountains.
70,000,000—				
	Mesozoic	Cretaceous		Mountain building in Rockies (Laramide Orogeny). Extinction of dinosaurs. *Ancestral Sierra eroded by streams, reducing range to low hills.* First flowering plants.
135,000,000—		Jurassic		*Molten granite masses of Sierra batholith are pushed upward (Nevadan Orogeny).* First birds and mammals.
180,000,000—		Triassic		First dinosaurs. *Sierra trough is formed, then filled with volcanic and sedimentary debris.*
225,000,000—	Paleozoic	Permian		Appalachian and Ural mountains complete development.
270,000,000—		Pennsylvanian		Conifer forests appear. Coal swamps form. First reptiles.
305,000,000—		Mississippian		First insects.
350,000,000—		Devonian		First land vertebrates. First fish.
400,000,000—		Silurian		First land plants.
440,000,000—		Ordovician		Corals, sea urchins first appear.
500,000,000—		Cambrian		Mollusks, trilobites dominate.
600,000,000—		Precambrian		Oldest dated rocks.

comer, for the last of the great glacial ice which gave it its present distinctive variety of shapes and forms has been gone for only ten or twenty thousand years. The fifty or sixty small glacierets which now crowd against the northeast scoops of the highest peaks are not left over from the last real glacial period but are relatively new and are themselves disappearing. Some are so crowded with debris that they are more rock than ice. At the time of the gold rush there were one hundred fifty more; by the time John Muir made his renowned explorations and studies, there were fewer than that, since their decline seems to have been caused by a warming cycle which started around 1850. It is assumed these small individual glaciers occupying old cirques were formed about two thousand years before Christ (five hundred years after the building of the pyramids), reached their peak long after Columbus discovered America, and have been declining only during the past century or two. They have nothing of the grandeur and power of the great ice engine that ground over and through the Sierra three or four times during a million-year era that ended with worldwide temperatures three or four degrees higher than present averages. It is possible that about five thousand years ago there was no ice or snow year-round on the Sierra peaks, even in the high cirques where the sun rarely touches. Today's glaciers meet the definition of a mass of ice with definite lateral limits, with motion in a definite direction, originating from the compacting of snow by pressure. But beautiful though they may be, they are faint echoes, mere samples, small reproductions of Ice Age glaciers.

At their maximums, the great ice masses covered the highlands for perhaps three hundred miles along the crest, sloping as far as sixty miles to the west and dropping off more abruptly at the east. From the main mass, a mile thick in places and with only the highest peaks protruding, long tongues were shoved inexorably down the canyons, reaching as low as 2,000 feet above sea level, stopped at last by lessening pressure from above and behind and by the inevitable melting by sun and rain in the foothills.

As it moved under the huge pressure of its own mass, the ice carried a mixture of huge rocks, fine sand, and every size of material in between, using the lowermost layer and the studded edges to chisel and gouge where it could, to polish and grind where native resistance was greatest. The finest silt ran off at the front in milky meltwater; heavier material was laid down at the bottom and all but the largest boulders washed away later. Some rocks and much gravel were dropped finally in curved piles along the edges of the tongues, or in a sort of dam where the progress of the glacier stopped. These ridges of mixed material are the *moraines* which mark the longest stages of the successive rivers of ice, and some of their rocks can be identified as originating far up on top of the range. The great ice masses came and went four times during a million years or more, each leaving a moraine record of its farthest progress down the slope.

At times the frozen white cap must have extended almost the full length of the Sierra; at other times there may have been spaces beween specific glaciers. Each, at maximum, must have been a glittering white blanket at its highest point, the purity of the white changing down lower to a beribboned effect. Where a branch joined the main stream, it brought with it not only the material shoved along in front and suspended in the ice itself, but the dark rock scraped from the sides, so that each flow maintained its identity for many miles in the main stream. As the whole glacier slowly melted, the fragments of rock suspended in the ice subsided to the solid ground, piling up arm-like ridges at the sides (lateral moraines), dam-like ridges at the end (terminal moraines), and often long embankments like a highway right-of-way the length of the former flow (medial moraines).

The moraines remain today, although many have been covered by vegetation, eroded, or moved around by man's works. Their location, shape, and the material of which they are composed have been valuable clues in the study of the shaping of the present Sierra, and these rock-and-dirt piles have provided special habitats for plant and animal life. Often they serve as dams, impounding lakes which are homes for various kinds of aquatic life, and many of the flower-decked high meadows are the result of moraine dams against which sediment collected to form the soil of Sierran gardens.

So the U-shaped valleys like Yosemite, Kings, and Kern were scraped from V-shaped canyons by the bottom and sides of the glaciers as they inched along, widening the canyons and straightening them by grinding off salient spurs, slowly flowing around rock too

Important geological features of the Sierra Nevada:
(1) snow field, (2) tarn, or glacial lake, (3) U-shaped
glacial trough, (4) V-shaped valley, (5) escarpment,
(6) arete, (7) lateral moraine, (8) horn, (9) pater noster
lakes, (10) rock steps, (11) glacier, (12) cirque,
(13) cascades, and (14) terminal moraine.

hard to cut, with each successive glacier taking away material loosened by water, frost, chemicals, and gravity during the interglacial times. In addition to the grinding action, huge blocks of rock were plucked from canyon bottoms to make step-like terraces, each with a bowl-shaped center which became in time a clear lake or an amphitheater for a cascading stream.

The top of every glacier left a spectacular mark: the *cirque,* a tilted, hollowed-out bowl, open on one side, almost always now with a lake or snowpatch in it, usually with steep and jagged arms or *aretes* along two sides and a sharp peak at the top. At maximum size, the Sierra glaciers overtopped the crest and flowed in more than one direction, whittling the mountaintops beneath them into points and knife-like ridges which often became even more pronounced later by rockfalls and avalanches. Today's small glaciers and year-round snow patches are always in one of these cirques, on the

northeasterly side of the peak because that is where the sun's rays are weakest or do not reach at all, and because prevailing winds tend to blow loose snow there. The effects of the glaciers were universal throughout the Sierra, but the sharpest ice-sculpturing is along the crest from Sonora Pass southward.

The broad outline of the glacier story can best be filled in by reading and by personal observation. Only the most northerly part of the Sierra lacks the spectacular "gorges, gulches, and gouges" which the retreating glaciers left behind—the scenic and awesome carving of what basically is a tilted plain.

THE GREAT CONTINENTAL ICE SHEETS which carved out the Great Lakes and left Canadian boulders on New England hillsides came and went four times; and while it was "back North for another load of rock," as some New Englanders say, there were periods of almost tropical weather in which locust and pawpaw trees grew at Toronto. While the Sierra glaciers were not physically connected with the continental glaciers, they occurred at the same time and with similar intervals of warmth, during which vegetation and animal life followed the ice front higher and higher as it receded, only to be wiped out in the succeeding glacial period. Warm-climate trees flourished in the Sierra between glaciers, as did warm-country animals. The Sierra glaciers were much farther south than the ice sheets of Canada and the Great Lakes country, not shoved down from the arctic but formed by a combination of a high and cold land mass directly in line with a moving wet air mass; more snow fell than could melt between winters.

So, the surplus of snow in the Ice Age was the result, not of arctic air, but of ocean air. The Sierra's heaviest snowfall occurs in a band about a hundred and fifty miles from the Pacific Ocean. The winds sweeping across that great expanse flow through the Golden Gate and over the adjoining Coast Ranges, then blow unimpeded across the Great Valley and up the Sierra slope into colder elevations. A tremendous change in topography, occurring before the Ice Age and lasting at least ten times as long, made these mountains high enough to change rain to snow: a huge block 350 by 40 or 50 miles was tilted up, almost in one piece, not abruptly but over a long time.

Other mountains in other places have been formed by the lifting of the landscape, but there are none where this much land was lifted along one edge as a unit. There had been three Sierran uplifts before this, but four or five million years ago the most dramatic of all lifted the eastern side of the range 6,000 feet. About the same time the Pacific Ocean, which beached along the present foothills, receded to the westward, and the Coast Range folded up to form one side of the Great Valley, leaving an opening at the Golden Gate. Then the range was almost in its present basic form, ready for the ice sculpture to start, and lacking only one dramatic event: while the ice was at work, a long strip on the eastern side dropped as much as a mile, leaving the great eastern escarpment standing tall and rugged above a string of valleys.

The tilting of the Sierran block followed less dramatic but still huge changes. Perhaps 130 million years ago, the land lifted out of a sea, wrinkling itself into rolling but high hills and valleys trending northwest and southeast, while far below, rock, heated to a liquid, filled the cavities with a granite batholith. On the surface grew lush vegetation in which strange animals lived beside rivers flowing parallel to what is now the coast. Then erosion of this ancestral Sierra wore the old marine deposits down to the new granite in many places, and the cutting action of flowing water carved rolling hills into mountains and ridges on which warm-weather plants, redwoods, and deciduous trees grew. More bowing-up of the Sierra followed, and perhaps twenty million years ago volcanoes broke loose to spread mud and lava over the northern part and cause separated flows and extrusions farther south. Then, for at least ten million years, more uplifts alternated with long intervals of comparative quiet, while the rivers did their work to cut deep and broad valleys on the western slope.

Just before that great uplift that preceded the Ice Age, Mount Whitney was about seven thousand feet above sea level, and its top retained all the characteristics of the lowland hill which it once was. The rest of the range was at a comparable height, although in the north the top thousand feet may have been volcanic material. The block under Lake Tahoe had dropped, in what must have been a splendid earthquake and tumult. Between the mountains were broad valleys—much broader than the Sierran valleys of the present, each with a narrowed valley cut into it, and each of those with still narrower and steep-sided valley at the bottom.

Before that final tilt, about a million years ago, there were forests of sequoias, palms, and subtropical trees in which roamed sabertooth tigers, giant sloths, little camels, odd rhinoceroses, and others, living in a wet and warm climate. Grasses and cereals were appearing on the earth, the animals were becoming somewhat as they are now, and while time was moving the Sierra to its climax of tilt and ice, man was beginning to stir, a latecomer on earth and a million years, more or less, from walking the range of light.

No one knows if the ice will come back, or if that fourth great uplift can truly be called the final one, or if volcanoes will break out again, or if the rocks will shudder and move in great earthquakes and block movements. Perhaps those great events have given way for all time to changes more moderate, but the landscape does not remain static even when seemingly quiet. The broad sculpture of tilting, glacial gouging, and volcanic overlays has gained detail through the action of water, wind, ice, snow, and chemicals, and one winter may make discernible changes. In any year the constant attrition of flowing water etches deeper the thousands of miles of stream beds, and as the flowing water slows, it deposits silt in alpine lakes that will someday be meadowland and gardens. Under it all lies a great mass of granite, the root of the range, which astonish-

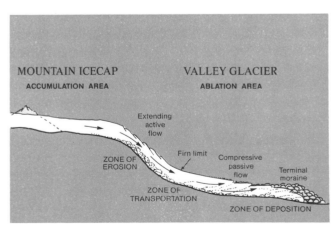

Profile of a glacier.

27

Moisture-laden air blows landward from the Pacific and rises over the west slope of the Sierra. There it cools and condenses into rain or snow, leaving the east slope high and dry in the rain shadow.

ingly keeps its position, not because of its huge weight, but because it is lighter than the earth in general and, in the lexicon of geologists, "floats" there with the Sierra Nevada on its back.

F OR WEEKS THE SKY has been clear—the sun warm through the middle hours of the day, the nights crisp at first and then cold. An occasional high, thin cloud has come and gone, but since the middle of September it has rained just once, and only a little then.

Picnic spots beside the highways have hardly been used for many weeks, and the deer hunters are almost invisible in small camps off the main, traveled ways. On seven of the eight roads through the mountains, occasional cars whiz up and down but only a few stop. On the eighth road, the interstate highway, it is business as usual—people just passing through a corridor to someplace else. Birds have been disappearing quietly. Deer, spooked by hunters by day and answering some herd memory by night, have been migrating down the slopes towards the foothills. Bear have nearly finished their autumn gorging and are cruising the country for a wintering place. Small animals run busily but do not roam far.

Men who have been operating summer resorts nail up the last shutters; men who will operate winter resorts are taking their shutters down. Road crews have bolted blades onto their trucks and oiled up the big rotary snow-throwers. Lake tenders for power companies and irrigation districts have finished their chores, and the ditch and highline crews are checking foul-weather gear. Logging equipment has been taken to the lowlands; forest fire crews are gone; lookout towers are locked; all over the range the scattered but numerous business and pleasure buildings have been boarded up—all but those in the ski areas. The annual winter drama of the Sierra Nevada is about to begin.

It is routine enough. Winds from the southwest sweep across the lower Pacific, picking up moisture. In late October and early November, most years, the winds are not strong on the surface, and the mass of wet air does not move swiftly, but it moves steadily. (Later will come the storms out of the North Pacific, a different kind of a storm with a different kind of power.) As the mass starts lifting along the foothills, impelled by pressure from behind and forced up by the terrain, the temperature is around 40 degrees at ground level, the moisture still in the form of vapor, visible now as an increasing cloudiness. But the bottom of the mass is

Giant cumuli, borne on westerly winds, pour precipitation onto the peaks. There the moisture is held in cold storage until spring thaws release it to water high meadows, mid-slope forests, and man's crops in the valleys.

sliding up the slope, climbing 150 to 300 feet in each mile of travel, and the clouds are being lifted and compressed, getting thicker. The wind at valley level is about 20 miles an hour.

At 5,000 feet above sea level, in the pine and fir forest, the air is below freezing, the wind about 35 miles an hour. At 10,000 feet, above the level of the main highway passes, the air is 20 degrees, wind 50 miles an hour. Up near the top of the storm, higher than the topmost peaks, the temperature is around zero, and wind may be moving at 75 or 80 miles an hour.

Water vapor cannot remain vapor at low temperatures like these. As it cools, rain starts falling while the mass is still moving. At around 32 degrees, the vapor snaps directly into snow, crystallizing into tiny six-sided drops which then lock together into larger florets, each floret made up of many drops and infinitely varied in design, but always with six points. In the foothills rain is noisily drumming on the roofs and bounding off the pavements. In the mountans snow is falling quietly and steadily. It will not pile up immediately unless the ground has been frozen earlier, but even as it melts and is absorbed into the summer-dry ground, it starts its timeless work of growth and change.

The last widespread volcanic action ended in the Sierra perhaps a million years ago. The last major glaciers withdrew to small, protected cirques or disappeared possibly ten or twenty thousand years ago. It has been millions of years since sediments were deposited by lakes and seas, and rocks were formed by settling, heat, and pressure. So, except for some wind erosion, the silent chemical work of lichens, and the levering of rocks by roots throughout the year, the shaping of the mountains is now done mostly by winter and the runoff that follows it.

The first rains wet the ground. Moisture seeps into cracks and crannies. Freezing comes, sometimes before and sometimes after the first snow (parts of the Sierra have fewer than two months of frost-free days). When water freezes to ice, it expands, exerting force sufficient to crack boulders. On some of the onion-skin domes, ice pries loose slabs bigger than houses, which crash down the slopes shattering as they go. The process is seldom so spectacular, but year after year it changes the shape of the mountains. In the new cracks and crevices, small pockets of soil start to form; plants will grow there eventually. The plants will add to the habitat of insects or rodents or birds; the smaller creatures will be food for larger ones; the cycle of life continues, altered ever so slightly by each change in the terrain.

29

Spring comes late to the high country, and winter arrives early. Gale-velocity winds whip the summits, driving clouds and powdered snow before them, as here on Mount Morrison after an October storm.

Some of the early snow melts; some of it stays and becomes the base on which later storms build the tremendous snow packs of January, February and March. More than seventy feet piles up in some places. The first melting makes small rivulets; these move soil, gravel, and pebbles. Later runoff will pour great floods of water down every draw, every gulley, every valley, and at its crest huge boulders will be rolled and jolted along, moved by the great force. Some years bridges, highways, and cities are moved, too.

As the storms increase in frequency and power, the snow piles deeper and deeper. The permanent snow fields that lasted all summer merge with the overall white covering, and the fifty or sixty small glaciers start to grow again. When new snow falls on packed and slicked old snow, or when the wind whips cornices on the lee side of a high ridge, avalanches are born—avalanches which may move tons of rock and soil as well as snow and which can sheer the top from a sizable grove of trees or fill a lake with debris. Contours of the slopes may change in winter because of this, and most of the soil which gradually changes high lakes to meadows comes down in the heavy runoff period.

Lakes freeze, but never all the way to the bottom, and snow piles on the ice. The snow gets deeper and deeper—ten feet, twenty feet, thirty feet or more, except on the highest and barest places where the wind

blows most. Unless an unusual warm rain comes, there is little melting in the winter months, even on the frequent sunny days when skiers and snowmobilers get sunburned noses while their feet are freezing, because the sun's rays are reflected from the dazzling surface.

From a distance the snowbound Sierra seems still and motionless. But there is constant movement, greatest along the highways and at ski slopes, where people and their appurtenances snort, smoke, grind, squawk, roar, pop, and screech—lesser but just as significant farther out, where a limber fir tree slips loose a branchload of wet snow, a rodent squeaks once just before the hawk strikes, the wind whispers or howls through the forest, an overburdened tree breaks and falls, or an avalanche thunders down a high slope with a tremendous roar.

While the first few snowfalls are setting the stage, however, not much moves. Hibernating animals are denned up, and the non-hibernators are sleeping until a break in the weather comes. It snows hardest at middle elevations, even more than at the crest; and once the snow starts to stick, the drifts and pack pile up astonishingly fast. For a day or two the soft white layer may be almost untracked; typical Sierra snow is light and fluffy, and moving in it is difficult. Then, as it compacts and hardens, a rabbit ventures forth, and other small animals such as squirrels, chickarees, and perhaps mice. When they are out, a coyote or bobcat or marten is sure to follow. Coyote tracks are the most common, tracing an erratic hunt from a tree base, along a partly buried rail fence, around base of a boulder, in and out of the branches of a fallen pine. At lower elevations, deer yard up and eat what they can reach, handicapped in snow by their slender feet; winter is hard on deer, especially if they have not gone low enough on the slopes or if the snow falls below its usual line.

In the inevitable spell of clear, sunny weather, skiers flock to the civilized slopes, and farther out the modest number of ski-tourers in pairs and small groups start leaving their slim tracks in a climbing pattern up the ridges, then in long sweeping paths down the steep hillsides. An occasional snowshoer makes his trudging marks up along the contours. Then the snowmobiles come out, penetrating farther back than the others, leaving deep marks in the snow and a scent of gasoline and oil in the air. Workmen, using all kinds of transportation from snowshoes through large tracked vehicles to helicopters, go to their maintenance and repair work on power lines, communication wires, water canals, dam installations, microwave stations, and airway beacons. All people on the surface are playing or working within a reasonable distance of a road end, perhaps ten or twenty miles at the most, although the helicopters may go in more deeply. Even in midwinter there are as many open, sunny days as there are stormy days, making life and activity possible.

Winter starts changing to spring in March or April, although it may snow in May or June, and some spring flowers do not appear at alpine elevations until August, for the Sierra is a complex place and does not lend itself to generalities. On an Easter Sunday, garden and wildflowers may be in full bloom in the foothills at 2,500 feet while at 7,000 feet there may be twenty feet of snow, and the airline distance between the two elevations may be only twenty or thirty miles.

While the snow is soft and melting, human activity slows down and plant and animal life picks up. Small animals are out every day; insects of special kinds appear at the edges of snow banks and birds come to eat them. Where water trickles out from the melting edge, plants start to grow—but almost imperceptibly because the temperature drops below freezing in the early hours of every morning; differences of forty to fifty degrees are recorded in the same day. The changes in temperature affect the streams: fast melting in mid-afternoon raises the water level and velocity for a few hours, and the night's freeze cuts it back, so that sometimes waterfalls start and stop on a daily schedule. Farther down the mountain, aquatic life in the rivers adjusts to the daily rise and fall. During the spring, the big dams in the foothills fill to carry the state through the arid summer.

If Memorial Day is marked by good weather, and particularly if it comes at the end or beginning of a week and makes a three-day holiday possible, the influx of human beings into the mountains begins. Fishermen have been in and out since earlier in the month, but for the cabin owner and resort owner, Memorial Day is an aiming point. June, July, and August, all with benign weather, bring human and non-human activity to a peak; then, in the beautiful Indian summer before the storms start again, human activity tapers off and the animals and plants are busy once more beating the deadline of the snow.

SUCH ARE THE CYCLES of time and season in the Sierra Nevada, a mountain range that includes most of the geological and climatic zones of the earth; a knowledge of the Sierra is in part a knowledge of the planet. Although geologically a unit—one of the greatest single ranges in the world—it is really many different localities, each with its own characteristics distinct from, but sometimes shared with, the rest of the range.

The localities and regions, the life zones and elevations, and even the shapes of the peaks and canyons may vary, but there is one constant and immeasurably important function: the Sierra Nevada is the lungs of California. Certainly, the prevailing winds from off the Pacific bring fresh air; certainly the lush fog-belt foliage of the Coast Range and the green crops of the Great Valley give up vast amounts of oxygen. But just as certainly, the great forests and brushlands of the Sierra pump a huge quantity of oxygen into the air in its part of the cycle in which plants and animals, including man, live side by side—*must* live side by side. The Sierra Nevada provides not only breathing space for the cities and their suburbs, but the breath of life itself.

Chapter 2

STILL BLUE WATERS

Those marvelous mountain lakes—some caught in glacier-carved bowls, some dammed by avalanche, beaver, or man

YOU FLY OVER THE SIERRA NEVADA and you notice them—a scattering of sudden blue surprises tucked into nooks and crannies of the range from north to south, like a fat handful of azure bits tossed at random into a wrinkled carpet of brown and green and gray. These are the lakes, and they are as various as the mountains themselves.

Some Sierra lakes are held entirely by rock, with no beaches, no marshes, no overhanging trees or bushes. Some are little more than ponds in the middle or at the end of a meadow, surrounded by sedges, rushes, and willows, with banks soft and sloping or sharply undercut. Many are a combination, with steep rock at the upper end, rock walls or boulder piles along part of the sides, and softer sloping ground where streams come in or where an end is blocked by a moraine. Some are deep and dark; many are shallow and clearly lighted to the bottom. Some support fish, many do not.

In the northern part of the range, an elevation of 3,500 feet is halfway up to the crest, unlike the southern part where that elevation is only a third of the way up on the west and would be underground in the high valleys on the east. Many of the lakes in the middle heights between the foothills and the high country are either artificial or partly so; it is only at the highest elevations that most lakes are entirely natural.

Consider a man-made lake. It was once a meadow with meandering streams which came together above a narrow opening. Economics dictates that dams are best built in a defile, but more water can be stored in a wide valley, so a combination of the two is desirable.

The former creeks in the meadow supported fairly large populations of native fish, and the water edges supported frogs and smaller fishes. Sedges and rushes were shelter and food for insects and small animals; large animals came and went for food and water, and there were migration trails across the meadow. Large numbers of waterfowl stopped by, many of them nesting there.

When the lake rose behind the dam, the fish population surged for a time, then leveled off, and in recent years annual plantings have been required. The manicured banks provided little food or protection for animals until vegetation grew back; large animals found their habits changed or impossible, with trails and feeding grounds flooded over. Soon simple cabins and then elaborate homes were built around the edge. The lake now is collecting effluent from septic tanks, absorbing altered runoff from nearby streets and gutters, silting more and more where entering streams slow down and drop their loads of sand and mud. There are some waterfowl, and to some extent their nesting grounds are protected, but they are not as extensive and protected as before.

For several miles below the dam, the stream is a bare trickle, for the water is impounded for hydroelectric generation and bypasses its normal channel so it can be diverted through ditches and tunnels to the penstocks and turbines. The large expanse of surface (and these lakes are usually judged by their surface acreage) is just right for motorboats and water skiers. At dawn or sunset the view is great, and fine photographs can be

Convict Lake, on the east slope of the Sierra, rests between two arms of glacial debris. In the foreground, a third, lateral moraine forms a natural dam.

Honeymoon Lake, at 10,500 feet, is just below timberline, and lodgepole pines find a last foothold along its shore.

taken right out of the window of a car. An example of this is Lake Almanor.

Another kind of lake in the northern Sierra is a hybrid. For years it was a large, quiet pond, with no visible running streams going into it—just seeps and springs which fed out accumulated snow melt. Beavers found it attractive and built a dam at the outlet, so that the level of the water was raised a few feet; this caused the water to spread out many feet horizontally because of the low profile of the meadow, and the pond became a respectable lake. Gold miners improved the work of the beavers (who moved farther downstream and made new ponds) with a durable dam; much later, sportsmen's groups and the county improved that dam to preserve the fishing. The fish are crappie, bluegills, and catfish, all adapted to warm water with much vegetation, for this lake heats up in the summer and has less oxygen than some because of the lack of flowing tributaries. Without paved roads to it, and with a surface

so small that water sports are impractical, this remains a quiet water, a pleasant place—like Snake Lake in Plumas County.

There are deer, bear, raccoon, and bobcat tracks around the edges; the mixed forest of pine, fir, and oak is full of squirrels and other small animals; hundreds of ducks and geese stop here on their restless routes, and some stay the year around. Occasional attempts are made to clear out some of the lilies and other water plants to make the fishing easier, but so far the lake has defeated the fairly low-key chemical and mechanical attacks. No mountains surround this lake—just rounded hills, steep enough for the walker, high enough to hold snow, wooded enough to catch and slowly feed out the moisture—but no great crags, for at this latitude the Sierra is starting to merge with the Cascades, and the great jagged ridges are scarce.

A third kind of lake in the northern Sierra is more like those near timberline farther south. It is small.

In the background, beyond the first ridge, looms Mount Humphreys.

It has no name on the map. It is above six thousand feet on Bald Eagle mountain. And it is a walk-in lake, requiring some climbing and some endurance to reach, so it is not often visited. It occupies a small pocket high on the mountain side, where dark basic-intrusive cliffs of the Mesozoic time, possibly 140 million years old, have broken and fallen into talus piles of huge boulders.

The blackish rock was an almost-volcano, but did not break through the surface; then over the years the overlying material eroded away, leaving the hardened almost-lava standing there. Without support and with a weak structure, the face of the cliff collapsed—perhaps with the help of earthquakes—and some of the chunks rolled almost to the river, two or three thousand feet below. Most of the boulders, however, being sharp and irregular, collected at the bottom of the remaining cliffs.

There was no room there for a lake, but during the past million years, when the climate was cold and the precipitation high, a small glacier came and went on the north side of this mountain. It shoved the blocky boulders a short distance, a few more of them rolling down toward the river, but most staying together because of their interlocking angles and points. Up against this pile of boulders, the melting glacier dropped a load of sand, gravel and silt—a moraine—very small by glacial standards, but an effective dam, for behind this compact rim there was a hollow which filled with water and remains filled today, each year's surplus trickling through a natural spillway at a low place in the moraine.

At the upper end of this lake remain big black blocks of the cliff material; on the west side are some granite boulders, brought a short distance laterally by the ice; on the east side, where most of the spring snow melt trickles in, there is an accumulation of alluvial soil built up particle by particle over thousands of years

Tiny Thompson Lake, at 12,200 feet, is one of the highest in the range. It is just a rocky pocket of snowmelt, with neither vegetation nor apparent outlet. On the shady southern side snow remains all summer.

and still not amounting to much in volume.

In that soil grow willows and other marsh plants, extending out into the little lake a few inches more each year. A half mile away there is a small red fir woods, somewhat sparse on this dry mountain; but closer around the lake the earth is rocky and barren, so that the lake is a small oasis, wet and green, a community of insects, algae, grasses, shrubs, sedges, rushes, rock plants, rodents, and birds—and in the lake is a colony of eastern brook trout, probably descendants of some planted by an early fisherman, for there is no way an ancestor could have reached this point unaided. The "brookie" can spawn in the closed waters of the lake and finds nourishment in the minute water plants and animals, with bugs that drop off the willows for

dessert.

There are no deer tracks in the few impressionable places on the moraine but occasional evidence of a bobcat and possibly a mountain lion. Redtailed hawks and golden eagles slide over the thermal updrafts and sometimes swoop down near the lake; an occasional pair of ducks stops off for a season. It is a private community, quiet and natural, most of the activity small and concealed; the sparks of energy which mark birth, life, death, and change are tiny, remote, unobserved, and unmeddled with—a rare circumstance in the twentieth century.

There is more granite in the middle Sierra than in the north, and the glaciers are more active. Wherever the glaciers came and went, pockets were left in the

Small glacial lakes like this one below Temple Crags abound in the High Sierra, many of them secluded where only the hardiest knapsackers and peak climbers can appreciate their beauty.

granite, and morainal dams were pushed into place—so glacier country is lake country.

Consider one square mile for example: there are fifteen lakes, all small, all natural, so close together and so closely related that one name takes care of all of them: Eagle Lakes. When they overflow in the spring, the surplus runs from one to another until it reaches a large stream; for some months in the summer (depending on the snow melt up above) there seems to be no overflow at all. In this square mile of lakes, the highest point is 5,722 feet, the lowest only about 250 feet less, so that these are pockets in a larger basin. Peaks and ridges within view, 2,000 feet higher, make it plain that this is mountain country, however.

The tranquil nature of these lakes, and an absence of scouring action because incoming trickles are of low velocity, lets mushy silt and organic material gather in the bottoms of the granite pockets and around the edges where rushes and other aquatic plants grow. Pine and fir needles, broken branches, and occasional tree trunks fall into them, and slowly become part of the muck. As the glacier retreated, it left patches of soil in its moraines, so that around each pond is a rim of green. These fifteen lakes, with much shade, shadow, and protection around them, are natural stopping and breeding places for waterfowl, and all along their edges is a heavy traffic of four-footed creatures intent on making a living. Deer wander through the basin, and around the fringes of the summer herd move one or two mountain lions.

A ROUGH ROAD AND SOME TRAILS come in from the highway, each cutting diagonally across the face of a moraine to reach the next shelf above. Clearly evident in these low ridges is the mixed cargo brought down by the glacier—boulders as big as a house, and fine grains of sand. Enough time has passed so that the exposed granite has begun to weather and partly disintegrate; cracks have appeared in the bigger rocks, and small trees and shrubs have found footholds. The surface of some of the granite has flaked away, exfoliating on a small scale; the flakes are nearby but are slowly being moved away by snow. Some of the shelves are entirely of the rounded granite on which this basin is set, and the marks of weathering are everywhere.

Red firs and lodgepoles grow to the water's edge and even on the rocky barrier that, were it not for this channel, would make Echo two lakes instead of one.

In the main stream which threads the larger basin there are vigorous rainbow trout, but in most of the small lakes there is no sign of game fish. This is understandable, for trout do not usually live in water which is not attractive to human swimmers, and these lakes are murky, unclear most of the year, and without sandy beaches. They are habitat for many living things but are not the sparkling lakes usually associated with the Sierra—although there are many of those within a few miles.

Five or ten miles away, there is another lake—also in a basin formed by a glacier but entirely different from the chain of ponds. Crystal Lake is clear, as there has been less erosion above it and so less material in the water. There are a few trout, and numerous bluegill. Where a small stream comes down through a side moraine, an alluvial meadow has been formed, and on the sloping meadow are the usual willows and hundreds of small incense cedars growing out of the grass. Where

Echo Lake is high above Lake Tahoe and an easy hike south of Desolation Valley.
It occupies a pair of natural granite bowls, connected by a narrow channel.

the meadow meets the water, the willows grow thickly; in late summer their catkins burst and put out great quantities of white fluff. On the westerly side of the lake, a fringe of red fir and cedar occupies a strip of soil between a granite dome and the water, the trees growing right down to the edge; but on the opposite side the rounded granite with no soil on it affords a roothold for only a few small twisted trees, and the rock curves down, bare and hard, into the lake making this side a fine, clear place to swim.

A low concrete dam has raised the natural outlet by a few feet, installed so long ago that it seems almost natural itself—especially since extensive weathering of the concrete has taken place. There are smaller and more vegetated ponds nearby which seem more attractive to waterfowl, but one or two pair paddle around on this one, perhaps not nesting but feeding. Ducks which eat near the surface, tipping and dipping, fly right up off the water when startled—but the usual ducks on this lake are the kind that dive deeply for food and, when alarmed, clatter along the water as if trying to run on the surface before breaking free into strong and purposeful flight.

A third lake in the middle Sierra has many counterparts and is typical of those which are part of the electricity factory. This was once two lakes, separated by the characteristic low ridge left by the glaciers. The upper one did not drain into the lower one, however, and each had its own outlet, the two streams coming together a short distance away. Then each outlet was dammed, the tops of the dams being equal in height, and a lake with a much larger area than the two inefficient ones was created.

In the spring the lake is brimful and the spillways are busy; in the summer, this expanse of water, with an island or two in the middle where the old dividing ridge was, reflects the volcanic cliffs above it and supports two small resorts and a couple of group camps, along with a public camp and a picnic ground. It is a beautiful place, and the fishing is good; there are many birds, but not much other wildlife around the edges. The reason for this shows up in the late fall, after the tourist season but before the winter rain and snow: Like all hydroelectric lakes, Caples Lake is drawn down to a bare minimum to keep the turbines turning. The gravelly bottom is exposed for several feet vertically and many yards horizontally, so aquatic plants cannot survive. The boat docks, launching ramps, and swimming floats are far from the water's edge; resorts are boarded up; access roads to the camps are blocked with a pole gate or, sometimes, a padlocked chain on which bright wisps of cloth or strips of red tape are tied to show the late-season visitor that there is indeed a right time for all things, including visits to the Sierra Nevada.

FARTHER SOUTH ALONG THE RANGE, where the crest is higher and the access increasingly difficult, there are more wild lakes, and many tame ones. Each is different, but all take on the characteristics of their position and elevation. There are large man-made reservoirs on the Tuolumne, Merced, and San Joaquin, on the Kings and the Kern; there are smaller dams on lesser streams, and some of the natural lakes have been raised by low obstructions to serve man's purposes.

At the lower elevations, the water is warmer and more turbid, and the fish are bass more often than trout. There is more plankton in the water, those microscopic plants and animals which are the basis of the aquatic food chain, eaten by clams, snails, insect larvae, and small swimmers, which are in turn eaten by increasingly larger animals. In the low and middle elevations, the lakes are often surrounded by forests, and sometimes have marshlands of various sizes beside them. These are busy places, and the lake becomes the hub of a community of creatures large and small making a living in a world of multiple kinds of vegetation, in a reasonably stable environment where the patterns of life can be expected to continue from season to season and year to year in an orderly way—subject to nature's vicissitudes and vulnerable to man's intercession, but still reasonably stable.

The Sierra's lakes are infinitely varied, and no brief summary can define them all. Whether pocketed in bowls of high rock by processes as old as time itself or crammed into narrow canyons by the contrivances of modern man, the lakes of the range are rewarding—to the naturalist, to the artist, to the recreationist. And big or small, shallow or deep, clouded with sediment or as clear as the eyes of a child, the lakes are the gems of the Sierra.

In summer great clouds often form in late afternoon over the Sierra crest.
If the air aloft is cold enough, there may be brief thunderstorms with heavy
rain. But the chances are that the day will end, as it began, with golden
sunshine casting long shadows over the peaks.

Water is everywhere part of the mountain scene—drifting overhead as a billowing cumulus;
roaring down cataracts or lying placidly in mountain lakes; deposited in massive snowbanks, to be
withdrawn when reawakening life needs it in the spring. The Sierra seizes the water from the
clouds, stores it, and distributes it. Were there no mountains at this particular spot, the Great Basin
might be a garden and California a desert.

Raging storms alternate with bright, sunny days, even in the middle of winter. In the warm sunshine deeply drifted snow melts slightly to form small cascades; with the chill of night they freeze into icicles.

The morning after the first storm of winter finds the slopes below Sonora Pass covered with a few inches of snow. As the snows get heavier, limber saplings will bend to the ground and tree branches dip to let the snow slide off.

Vegetation takes a foothold wherever it can, encroaching on lake and stream and solid rock. Its lush growth harbors birds, animals, and insects, and silent fungi live beneath its fallen leaves.

Red Lake, just east of Carson Pass, was visited early by explorers and emigrants. From a peak north of the lake, John Frémont made the first recorded sighting of Lake Tahoe.

Melting snows fill shallow Oriole Lake in Sequoia National Park. Scarcely more than a pond, it shrinks in summer but retains some water all year, sheltering many forms of aquatic life and providing water and food for land animals as well.

Throughout the Sierra, glaciers have left signs of their passing. Here one deposited a low moraine that now dams a small pocket of water. The ice may also have scraped soil from the boulder, foreground, exposing it to frost splitting.

Donner Lake, lying cold and blue on the east side of Donner Pass, was named in memory of the emigrant party that lost thirty-six of its members there in the winter of 1846-47.

Chapter 3

ROCKS AND RILLS

Sierra streams—now plunging down a cascade, now swirling white over boulders, now shining quietly in a mirror pool

THE RIVERS OF THE SIERRA NEVADA can be tallied and catalogued, each with a name and a place and a description. But the lesser streams, from tiny trickles to large flows, are more numerous; most have names, at least locally, but many are so small and some so transient that they do not even have this dignity.

In the Sierra, anything less than a river is called a creek (most often pronounced "crick"), and the only streams that are called "brooks" are those flowing through fancy subdivisions. Rivers are usually a combination of two or more "forks," and sometimes there is a "branch" of a fork—but a creek is a creek, not a branch. Thus in a more or less typical sequence, there is tiny Jacks Creek running into larger Silver Creek, which joins Spanish Creek, which continues to grow as it takes in numerous other tributaries. After ten or fifteen miles of growth, Spanish Creek joins Indian Creek (which has come from an entirely different drainage area), and the two together are the East Branch of the North Fork of the Feather River. Still growing, picking up contributions from both sides, the East Branch moves down its canyon until it swirls in against the heavier flow of the North Fork proper. In some seasons, the color of the water of each branch is different, and each keeps a diminishing identity for some yards until the rough bottom and the boulders in the middle and along the edges combine with the momentum of the flow to churn it all into one.

The North Fork continues down toward the Great Valley, gathering in trickles and creeks—some coming for several miles down side canyons from upland meadows, some just short-lived cascades from the main canyon walls. Several miles farther west, the West Branch of the North Fork comes in, the product of another major drainage area. Meanwhile, the Middle Fork and the South Fork have been gathering tribute from two other watersheds and have joined together and flowed as one for a few miles to their junction with the North Fork, where for the first time the Feather is one river, becoming one only after reaching the lower edge of the Sierra.

At least, that is the way it is in memory and on the old maps; but now the Feather is full of dams and diversions, and much of it squeezes through tunnels, penstocks and generators. Where the three forks used to come together in waves and spray and foam and great blue and green eddies, they now silently merge in a great amorphous pool behind the giant Oroville Dam. The Feather serves to illustrate the nomenclature of Sierra Nevada streams and also provides a parable the point of which may not be fully known for many years.

Turbulence is an essential factor in the life of the Sierra creeks and the smaller branches and forks of the rivers. Although there are many deep pools and quiet stretches, the hallmarks are the bright and busy riffles, the churning and curling of water against a midstream boulder, and the roaring of falls and cascades. The almost constant agitation of the water keeps it full of oxygen, and because of the dissolved oxygen, aquatic life flourishes. As in all balanced systems, there is an incredible amount of minute life on which larger things

The music, the sparkle, the cooling taste of mountain water can be enjoyed along any of a hundred streams. This one is on the west side of Sonora Pass.

WHITE WATER CREATURES

SPECIES	DESCRIPTION	HABITAT	SPECIAL ADAPTATION
FISH			
Trout	Strong, streamlined swimmers; up to 30 pounds	Varies with species; all require fresh, moving water	Takes advantage of eddies and backwashes where he can rest with a minimum of motion yet watch for passing morsels
Sculpin	Grows to 5 inches long	Gravel bottom of flowing streams	Extends ear-like front fins and "hangs by his ears" between two rocks, camouflaged by his resemblance to stream bottom
CRUSTACEANS			
Crayfish	Up to 6 inches long; looks like small lobster	Quiet pools, under an overhang	Fast swimmer with stout pincers
INSECTS			
Black fly larvae	About ½ inch long; when densely packed look more like dark moss than animals	Fast-flowing water	Have hooks and suckers on one end to fasten to rocks, fans on the other end to catch floating food; when they emerge as flies, they float to the surface in a bubble of air that keeps their new wings dry
Water penny	½-inch oval shell	Fast-flowing water	Sealed to rock by suction; so thin it offers little resistance to moving water
Midge larva	Less than ½ inch long	Roughest water or waterfalls	Holds to rock with seven pairs of fingers, each with multiple small hooks; moves through fast flows by disengaging a few fingers at a time, moving them to a new grip
Hellgrammite	Grows to 2 inches as larva; becomes dobsonfly as an adult	Stream bottom	Takes advantage of fact that water flows more slowly just above streambed; walks in partial shelter of stream-bottom rocks
Caddis worm	Grub-like larva in protective device	Stream bottoms, swift water	Covers self with armor of sand or rock grains (in ponds, stick fragments) stuck to a silken tube; one variety forms a net to catch passing food
Mayfly nymph	Flattish body with three "tails"	Fast-moving water	Have rounded or domed backs so water flows over; move on long, strong legs
Stonefly nymph	Two "tails" and six prominent legs		

feed; those in turn are eaten by still larger (but fewer) animals, and so on up the familiar chain—which has many links in this liquid environment, from a tiny bit of algae to a hulking black bear.

Along with the usual life problems of food, reproduction, and avoidance of being eaten, the small creature in the Sierra stream has another major endeavor, staying in one place. Even in the busiest riffles or the roughest cascades, creatures live, holding on with special devices against the incessant attempts of the water to pull them loose.

Many Sierra creeks live brief lives, tumbling swiftly down a mountainside to the river, or plunging hundreds of feet over the rim of a glacial canyon. The rivers, however, average only a foot or two drop for each hundred feet of flow (steeper near the top of the range, more nearly level near the bottom).

The swiftest water is the brightest, glinting with reflected sunshine or throwing up rainbow-lit spray. But pools, too, have a compelling attraction, sometimes mysterious in their depths, each one with a different arrangement of rocks and beaches, all infinitely varied in the patterns of their surfaces. There are eddies, backwaters, and whirlpools—and long stretches where the water does not seem to move at all, though a twig thrown in at the upper end very soon slips over the accelerating flow at the lower end.

Besides the specially adapted species listed in the

Evolution Creek tumbles down steps of granite within a mile or two of the crest of the Sierra. Many living things have evolved ways to live in such turbulent white-water homes.

SOME INHABITANTS OF SIERRA STREAMS AND BANKS

SPECIES	HABITAT	INTERESTING CHARACTERISTICS
MAMMALS		
Beaver	Slow-running streams of lower elevations; a few at higher levels but food supply scarcer there	Eats inner bark of willows, aspens, and cottonwoods, which grow along streams at lower elevations
Aplodontia ("mountain beaver")	Burrows along creek banks from 6,000 to 11,000 feet elevation	Not a true beaver; smaller than beaver, which it does not even resemble; does have similar eating habits, cutting twigs and green plants for food; seldom seen in daytime and only a little oftener at night
Water shrew	In streams	Eats its weight in insects, worms, and small animals every day; swims, dives, walks on bottom of stream, and sometimes skitters along the surface for short distances
Mink & weasel	Along stream banks and in nearby forests and brush	Hunt prey along streams but are seldom seen
Raccoon	Along stream banks and in nearby forests and brush	Searches for almost anything it can pick up in handlike paws and put into its mouth; nocturnal, but tracks are common in mud and sand along streams
Ring-tailed cat	Along stream banks up to middle elevations	Tail almost as long as its body; eats rodents, birds, sometimes berries; so shy that neither it nor its tracks are often seen
Also: skunks, foxes, coyotes, bear, deer, bobcats, mountain lions		
REPTILES		
Rubber boa	Along stream banks and under moist, rotting logs	Has tail the same shape as its head; occasionally grows to two feet in length; eats small animals and reptiles; nonpoisonous
Garter snake (3 varieties)	Along stream banks and in adjacent meadows	Brightly colored, grows to two feet and occasionally four feet long; eats slugs, salamanders, and mice ashore; small fish, amphibians, and water insects afloat; nonpoisonous
Mountain kingsnake	Along streams and in forested areas	Bright red, white, and black; eats small rodents; nonpoisonous
Western rattlesnake	Usually found from Lodgepole Belt down, though recorded as high as 11,000 feet (contrary to folklore)	Thick-bodied, up to five feet long; feeds on rodents, lizards, and birds; not aggressively vicious, prefers to be left alone, but is equipped with fangs and poisonous venom which it uses if cornered
Gopher snake	Grasslands and other open places	Appearance, diet, behavior all resemble rattlesnake, but head is less triangular and tail less blunt; *nonpoisonous*
BIRDS		
Kingfisher	Can be found up to high elevations in summer	Perches on branches overhanging the stream, then plunges in after a small fish or insect; fishermen consider him a competitor, so man is his worst enemy
Ouzel	Along the most turbulent streams, at any elevation where creeks do not freeze over	Dives into water where he can swim with his wings or walk along the bottom; builds nest of growing moss behind a waterfall
Spotted sandpiper	Up to high elevations	Brown and white; forages singly or in pairs along pebbly stream edges; startles easily and will fly away quickly; builds sparse nest on ground
Black phoebe	As high as Yellow Pine Belt, living all year in the Sierra (other species of flycatcher are seasonal visitors only)	A flycatcher that perches out in the open, making occasional forays to pick insects off stream surface or out of the air; builds nest of mud pellets and grass on a rocky ledge near a creek
Calliope hummingbird	Nests in Yellow Pine and Red Fir belts, moves to higher elevations as flowers begin to bloom along streams	Very small; leaves mountains in winter for warmer climate

SOME INHABITANTS OF SIERRA STREAMS AND BANKS (continued)

SPECIES	HABITAT	INTERESTING CHARACTERISTICS
Downy woodpecker	Streamside willows and cottonwoods as high as 4,000 feet	Quiet and shy
Yellow-bellied sapsucker	Along stream banks	Pecks holes in parallel rows in bark of softwood trees, to establish "food bank"; sap oozes through holes, insects get caught in it, and sapsucker eats both trap and trapped
Also: chats, orioles, grosbeaks, goldfinches, towhees, sparrows, vireos, warblers, all of which are permanent residents; other varieties come and go		
INSECTS		
Water boatman	Quiet pools in stream	Has hind legs shaped like oars
Backswimmer	Quiet pools in stream	Swims upside down; picks up air by poking tip of his abdomen through the surface of the water
Giant water bug	Quiet pools	Grows to three inches long; can eat a young fish or bite fishermen
Water scorpion	Quiet pools	Breathes through a pair of snorkels
Toad bug	Quiet pools	Looks like frog but is only ½ inch long
Water strider	Quiet pools	Weight is spread out on widely placed legs, and on each leg further spread to many waxy hairs, so thin "skin" on top of water (created by surface tension) supports him; claws are high on leg so they don't break surface tension; legs create shallow dimples in surface, which appear as magnified shadows on stream bottom
Whirligig beetle	Surface of pools	Can both swim and fly; uses upper half of divided eyes to see in air, lower half to see underwater; usually found with many others of his kind
Predacious diving beetle	Quiet pools	Picks up air and stores it under wing covers while he swims down to catch insects; uses back legs for oars
MOLLUSKS		
Water snails	Quiet waters at all elevations	Comes to surface to breathe; some varieties can glide along on under side of film created by surface tension of water
Keel shell	Under stones in streambed	
Fingernail clam	In mud of streambed	Tiny
Freshwater clam		Grows to more than three inches in length; young clip themselves to fins of passing fish and embed themselves in the flesh, living for several weeks as a parasite before detaching themselves

table on page 50, there are many other unseen but essential tiny creatures; their enormous numbers provide the guarantee that each species will survive predators, changes of water level, surges of velocity, shifting of the streambed, and all the other hazards inherent in life in a mountain stream. While the animals which merely live or forage along the creek edges or come to the stream to drink are less affected by those hazards, they are still dependent on the flow of water for their comfort or their livelihood.

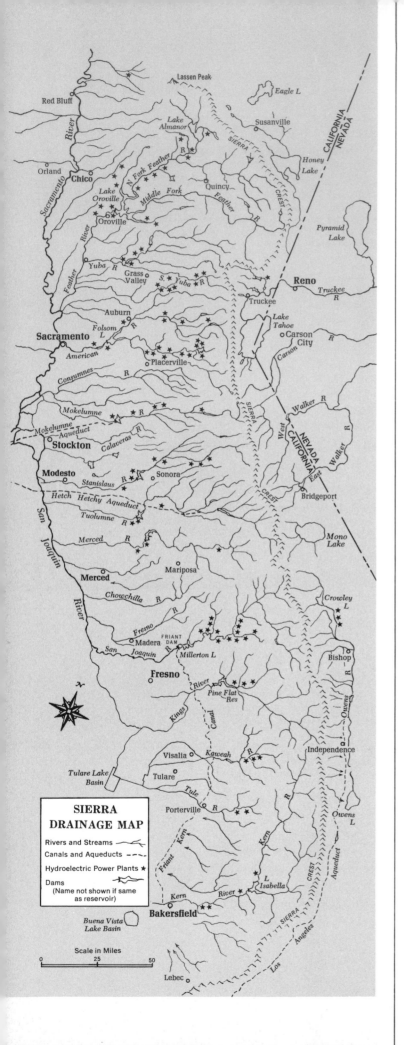

SIERRA DRAINAGE MAP

Rivers and Streams
Canals and Aqueducts
Hydroelectric Power Plants ★
Dams
(Name not shown if same as reservoir)

Scale in Miles
0   25   50

Fourteen kinds of willows grow in the Sierra, many of them in the stream bottoms wherever there is a patch of soil. Red willow and black willow range to 5,000 feet or so and are home to many of the birds; from 5,000 to 10,000 feet is the lemmon willow in dense clumps, and beside the highest streams at 12,000 feet or more is the alpine willow, growing only three or four inches above the ground. Along with the willows up to about 8,000 feet are black cottonwoods (tall, open, heart-shaped leaves) and white alders (tall, slender, more shade-tolerant, with whitish bark). The slender water birch is more common on the east side above Owens Valley but is sometimes found on the west slope up to about 8,000 feet.

Along with the trees are numerous ferns and other water-edge plants—sometimes so dense that human passage along a stream is difficult or impossible. Mosses grow thickly on the rocks in many places, especially where there is spray from a waterfall. In and around these growing plants, insects thrive; the millions of leaves in the summer break the wind, provide shade, and afford privacy for bird nests; and the dead leaves on the ground in the thicket are home for many other creatures.

Life in and around Sierra streams is tuned to alternate tumult and calm—falls and rapids, then pools; spring runoff and flood, then periods of tranquility or frozen silence. Creatures come and go in accordance with the cycles that have developed in the thousands of years since the Ice Age; some fall victim to the changes, but enough of each essential species live on. If a bank is undercut and collapses into the creek, the silt may block some of the spawning beds for trout, but upstream another gravel bed is still open, and farther down the silt does not reach. Adjustments are made to flooding and drought; catastrophe is common in local habitats but uncommon along the entire length of a stream. Season to season and year to year, the picture constantly changes—but over the centuries there has been relative stability.

Indians came and went, living along the streams at lower elevations, hunting and fishing up higher as the weather permitted; but they were few in number and natural in approach, and their presence required only minor adjustments by their fellow tenants. They had no shovels, no explosives, no earth-moving machinery,

In the two spectacular cascades of Yosemite Falls, a tributary of the Merced River drops almost half a mile.

The Tuolumne River meanders quietly through Tuolumne Meadows before plunging down into a reservoir in

no trucks to haul sand and gravel, and no reason to haul it; they had no concrete and no steel; there was no market for trees or animal skins, and they were not angry at snakes, coyotes, bobcats, and mountain lions. It was to the Indian's advantage to leave little trace of his passing, and to leave living shelter and food for his return. If he made "permanent" installations, they were of wood, skin, or bark, which eventually decayed and returned to the earth; so there are few evidences of his occupation except grinding holes in rocks, a few petroglyphs, and occasionally a circle of stones and a depression in the earth where a hut stood.

Hetch Hetchy canyon to become part of the San Francisco water supply. Cathedral Range is in the background.

But, in the lower elevations, there is not one stream unaltered by man in the past hundred and fifty years; in the middle elevations, there are only a few with fairly long stretches free of dams, culverts, or bridges; only at the highest elevations are there many small creeks and headwaters of rivers where the water runs for many miles unobstructed and almost uncrossed except for down logs and hopping-rocks—where the march of time is to the drumbeat of nature, not man. Part of the attraction of the Sierra is its running waters; only in the highest Sierra do the waters run free; but where they do, they are magnificent.

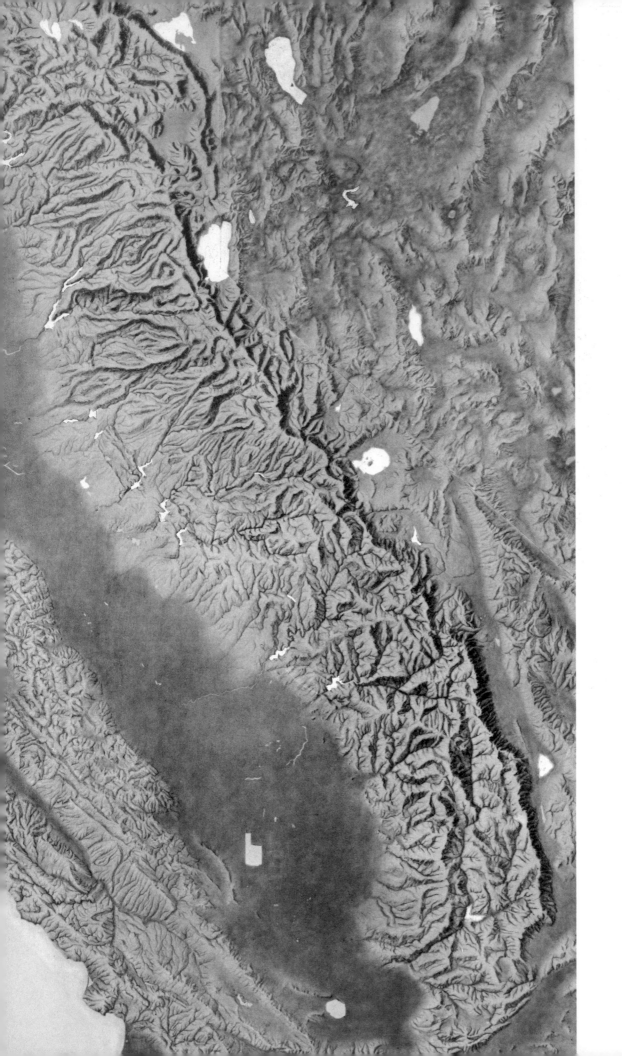

A
PORTFOLIO
OF
MAPS

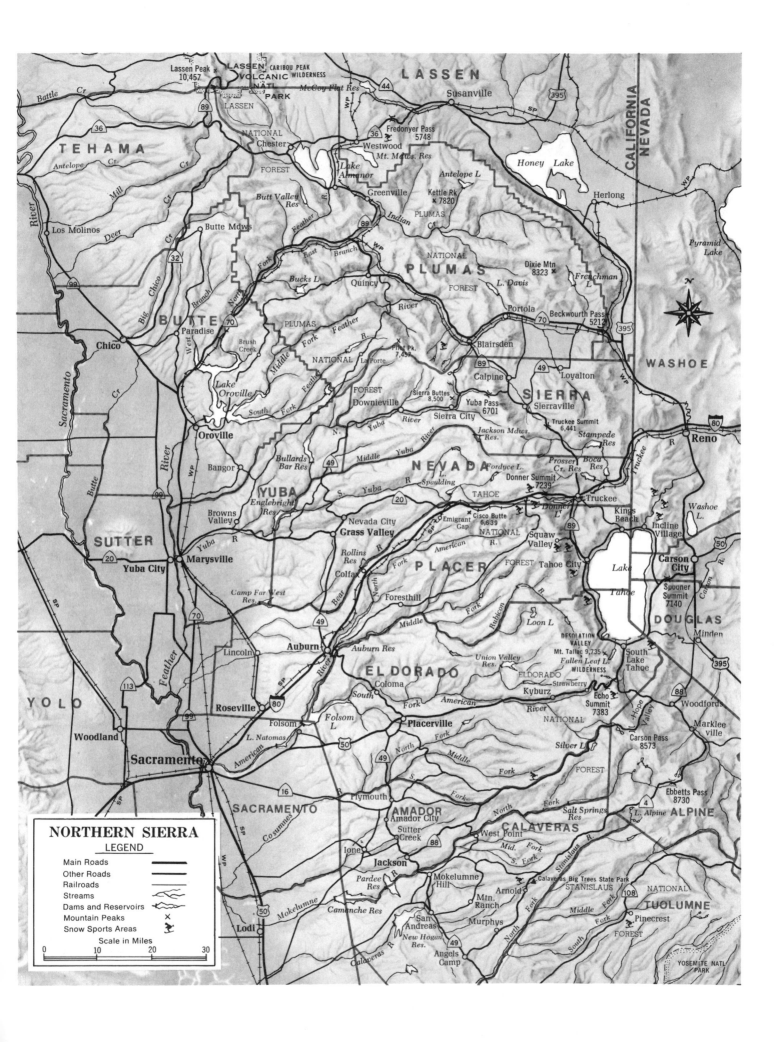

NORTHERN SIERRA

LEGEND

Main Roads
Other Roads
Railroads
Streams
Dams and Reservoirs
Mountain Peaks ×
Snow Sports Areas

Scale in Miles

0   10   20   30

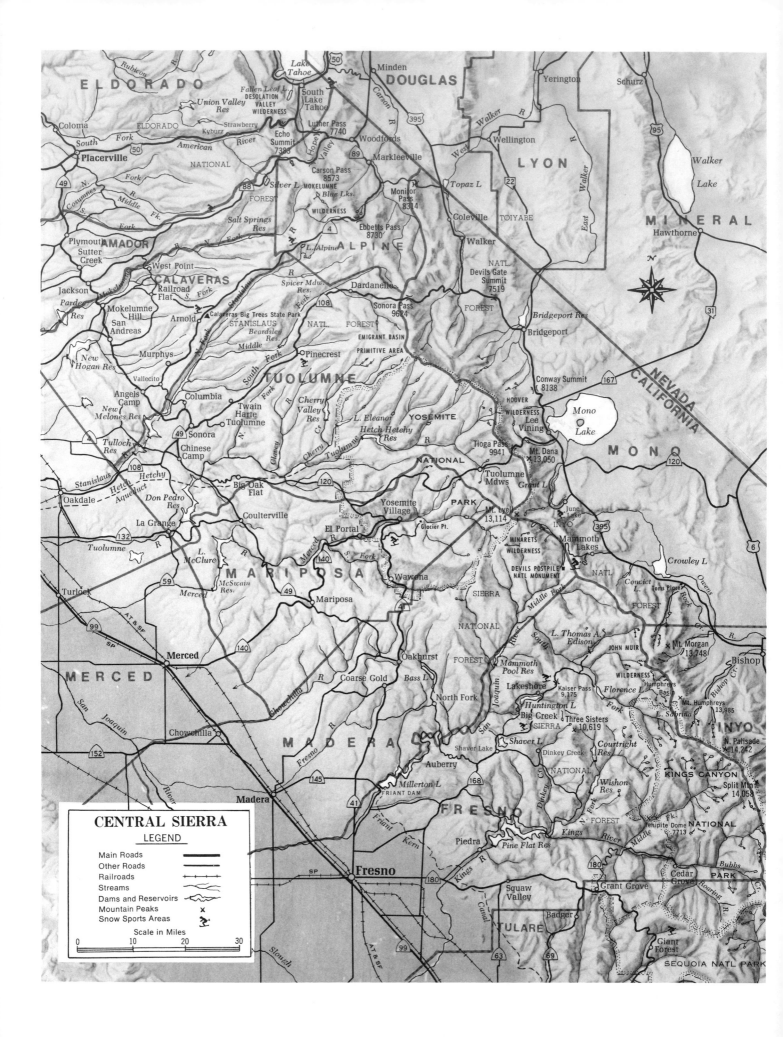

CENTRAL SIERRA

LEGEND

Main Roads	
Other Roads	
Railroads	
Streams	
Dams and Reservoirs	
Mountain Peaks	×
Snow Sports Areas	

Scale in Miles

0   10   20   30

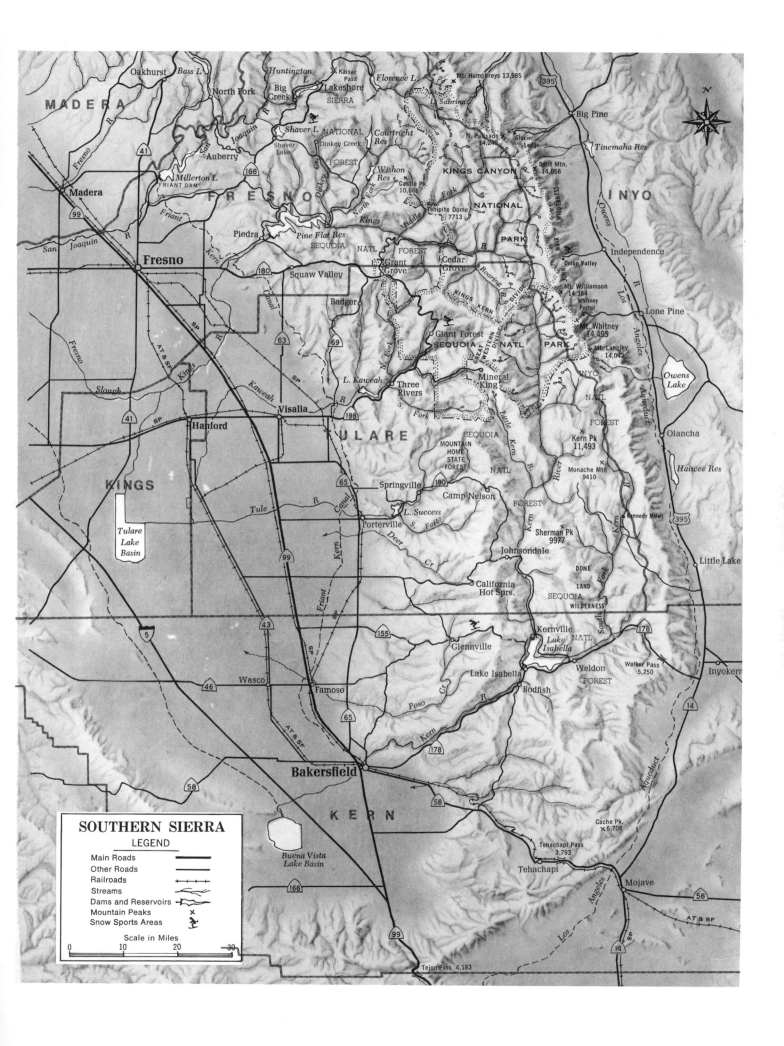

THE INDIANS

In the beginning the world was rock. Every year the rains came and fell on the rock and washed off a little; this made earth. By and by, plants grew on the earth, and their leaves fell and made more earth. Then pine trees grew, and their needles and cones fell off every year and with the other leaves and bark made more earth and covered more of the rock.

If you look closely at the ground in the woods, you will see how the top is leaves and bark and pine needles and cones, and how a little below the top these are matted together, and a little deeper are rotting and breaking up into earth. This is the way the world grew—and is growing still.

—Northern Miwok Creation Myth

Indians came and went throughout the Sierra Nevada, and lived year-round in the northern portion—but they left little trace: only forerunners of the present roads and trails, a few pitted stones where meal was ground, some scattered rock markings and a few places where depressions in the ground mark sites of round houses. There are some Indian names on streams, peaks, and valleys, but few of them are the original ones; most are either corruptions of the terms used by the Indians, or were arbitrarily applied to indicate the supposed name of the tribe living there (usually wrong) or the name of some individual Indian either admired or feared.

Among the best known examples is Yosemite—supposedly, according to much of the early literature, "the name of the tribe that lived there." But there probably was no tribe living there with a name even remotely resembling that. There were probably seven to nine villages, perhaps more, the major one called something like Ahwanee; the closest thing to Yosemite in sound was a word for grizzly bear, so perhaps the valley was referred to in the presence of whites as a place of grizzly bears; or perhaps there was a reference to a village named after bears, since the animal loomed large in the stories and myths of the Indians all over California. Tenaya Lake and Canyon in the park, however, were named for the chief who was leader when the Indians of Yosemite were giving the whites a great deal of trouble—but the name was applied by the whites, not by the Indians, who insisted they had their own name for that lake: Pyweack, meaning something like "lake of the shining rocks," because of the high glacial polish on the bright granite all around it.

On the California side of the Sierra, the density of Indians was higher than in other parts of the United

For the Indians, the native plants of the Sierra provided a bountiful harvest. Here a Seraku woman grinds manzanita berries in a bedrock mortar (photographed in 1918).

States. A reasonable estimate of their number in 1770 seems to be about 133,000, although there have been guesses as high as 250,000. Perhaps one out of five or six U.S. Indians lived within a hundred miles or so of the Sierra, and of those it can be assumed a third lived close enough to walk in and out on hunting or trading expeditions. Many of the foothill people just moved up higher in the summer to avoid the heat. Despite California's long dry season, there was plenty of water and food in the form of acorns, other seeds, deer, waterfowl, fish, and other game, so that the Indians were well fed and numerous. On the Nevada side of the range and in the high valleys, there was a harsher climate and more austere food supply, but except for some bad years the Indians still did well.

After all the pressures of time and Spanish, Mexican, and American contact, little has remained of Sierran Indian culture—barely enough to show that these were gentle, family-minded people, rather precisely tuned to their natural surroundings, with a wonderful imaginative folklore, deep religious feelings, and certainly the weaknesses of human beings individually and as a people.

Anthropologists have a system of sorting Indians into various kinds of groupings that is a help to anthropologists but not particularly reflective of the people themselves, who seemed to be concerned first with their immediate households and the households right around them, then perhaps with a larger grouping. "Tribes" or "nations" in the eastern sense were not found around the Sierra. A broad division of the Indians of the United States puts the Indians who used the Sierra among the "seed-gatherers." Early settlers called them "diggers," a term which came to indicate a degree of scorn.

Indians are also sorted out according to broad language families, in which common roots of words seem to show some common genetic possibilities. The Indians around the Sierra fall into three of these. A further grouping within each language group is by dialects; around the Sierra are a number of these.

The Yokuts lived in the foothills and valleys west of the southern Sierra, moving upward to the mountains in hot weather and sometimes going around Walker Pass for arrow point material and other items of trade. They were easygoing and peaceful, well fed most of the time, needing only scant protection against the elements. They had seven dialect groups, four of them close to the Sierra and extending into it: the Northern Hill or Chukchansi; the Kings River or Choinimne and others; the Tule-Kaweah or Yaudanchi and others; and perhaps the Poso Creek or Paleuyami. All the Yokuts are in the Penutian language family, which included most of the California Indians.

Next to the north were the Miwok, between the Fresno and American rivers, a land of many oaks, much wildlife, and abundant water. Their trails led up into the high country, and there were many trips over the crest to trade for obsidian and other items. They too were peaceful, although they may have edged into the Yokuts' territory to some degree with a now unknown amount of friction. Of the five Miwok dialect groups, three lived in and adjacent to the Sierra, and are classified by white anthropologists simply as northern, central, and southern Miwok. They, too, were in the Penutian language family.

The Maidu inhabited the northern foothills and many lived year-round in the fairly sheltered mountain valleys of the Feather River country. This part of the range has lower passes and milder winters, so of the three main California groups involved with the Sierra, the Maidu (my-doo) made most use of the mountains. There were three dialect groups in the Sierra part of their land, classified now as northeastern, northwestern, and southern. The Maidu, too, are in the Penutian language family.

East of the northern Sierra, along the Truckee, Carson, and Walker rivers, the Washo lived a tougher life, with less abundance and more cold. Many of them moved up to Lake Tahoe for the summer and probably farther over the crest as well. They were of the Hokan language family, the only Sierra Indians in that category.

The Mono ranged widely east of the highest Sierra, around Mono Lake and Owens Valley, going up and over the crest to hunt and to trade their obsidian and pine nuts for goods from California. Around the end of the southern Sierra they were in contact with the Yokuts, and in fact some Monos lived quite close to the southwestern base. The Mono were in the Plateau branch of the Uto-Azetekan or Shoshonean language family, and are divided now into eastern and western dialect groups.

The natural fish supply in Sierra streams was more than ample for the Miwok and Maidu population of the foothills, who caught them with primitive devices like the fish trap pictured here.

Although not strictly Sierra Indians, the Yana of the Deer Creek and Mill Creek country southwest of Lassen Peak at the extreme northern end of the range—the Indians of whom Ishi is the most famous—are in the same language group as the Washo on the east side of the ridges; but their dialects have removed them far from the ability to converse with a Washo of the same generation.

Within each of the five groups of the main Sierra (Yokuts, Miwok, Maidu, Washo, Mono) smaller groups had more specific names, actually as tribes or tribelets and in some cases just families—for example, the Oustamahs of the Maidu around the present Nevada City. To the white man, the names of groups seem complicated; but they were not so to the Indian, for they were usually descriptive of the place where a certain group lived or of some physical or social characteristic of the group. The present-day name may be a Spanish-influenced spelling of words picked up by early explorers, further modified by English-speaking settlers or scholars. For example, **Cosumnes** may have come from a root meaning "salmon" and an ending meaning "people" (the "salmon-people" of the Miwok); but the Indian never wrote anything down nor made any map more permanent than a diagram in the sand, so it will never be known precisely what the people who lived along the Cosumnes River really called themselves a few hundred years ago. In many places, the Indians called their immediate group or band simply "the people" and had names for the other tribes; they had no real need to name themselves, for they knew who they were; only the "others" had to have names for identification or description.

The languages and dialects spoken may have appeared sparse to English-speaking inquirers, but there is a general misunderstanding about this, derived no doubt from stories and movies in which the Big Chief grunts "Me—go—now—ugh"! How the Indians would have written or dramatized the white man's attempts at the Indian's language would be interesting—the complicated workings of English, where many words are used to convey one specific meaning, preferably without repeating a word. In English one stone is singular, two or more stones, plural; and it takes another sentence or two to tell about the stones; in some Indian languages, one stone alone has a word; stones scattered around may have another word; stones in a pile may have still another.

The Maidu have four words for the third person singular: person-near-me, person-near-you; person-far-away-but-in-sight; person-far-away-out-of-sight. If that sounds complicated, consider the fact that the Maidu communicates that information in four words while the English speaker requires at least eighteen.

The Indians around the Sierra were "silent and taciturn" only (if at all) in their contacts with the whites—and then only because (a) Indian ideas were not easily translated into English words, (b) the Indians did not have much to say to the whites, and (c) the whites didn't want to listen anyway. Among themselves they talked a great deal, and within their constant communication was the essential element of their government, which was very close to a true democracy. They talked things over, often at great length, and ultimately did what there was little opposition to, without the formal necessity of taking a vote or bowing to the will of a chief. If there was real opposition to a proposal, it usually was dropped, for the time being or forever, because almost everyone knew what almost everybody else thought of it. In occasional wars or skirmishes there probably was leadership by a single man, but in everyday affairs life was probably a relatively tension-free consensus, subject ultimately to powers over which the Indian had little control.

Chiefs were chosen in various ways, sometimes by inheritance, sometimes by wealth, sometimes by personality, and usually led by influence rather than command; there was no super-chief over all the Maidu or over all the Miwok, for example, but several chiefs in various places. The shaman, who in some stories is given leadership power, actually served as a doctor rather than judge or enforcer; among most Indians, it was believed he could remove a foreign body which had entered a sick person to make him ill. In some places, he could make people sick as well as cure them.

The Indians who lived at the low elevations were "richer" than those who lived higher in the hills. Life was easier, there was more leisure, and the shells or beads or other possessions which marked wealth were easier to come by. Among the Maidu, for example,

The basic food of Indians in the oak-covered foothills was acorns, which they ground in holes hollowed out of solid granite. Some of these holes can still be seen at Indian Grinding Rock State Park.

those who lived in the uplands around what are now Quincy and Greenville were considered poorer than those who lived around, say, Brown's Valley.

Indians near the Sierra traded with each other extensively, going around the low ends of the mountains or over the crest when necessary. Inevitably, the trails they used for centuries became heavily traveled also by Americans, and to some extent present roads follow the same general courses; there are only so many passes over the crest, and they have been used by animals, Indians and whites.

Most of the trading was value for value—Washo salt for Miwok acorns, for example—although there was some buying and selling, such as Yokuts shell beads (used as money) for Mono sinew-backed bows. Some of the trade went back thousands of years, for the Indians were truly "early settlers" of the California and western Nevada region; other trade was less ancient, such as the brisk business in obsidian from Glass Mountain, which is only 900 years old.

The Miwok lived west of the highest part of the Sierra; the Mono lived in a corresponding position east of the crest. The trails, which were used by both, led over some of the highest passes above the Yosemite country and elsewhere. The trade eastward consisted of shell beads, acorns, berries, a fungus used in paint, baskets, seashells, and arrows; the trade westward was in pine nuts, caterpillars, fly pupae, baskets, red and white paint, salt, pumice stone, buffalo robes, and rabbit-skin blankets. Some of the trade goods did not originate with the sellers. The Miwok acquired sea shells for the purpose of trading them and the Mono did the same with buffalo robes. How far east did the sea shells finally get? Did the buffalo robes ever reach the shore of the Pacific?

The trade was not all across the mountains, of course; much of it was closer. The Kings River Yokuts provided clay for pottery, black paint, and certain basket materials in exchange for Tule-Kaweah Yokuts roots and herbs, salt, baskets and basket material. Within the Maidu, there was traffic in pine nuts: those from the digger pine of the low country for those of the sugar pine from the highlands.

There is some indication that there was a class of traders—that the same general group of men and women went each year, so that there would be familiar faces

and so the trading would be sharp and informed. Undoubtedly, some individuals elected to stay with the foreign tribe; most of the Indians who occupied Yosemite Valley in the many years before the white man came were Monos from the other side of the crest who had moved in.

Much has been written about the Yosemite Indians; about the long centuries in the incomparable valley, a plague which left it empty for decades, new settlers who came in from the other side of the mountains, the valley as a sort of refuge for renegades from many tribes, the final one-sided battles with the whites. Some of the stories are pure fiction, some are true—some are white fantasies, some are Indian lore. But whatever the stories, the fact remains: there were Indians in Yosemite for a long time, perhaps all the way back to the receding of the glaciers. The rock of their sheltering caves is black with the smoke of centuries.

I*t is hardly surprising to learn that when this simple, gentle culture met that of the white man, conflict resulted; such had been the case between Stone Age and civilization for centuries on the North American continent. What is surprising—or at least unusual—is that the conflict was such a one-sided affair. Unlike Indians of the Atlantic seacoast and the Plains, the native peoples of California, except when backed to the wall, were not aggressive or warlike. They had little heart for fighting and almost no strength to resist one of the most vicious, single-minded, and effective assaults of one culture on another in the history of man.*

Although it came close to destroying the Indian cultures of the coastal and interior valley regions, the Spanish and Mexican occupancy of California bothered the foothill and Sierra Indians comparatively little, except to provide them with new sicknesses and a considerable amount of tasty horseflesh—and to cause readjustments when refugees from the missions sought sanctuary and were pursued.

That pleasant situation deteriorated rapidly after 1848, when the discovery of gold inspired an awesome rush of greedy Americans to the foothill country—a land previously viewed with thundering disinterest by the Spanish and Mexicans. Although the Indians had property rights among themselves, varying from group to group, they did not understand the white viewpoint, particularly in four-legged food supplies and other items, and this was a cause of friction in the years of their extermination. Most of the real trouble, however, resulted from invasion, preemption of land, and utter disregard for human rights. At first, the Indians tried to accommodate this new factor, just as they had always adapted to early snowstorms, periods of drought, poor acorn harvests, and the like—as a sort of natural disaster. But as the pressure intensified and the accommodation was all one-sided, many of the Indians fought back; and, of course, they lost—lost miserably.

Apparently the Indians who survived the western invasion were those who had had an easier life and adapted more easily to the whites, who had more to fall back on than some of the upland tribes which were in a precarious position anyway. According to R. F. Heizer and M. A. Whipple of the University of California, these ". . . were rude even in native culture; which is equivalent to saying that they were poor; in short, that the margin which they had established between themselves and the minimum limit of existence was narrower than those of other tribes. Thus, the maladjustment caused by even a light immigration of Americans was enough to push them over the precipice."

Survival against the Caucasian invasion of the 1800s was probably better among the Sierra-oriented people than among those around the missions, for many mission tribes are extinct while many descendants of Maidu, Yokuts, Mono, Miwok, and Washo have been more or less integrated into the present mode of life. The attrition was tremendous, though, and between 1770 and 1910 the overall population dropped almost 90 percent. Some of the Indians lived in places less coveted by whites and were less drastically disturbed.

In general, however, the miners and later the stockmen considered all Indians to be pests who stole food and livestock, and they set out to exterminate them as they would have poisoned coyotes or shot mountain lions. It was a very deliberate (if not exactly official) procedure, well organized and extending to the massacre of women and children. Between 1848 and 1870, Indian deaths numbered 48,000; not all of these were shot down like dogs (some simply died of disease or starvation), but it was not for a lack of trying. The result cannot be called genocide, since it did not reflect an official practice of the United States government— or even of the state—but it came close enough to that dismal level so that no white Californian can rest too smugly in the shadow of its memory.

Those not actively engaged in hunting down Indians in this period viewed the activity variously. Many deplored it vigorously and vocally, many others thoroughly approved, and most simply paid no attention to it. Some simply considered it part of the course of history, as did California's Governor Peter H. Burnett in 1851: "That a war of extermination will continue to be waged between the two races until the Indian race becomes extinct must be expected; while we cannot anticipate this result with but painful regret, the inevitable destiny of the race is beyond the power and wisdom of man to avert."

Those who did the hunting were considerably more blunt about it. Consider the words of T. T. Waterman, a University of California anthropologist, telling about stockmen who sought out some Yana and surrounded them in an open-fronted cave, where there were many children: "The hero of the occasion, being a humane man, a person of fine sensibilities and delicacy of feeling, could not bear to kill those babies—at any rate, not with the heavy 56-calibre Spencer rifle he was carrying. 'It tore them up too bad.' So he shot them with his 38-calibre Smith and Wesson revolver."

The Indians were the gentlest of all the peoples who have known the Sierra Nevada. The great range was part of the land, and the land was their heritage, their legacy, their life. It was to be used, but not used up. They gathered acorns in the foothills, pine nuts on the east side, seeds in the meadows where grasses grew head high before the white man's sheep arrived; they hunted deer, rabbits, and lesser animals wherever they could be found, and stalked mountain sheep up in the great crags; they walked the summer trails eastward with skins and salt, westward with obsidian and brine flies; they moved whole villages to better places during the change of seasons but had an ancestral home regardless of temporary abode; they adjusted, constantly adjusted, to nature's whims and powers, and told about these in stories and myths going back thousands of years. The Indians used the Sierra, but unlike those who came after them, they left it virtually untouched; footprints mar nothing for posterity.

PART TWO

COMMUNITIES
OF LIFE

*This grove of pines on the shore of **Tenaya Lake**
is just one of many separate environments in the Sierra
where a variety of living things—plants, animals,
birds, insects, and fungi—have achieved a
harmonious coexistence.*

71

Chapter 4

NEIGHBORHOODS ON THE SLOPES

*A guided tour of the zones of life, from foothills and forests
to the spare alpine subsistence above timberline*

THE WEB OF LIFE spun over the Sierra Nevada is bright and shimmering in some places, dull and drab in others—tough and seemingly unbreakable here, delicate and tenuous there—securely anchored in time and space at one point, at the mercy of the slightest breeze just a few feet away. But the web is there, although almost invisible most of the time, and it endures over the range even while it changes with each particular locality.

The changes of rocks and ridges may be measured in the millennia of vulcanism and glaciation; the mayfly lives only a few hours. But each contributes somehow to the other, and each is a part of all else. The stream splashes or glides because the rocks are just where they are and shaped just so, the rocks are so because of ancient heat or cold or stresses from within the earth, or because of radiant heat from the sun or lack of it. The moon's reflected light gives enough illumination to insure the death of this creature for the life of that predator, and the moon's rhythms are mysteriously reflected in the life cycles of subterranean organisms. Even the distant stars have an influence, not in the ways of astrologers, but as guideposts or navigating beacons and, when sun and moon are down, as a faint light to help noctural hunters.

The largest growing things in the Sierra are the trees, and some of the trees are large indeed. The giant sequoia can reach 30 feet thick and 330 feet high, and some standing trees are as old as 3,500 years. But this is not the typical tree of the Sierra, for it grows in only thirty-two groves, scattered from Placer to Tulare County at middle elevations of 4,500 to 7,500 feet.

The pines are the dominant trees, standing sometimes as single statuesque individuals, more often in extended groves, less commonly in dense forests. The pine pattern has changed in the past hundred years, probably because large crown fires have taken the place of small ground fires, permitting more undergrowth where anything at all has been left. In earlier days John Muir said: "The inviting openness of the Sierra woods is one of their most distinguishing characteristics. The trees of all the species stand more or less apart in groves, or in small irregular groups, enabling one to find a way nearly everywhere, along sunny colonnades and through openings that have a smooth, park-like surface, strewn with brown needles and burrs. . . . One would experience but little difficulty in riding a horse through the successive belts all the way up to the storm-beaten fringes of the icy peaks."

And Clarence King said: "The whole sensation is of being roofed and enclosed. You are never tired of gazing down long vistas where, in stately groups, stand tall shafts of pine. Columns they are, each with its own characteristic tinting and finish, yet all standing together with the air of relationship and harmony. . . . Here and there are wide open spaces around which the trees group themselves in majestic ranks."

A broad strip of forest clothes the full length of the western slope of the Sierra, and a narrower forest runs intermittently along the eastern slope. The main forest is pleasingly confusing in its arrangement of species, for there is no distinct line at which this kind stops and

*The trunk of this incense cedar has been riddled by woodpeckers looking for insects in the thick bark.
Although the dead lower branches are hosts to moss, there may be live branches higher up.*

that kind starts; nor, for that matter, is there a clear-cut distinction as to the lower and the upper edge of the forest. In the northern Sierra, the tree bands are narrower and go over the top of the crest in many places; in the southern Sierra, the bands are wider and there are miles of mountains without any forests at all.

At one time there was an effort to build a road the length of the Sierra at the lowest edge of the main forest, to provide fire protection and timber access and, in a way, to delineate the line between the foothills (with their widely spaced oaks and scrawny digger pines) and the mountains (with their merchantable timber forests). The road was built in some places and, where it exists, is called Ponderosa Way. It winds in and out of canyons, crosses creeks and rivers on thin bridges or through rough fords, disappears into thickets of willow or dogwood in some places and manzanita in others, swings out onto dry promontories, wanders through recent subdivisions, and occasionally ends at some stream where the bridge never got built. Parts of Ponderosa Way are heavily used, parts are just a bulldozed trail with the brush closing in more and more each year. It never did segregate the digger pines from the ponderosas, and it never did quite find the precise line where the forest really begins, because there is no such line.

THE TREES and all the plant and animal life sheltered and fed by them are not concerned with boundary lines, but with sun, water, soil, wind, frost, and elevation. Scholars, however, are concerned with definitions and boundaries, and have applied some to the mountains. The simplest way to classify the Sierra is to divide it into six belts:

The Digger Pine/Chaparral Belt. This foothill zone exists only on the west side, not on the east. The lower edge may be around 500 feet in the north, 1,200 feet in the south; the upper edge 2,500 to 3,000 feet in the north, 4,000 to 5,000 feet farther south. One of the paradoxes of the Sierra is the fact that at one end the crest is not much higher than an elevation considered foothill country at the other end. Going farther afield, some of the foothill summits no one has bothered to name are higher than the storied peaks of Vermont, New York, Maine, Massachusetts, and Georgia. The

light, airy, gray-green digger pine is widely spaced among live oak and blue oak, with California buckeye and willow along the streams and redbud on the hillsides; closer to the ground are the many shrubs, sometimes in dense thickets, that make up the chaparral, or elfin forest.

The Yellow Pine Belt. This zone, along the western slope, is where most of the commercial timber is cut and much other commercial activity takes place. The lower edge mixes into the foothills at 1,200 or 1,500 feet in the north, 2,000 to 2,500 feet in the south; the upper edge blends into the Red Fir Belt at perhaps 5,500 feet in the north, 9,000 feet in the south. There are four major evergreens in addition to yellow pine (often called "ponderosa"), and many other trees and plants; numerous year-round birds and animals are joined in the warm weather by others from lower elevations. There is heavy precipitation in the winter in the form of rain or snow, but almost no rain in the summer. This zone is described in more detail later in this chapter.

The Red Fir/Lodgepole Pine Belt. Just above the yellow pines, this zone extends, in the north, from about 5,500 to 7,500 feet, often overtopping the crest at that latitude; in the center, from 6,500 to 8,000 feet, higher than Donner Pass; in the south, from 8,000 to 10,000 feet. This belt appears on the east side of the Sierra, too, but usually at somewhat higher elevations. The growing season is three to five months, somewhat limiting the growth of trees and plants, but in most places the forest has found ways to grow densely—including not just the two trees that give it its name, but many others, some from lower elevations, some from higher elevations, and some almost unique to this zone. The habits of birds and animals are adapted to the elevation and the climate, and are described in more detail later in the chapter.

The Subalpine Belt. This is the indefinite zone of timberline, not really forested but not really bare, extending from the lodgepole level up to 10,000 or 11,000 feet. The trees are tough, slow-growing whitebark and foxtail pines, with some lodgepoles and mountain hemlock—a pleasant tree which makes groves in sheltered places almost at timberline.

The Alpine Belt. This is the real "High Sierra." Even willows have met their match here; where they

Stands of dead lodgepole pines testify to the power of the little needleminer moth, whose larvae ate away their needles. But the pines have their own power: a new generation always rises.

The golden-mantled ground squirrel is often confused with its smaller cousin, the chipmunk. Common to the Lodgepole and Subalpine belts, it is preyed upon by weasels, coyotes, and hawks.

get a toehold at all, they may grow only six inches high, sharing the scarce soil with perhaps forty low-growing grasses, sedges, and tiny flowering plants. The little flowers grow singly or in miniature gardens, a delight to the few hardy climbers who behold them. Few weather records are kept up here; the growing season may be measured in days.

(The Subalpine and Alpine belts are mostly in the southern Sierra, and are a world in themselves. See Chapters 6, 11, and 14.)

The Sagebrush Belt, an extension of the Great Basin desert type of growth, is almost entirely limited to the east side of the range, although it penetrates partly into Sierra Valley in the north. Here are the piñon pines and Utah juniper, low growing and hardy. The piñon is nearly covered with needles which conceal the bark and branches, with nuts that were a staple in the Indian diet; the juniper is thin, crooked, and sparsely

scattered. Both grow in the open, often sticking up among bitterbrush and sagebrush. Though trees, they are sometimes not as tall as a companion shrub, the mountain or desert mahogany. The growing season may be two to five months, depending on elevation and exposure.

THE MOST ACCESSIBLE PART of the Sierra is the Yellow Pine Belt, so this has become, with time and travel, the best known and, to most persons, the most typical. With the yellow pines or near them grow sugar pine, Douglas fir, white fir, and incense cedar, all evergreen conifers; also black oak, cottonwood, broadleaf maple, and California dogwood—chastely beautiful with white blossom-like leaves in the spring but a brazen hussy of red and gold in the fall. In wet places the bushy azalea blooms, brilliant and fragrant in summer, and on the

The ringtail, sometimes called the miner's cat, lives near water in the rocks or brush of the foothills and lower Yellow Pine Belt. A night-time predator, it helps to keep down the population of mice and other rodents.

dry slopes the low-lying, tarry mountain-misery creeps. Interspersed with all, especially where a hillside has been burned, is manzanita. A great variety of other plants is here, and in these elevations also grows the *Sequoia gigantea*—the "Big Tree" or giant redwood. (See Chapter Five.)

It would seem simple to walk for miles cross-country through such open woods, but it is not. One obstacle to free roaming is the terrain itself—a pleasant, carefree walk may end at a steep canyon or a stream bank of broken rock, difficult to climb down and often blocked by undergrowth along the streambed. Even where the terrain is somewhat level, as on the long finger ridges, the pine forest is interrupted by patches of brush—sometimes the spiny whitethorn, more often one of the six kinds of Sierran manzanita. The thorn bush can be navigated with some difficulty and only a little loss of blood, for it grows only knee or hip high, and it is pos-

sible to step on its springy branches and so make one's way; but the manzanita is head high or higher, and its stiff multiple trunks and brittle, thin branches make an almost impossible barrier in many places. In Spanish, *manzanita* means "little apple," named for its berry, which is relished by many animals including bears (in some localities, it is called "bear berry") . It grows well on old wildfire scars, and in some places the brushfields extend for miles. Under the canopy of leaves and below the thicket of small branches, life goes on, and low, tunnel-like trails lead here and there, invisible from outside.

Where there is a good trail, however, walking through the Yellow Pine Belt is refreshing and entertaining, filled with variety in plant and animal life and with the feel of many kinds of earth underfoot. There may be an unusual tree—perhaps a yew or a nutmeg, near a stream. Or there may be a glimpse of a large bird

CONES OF SIERRAN FORESTS

SPECIES	SIZE	DESCRIPTION
Yellow pine	3 to 5 inches long	Reddish-brown; egg-shaped with flat base showing but little stem; scales thicker near the tip, which ends in a small barb
Sugar pine	11 to 20 inches long	Often slightly curved, with stem at the rounded base; scales of nearly uniform thickness
White fir	2 to 5 inches long	Light-colored; cylindrical; many fan-shaped scales; cones found on ground are most often green, knocked down by wind or squirrels, because mature cone disintegrates on tree, losing its scales after seeds have dropped
Incense cedar	1 inch long	Tiny fruit (for such a big tree) has only two scales
Douglas-fir	2 to 3 inches long	Reddish-brown; oval; less hard and woody than other cones and more easily crushed
Sequoia	2 to 4 inches long	Oblong, with 34 to 40 thick scales and 150 to 250 seeds

sweeping over a canyon—a redtailed hawk or golden eagle. A group of dusky grouse may move away from the trail; they live all year in the conifer country, eating the tips of the needles when berries are not available, surviving the severe Sierra winter well insulated by their thick plumage.

If the snow has not been gone for long, and the duff and litter of the forest floor has not yet dried out, there may be a snowplant—bright red against the dark ground. It is a foot or so high, branchless and leafless but with overlapping bracts, tight against the stem at the bottom, loosely curling at the top. Sometimes it grows singly, sometimes in a cluster, but always so swiftly that it seems to burst forth full-bodied; where it comes out of the ground, the litter is often pushed up and displaced as if by a small explosion. Next year's plant is partly formed this year and awaits just the right combination of warmth and moisture to burst out. The snowplant lives on decaying material, as a fungus does, and has no chlorophyll. Another saprophyte growing in the forest humus is the pinedrop, not as bright or as red but much taller, more like a wand than a pineapple. This one does not disappear after flowering but stands sere until the next snow knocks it down.

Everywhere on the ground there are dried pine or fir cones from which the seeds are already missing, and sometimes a green one either intact or shredded by a small animal. They make an interesting collection.

The pine woods *smells* good, an aromatic blending of bark, pitch, and needles; it *feels* good, the mixture of sun and shade controlling the temperature, the ground underfoot carpeted with needles; it *looks* good, for a characteristic of this forest, besides the impressive appearance of the trees themselves, is its cleanliness.

Winged scavengers such as the vulture and four-footed scavengers such as the raccoon and coyote are constantly on the prowl to remove dead animals; ants, flies, bees, larvae, bacteria, and mold work on smaller bits of dead tissue; and very quietly, often unseen, the ever-present fungus does its work. A pervasive network of rootlike fungus threads laces the top layer of ground wherever there is dead plant tissue to provide nourishment, and eventually a mushroom will appear, or a bracket-like growth on the side of a trunk. From the visible part come millions of spores, which are spread by wind, water, or animals. The scavenging system is essential to the forest but seldom heeded by the visitor.

The lower edge of the area in which the red fir grows interweaves only a little with the yellow pines, so the transition is noted almost instantly; but the upper edge where it mixes with lodgepole is very indistinct, so that the two trees seem to grow together along one strip, but with more fir on the lower side, more lodgepole on the upper.

Red firs grow close together, and their crowns touch so less light penetrates to the floor; this, with the dark trunks, makes a less inviting woods. The ground is usually littered with broken branches and uprooted or broken-off trees, so for human beings walking is less comfortable; but there are many creatures who find this protection appealing. A characteristic of this woods is the abundance of burrows under down-logs and in

The pileated woodpecker may reach a foot and a half in length. When it digs ants and larvae from a tree trunk, chips fly two feet or more, and the sound can be heard for hundreds of yards.

the disturbed dirt around exposed roots where a tree has blown down. There seem to be more mold at work breaking down the fallen material, more fungi, and an abundance of spiders. While these may make the red fir forest unattractive to people—such things being enthusiastically kept out of homes in the cities and suburbs—they are really not offensive and are essential to this part of the woods.

The lodgepole (sometimes wrongly called tamarack, or tamrac) is one of the Sierra's most adaptive natives. It frequently grows along the edges of wet meadows, encroaching on grass and flowers, but it just as often grows on gravelly slopes which seem devoid of moisture. Where it forms dense forests or thickets, the trunks are slim and straight, making them indeed useful for poles or cabin building; but where it grows singly or in exposed locations, it may have divided trunks or a short, stubby base trunk with confusing outgrowths at the top, and under some kinds of stress it may wrap around a boulder to get away from the wind or snowslides. Lodgepole roots can crack huge blocks of granite.

Scattered along the upper part of this belt are silver pine, also called western white pine; Jeffrey pine, which looks much like a western yellow but the bark tastes different; and sometimes a stray sugar pine a little above its normal habitat. The Sierra juniper lives here, too, growing old but not tall and sometimes almost as thick as it is high, preferring the granite ridges where it is spectacularly deformed by wind, snow, and lightning; if trees possess courage, this one has it in abundance. By contrast, the quaking aspen (at similar elevations but in damper places) seems almost timid and gentle, trembling in the slightest wind—an impression which belies its tenacity in living through the winter when snowdrifts press it almost prostrate to the ground. The low plants at this elevation are the familiar manzanita, small shrubs such as chinquapin and snowbrush, and the odd huckleberry oak, which never stands taller than four feet and more often just hugs the rocks—an oak, but hardly the mighty oak of poets.

Major birds among the red fir and lodgepole are goshawks, a sapsucker, a flycatcher, two or three sparrows, a towhee with a green tail, and many others that come and go. Little brown bats invisible in the daytime come out at dusk, swinging through the air in search of insects. After dark, the flying squirrels start their rarely seen act of climbing up a tree, launching themselves into the air with legs wide to spread out a web of skin, gliding 75 to 100 feet through the air, and landing upright with a gentle *bump* on the lower bark of another tree only to repeat the process in search of nuts, seeds, insects, fungus, and perhaps small animals. There are many of these soft, big-eyed creatures, but they stay hidden by day and at night are just an unseen part of the quiet rustling in the woods.

Another hard-to-see animal is the pocket gopher. It spends most of its life underground, tunneling under the snow in winter, burrowing underground in summer and leaving mounds of dirt at the burrow entrances. Its chief foods are green vegetation, roots, and bulbs, which it carries in external pouches in its cheeks. In some parts of the forest, moles push around under the litter, too, seeking earthworms, insects, larvae, buried seeds, and occasionally some other smaller animal. Ferocious shrews run on the surface or in and out of the burrows of other animals, always hungry when awake, eating anything they can catch.

The snowshoe rabbit sleeps in a thicket by day and forages at night for grasses, herbs, and shrubs. It wears a dark brown coat in the summer and a white one in the winter. Golden-mantled ground squirrels, on the other hand, are anything but invisible; they seem to be everywhere. These vegetarians are much relished by weasels, coyotes, and hawks.

Deer mice and brush mice are common in the forest on both sides of the Sierra, reproducing rapidly and making a staple food for owls, snakes, and carnivores in general. Bushy-tailed wood rats carry on their trading activities, living in rockpiles in a nest much more casual than the one their foothill relatives build.

The trees and large shrubs are the most visible living things in the Sierra, but in them, under them, and around them life teems. The deer that poises for a second on the roadside and then leaps into the underbrush is spectacular, but no more important a part of the scene than the spider or the bacteria hidden away in the soil. There are more bacteria than insects, more insects than birds, more birds than deer, more deer than mountain lions . . . and the serene and quiet landscape is deceptive. Visible to those who will look, there is constant activity, for this great range is home to millions of living things, from microbes to mountain lions.

The mountain coyote is often heard but seldom seen. Usually a lone traveler, it keeps up a constant hunt for food. Coyotes are smaller than wolves, for which they are sometimes mistaken.

Chapter 5

THE BIG WOODS

*The largest and nearly the oldest of all living things,
the giant sequoia—found nowhere else on earth*

O F ALL THE LIVING THINGS which carpet and populate the slopes and crags of the Sierra Nevada, none has so profoundly captured the public imagination as the *Sequoia gigantea* (or Big Tree, or Sierra redwood)—the largest and almost the oldest living thing on earth. Hundreds of quivering poems have attempted to capture its awesome impact; songs have been written, movies made, and philosophers stricken with purple excess. It is understandable enough: not only is its sheer bulk overwhelming, but many of the sequoias we see today were struggling saplings before the rise of the Athenian Empire, before Aristotle, Pericles, or Socrates gave their gifts of mind to the world.

None was more impressed with these trees or loved them more than John Muir, who became the prose laureate of the sequoias in 1878: "The average stature attained by the Big Tree under favorable conditions is perhaps about 275 feet, with a diameter of twenty feet. . . . Yet so exquisitely harmonious are even the very mightiest of these monarchs in all their proportions and circumstances, there never is anything over-grown or huge-looking about them, not to say monstrous; and the first exclamation on coming upon a group for the first time is usually, 'See what beautiful trees!' Their real godlike grandeur in the meantime is invisible, but to the loving eye it will be manifested sooner or later, stealing slowly on the senses like the grandeur of Niagara, or of some lofty Yosemite dome. Even the mere arithmetical greatness is never guessed by the inexperienced as long as the tree is comprehended from a little distance in one harmonious view. When, however, we approach so near that only the lower portion of the trunk is seen, and walk round and round the wide bulging base, then we begin to wonder at their vastness, and seek a measuring rod.

"Sequoias bulge considerably at the base, yet not more than is required for beauty and safety; and the only reason that this bulging is so often remarked as excessive is because so small a section of the shaft is seen at once. The real taper of the trunk, beheld as a unit, is perfectly charming in its exquisite fineness, and the appreciative eye ranges the massive columns, from the swelling muscular instep to the lofty summit dissolving in a crown of verdure, rejoicing in the unrivaled display of giant grandeur and giant loveliness."

The Sierra redwood is related to the more numerous coast redwood but is much more massive. The mountain tree reaches 35 feet thick and 300 feet high, and some are as old as 4,000 years—second in age only to the bristlecone pine.

Several characteristics of the sequoia contribute to its long life. The protective layer of bark is very thick —as much as two feet in a mature tree—and is fireproof because it contains no resin. Being porous, the bark also insulates the growing layers of the tree from heat and cold. Since the bark is a poor conductor of electricity, frequent lightning strikes rarely succeed in killing the tree, even when they are direct enough to break off limbs or split the trunk. Under the bark, the sequoia manufactures chemicals that prevent or discourage disease, decay, and insect attacks. Because of its very

In sheer bulk, the General Sherman is the largest tree in the world—thirty-two feet in diameter at the base. Perhaps 3,500 years old, it is still living and producing fertile seeds.

The roots of a fallen sequoia may be as much as forty feet across.
It is not surprising that many of these giants fall; though towering to 300 feet and higher,
they have no tap root.

The sequoias in this group are fairly young. As they become older, the lowest branches break off.
the conical top often gives way to a dead stump, and the bark can become as thick as two feet. Sequoias
mingle with firs and pines in a mixed grove.

The Parker Group in Sequoia National Park has some of the finest specimens that can be reached by auto. They show the typical columnar shape, the swollen base, and the clear sweep to the first branches—sometimes 150 feet above the ground.

size, a mature tree may have so much sapwood and cambium that it can go on growing even after a large part of the tree has been destroyed. The most vulnerable part of the Big Tree is its roots; they are relatively shallow for the height and bulk of the tree, spreading over a broad area in order to draw nutrients from decaying leaves and soil chemicals near the surface. Even heavy foot traffic by visitors to a grove can damage the roots. It is believed that many down trees in sequoia groves did not die while standing but fell when their shallow roots lost their grip on the earth.

Once established, the sequoia seems to continue to grow forever, but getting started is a problem. This is in no way the fault of the tree itself, which is wonderfully fruitful. Each year the mature tree bursts out in tiny yellow blossoms, male and female on the same tree, between February and April. After a windstorm, the snow may be powered with golden pollen. By autumn the blossoms have developed into cones about the size of a hen's egg, each with from 150 to 250 winged seeds. A single branch of a large tree may contain two hundred or more cones, so literally billions of seeds find their way to the forest floor. But as John Muir wrote, "Nature takes care . . . that not one seed in a million shall germinate at all, and of those that do perhaps not one in ten thousand is suffered to live through the vicissitudes of storm, drought, fire and snow-crushing that beset their youth."

Even reaching an age where drought and such things *become* a problem is not easy. The seed must land on mineral soil to sprout, and in the sequoia groves there is little such soil; the forest floor is covered with a thick layer of organic material, decaying branches, and cones of many varieties. In Indian and prehistoric days, groundfires ran through the mountains, controlling the undergrowth and burning away the litter and duff so that patches of mineral soil were available. The marks of old fires are highly visible on the giant trees, the scars sometimes reaching forty or fifty feet up the trunk. Some trees are still alive though burned out in the center with cavities large enough to shelter sixteen cows or afford living space for a man.

Unlike their coastal cousins, Sierra redwoods do not live alone. Growing among the giants are immense sugar pines, huge in their own right but seeming slender beside the thick trunk of the sequoia; and there are incense cedars, only a little smaller than the sugar pines but a minor third in this company. White firs, which make spectacular forests when alone, seem like junior partners.

There are about seventy-five groves of Big Trees in the Sierra, along a 2,500-mile strip between 4,500 and 8,000 feet above sea level, most of them in Tulare and Fresno counties in the southern part of the range; most are in national parks, but two groves are in a state park.

The first widely known sequoia grove came into public knowledge in 1852, during the gold excitement, although there had been other reports of Big Trees earlier. This grove was between the Stanislaus and Mokelumne rivers, at about 5,000 feet elevation. By 1854, a hotel had been built to accommodate the hundreds of visitors, and that year the bark was stripped off one tree to a height of 116 feet for exhibit; the dead tree is still standing. Tourists kept coming, for these marvels were more accessible than those near Yosemite Valley. While the pilgrims gaped at huge columnar trunks or measured for themselves the sixty-foot circumferences, botanists on both sides of the Atlantic were trying to gain some national pride from the spectacular trees: the British wanted to name the species *Wellingtonia,* and the Americans wanted to name it *Washingtonia.* In the end, the Big Trees and their coastal cousins, the *sempervirens,* were named for an Indian chief from Oklahoma!

Not so long ago—four generations in the life of a man, a few inches in the growth of the mature trees— these huge sequoias were being destroyed. Some were cut for lumber (although, because of the coarse and generally weak grain of the wood, the sequoia was not a prime target for the lumber industry—particularly since the Sierra was rich in the various pines and the coast boasted immense stands of the eminently more durable coastal redwood, ripe for marketing).

Man made the Big Tree an object of curiosity, the subject of stunts. The stump of one tree (if such an enormous chunk of wood could ever be called a stump) became a dance floor; little two- and three-room cottages were constructed inside the bark of fallen giants and hauled about the country for citizens to gape at; and in the Mariposa Grove south of Yosemite, the Wawona Tree sported an archway carved through its base for the giggling delight of tourists, who drove their buggies and later their automobiles through it with persistent regularity. Undoubtedly weakened by the evisceration, the Wawona Tree has collapsed. Others were sacrificed for display (the outside of one was stripped and sent to England to prove that such a tree existed), or just for the novelty of it (a giant was felled after twenty-three days of labor just to see if it could be done; the crash was heard fifteen miles away).

If any sequoias were to be saved for future generations to marvel at, the groves had to be acquired, and so they were. At least one far-sighted lumber company cut all around its grove but not within it, waiting for a slow-moving state to take it over—which eventually it did.

Today a gray squirrel or a chickaree—that small, noisy, and fast-moving squirrel common in the Sierra —may dash up a redwood, tear off fibers of bark, and run back to line a new nest, but he is about the only Californian whose home can be built with the *Sequoia gigantea.* Though the squirrels leave scooped-out hollows in the thick bark of the trees, arousing the curiosity of observant visitors, they cause no harm, for the bark is one to three feet thick. The tree continues to grow as it has through fires, blizzards, and great winds since before the birth of Christ.

Some 99 percent of the remaining giant sequoias are preserved in 36,000 scattered acres of groves. In Calaveras State Park, for example, there are 158 sequoias in the north grove and 947 in the south grove. Like many of the others, some of these have been given names. Mrs. Grover Cleveland, for instance, is 200 inches around at six feet above the ground and would produce twelve sawlogs 16 feet long if logging were permitted; from her 264-foot height could be sawed 124,770 board feet of lumber (enough to build a small village of wooden houses), and there would be 4,740 substandard board feet left over for the chicken houses and other outbuildings.

Such statistics may convey some idea of the immensity of the Big Tree—of its relationship to the works and concerns of men. But the dignity of its grace and age deserves more than reduction to dimensions and board-feet, and reason insists that no more be cut down for curios or fence posts; for this is the tree that John Muir called "the master-existence of these unrivaled woods . . . a monarch of monarchs."

The most famous stands of "Big Trees" are in Sequoia National Park, but there are scattered groves as far north as Calaveras State Park. The group pictured here is in southern Yosemite.

Overleaf: A wet, clinging snow accents the fluted red bark of these sequoias, and drifts exaggerate the buttresses at the base of the trunks.

*This lonely sentinel atop Sentinel Dome is a Jeffrey pine,
close cousin of the tall Ponderosa, or yellow pine, of the lower
slopes. Its shape has been molded by the wind, and its trunk scarred
by the lightning that plays around these peaks. Jeffrey pines
prefer a well-drained soil with considerable moisture, where
they will grow as tall as two hundred feet; but they manage
to survive on dry slopes as high as 10,600 feet, and even on bare
granite ledges such as this.*

*At lower elevations, where living is easier, dozens of species crowd together,
competing for the more plentiful moisture and more hospitable soil. This
mixed forest is a good example. The two large trees at left are incense cedars,
named for their distinctive aroma; behind them are white firs, identifiable
by their large flat branches with needles growing upward; to the right
of the dead white fir is a Douglas-fir, the most important lumber tree
in North America. In the foreground are manzanita bushes, ubiquitous shrubs of
the Sierra slopes and foothills.*

93

Lichens make a showy splash on a boulder as they go about their business of breaking down the rock chemically. A partnership of an alga and a fungus, they work together, each dependent on the other.

From a distance the high country looks barren, but the visitor who is willing to take to the trail will find lush meadows tucked among the peaks, watered by many, often nameless streams and lakes.

High above Washburn Lake, the battered skeleton of an ancient juniper continues the struggle for life with one solitary branch of green thrust up to the sun.

*The weathered remains of two foxtail pines show clearly this tree's limited height
(from 20 to 50 feet) and thick, tapering trunk. Foxtails, named for their branch-hugging needle
pattern, are often mistaken for bristle-cone pines, which grow east of the Owens Valley.*

Many low-growing plants have adapted to the rigors of high country life, among them showy yellow wallflowers and red Indian paintbrush. Gray basin sagebrush, far right, finds living conditions here surprisingly like its native desert.

Overleaf: A timberline slope near the headwaters of Bishop Creek.

Golden eagle and eaglet.

Pika, an appealing alpine rodent.

Ladybird beetles.

Clark nutcracker.

Chipmunk on forest floor.

House wren at its nest.

Hummingbird and snowplant.

Satin bells.

Leopard lily.

Rose epilobium.

Prickly poppy.

Indian paintbrush.

Common camas.

Spice bush.

Red columbine.

Indian pink.

Pinedrop.

Western blue flag.

102

*Fields of purple camas are a common
sight in Yosemite and other
upland meadows.*

Chapter 6

HIGH-COUNTRY MEADOWS

*The harsh and beautiful home of bighorn sheep, gnarled
whitebark pines, and delicate flowering heather*

ABOVE THE THICK FOREST BELT, up where there is more rock than soil and where the wind is more insistent; in the harder country where the growing season is two months a year or less, and where there can be killing frosts in any month; up where snow comes before Thanksgiving and may still be on the ground on the Fourth of July—these are the Subalpine and Alpine belts. At this elevation and in these surroundings, the challenge of life and growth is formidable, but some plants and animals manage to prosper. This is a setting that challenges the hiker, too, and gives him some of the rewards in satisfaction and accomplishment known only to those who have been on the high places. Awareness seems intensified. John Muir, in *The Mountains of California,* said.

"I made my bed in the nook of the pine thicket, where the branches were pressed and crinkled overhead like a roof and bent down around the sides. These are the best bedchambers our Alps afford—snug as squirrel nests, well ventilated, full of spicy odors, and with plenty of wind-played needles to sing one asleep. I little expected company, but, creeping in through a low side door, I found five or six birds nestling among the tassels. The night wind began to blow soon after dark; at first, only a gentle breathing, but increasing toward midnight to a violent gale that fell upon my leafy roof in ragged surges, like a cascade, and bearing strange sounds from the crags overhead. The waterfall sang in chorus, filling the old ice fountain with its solemn roar, and seeming to increase in power as the night advanced —fit voice for such a landscape."

The lower edge of the Subalpine Belt may be anywhere from 7,000 to 9,000 feet, depending on latitude and such local conditions as topography and exposure; it blends into the red fir woods. The upper edge merges into the Alpine Belt, which continues upward until it runs out of peaks.

Rock, meadows, trees, and water intermingle, and there is no real forest. In this rare air, lodgepole pines give up their fraternal instincts and grow singly, usually stunted by cold, often pressed into picturesque shapes by snow; down lower their dense groves may have been formed by prolific seed germination after a forest fire, but on the heights there are no forest fires, so seeds must be transported by wind, water, birds, or animals —if not eaten first.

A few sugar pines may grace the ridges of the Subalpine Belt, and silver pines (or western white pines) grow in the lee of an outcropping of rock up to 11,000 feet or so, becoming big straight trees, either singly or in small groups.

Another pine, the whitebark, grows on more exposed places, occasionally reaching 35 or 40 feet. It may grow almost horizontally, and its dense branches make a shelter for small life. Nutcrackers and squirrels usually find the few seeds produced in short purplish-brown cones, so that there is little reproduction of the trees. Those seeds which do find a hospitable crack grow infinitely slowly, and the little tree behind which a hiker may take refuge from the wind is very, very old.

Two other pines grow at high elevations, but are not common and are not found in the northern Sierra at

*The high slopes burst into bloom all at once as dozens of species hurry to make
use of the short summer above timberline. In the distance are the Minarets.*

SOME PLANTS OF THE ALPINE BELT

SPECIES	DESCRIPTION	INTERESTING CHARACTERISTICS
HEATH FAMILY		
Red mountain heather (purple heather, alpine heather)	Dwarf evergreen 4 to 12 inches high; stems grow close together; produces small, rounded fruit	Grows in swampy places
White heather (western mountain heather or Cassiope)	Wiry stems and branches with small, bell-shaped white or pink flowers; small, round fruit	Branches form dense mat on rocky ledges
Alpine laurel	Pink or rosy-purple blossoms; small fruit capsules; evergreen	Found up to 12,000 feet in wet places; grows as tall as 6 feet at lower elevations but much smaller on peaks; fruit edible for livestock but leaves poisonous
Sierra laurel	Erect-growing, with hanging white blossoms	Only occasionally found higher than the Lodgepole Belt
Sierra primrose	2 to 4 inches high with reddish-purple flower	Creeps under overhanging rocks; the hiker's flower—found from 8,000 to 13,000 feet
ROSE FAMILY		
Wild strawberry	White blossoms on short stems	Found as high as 10,500 feet; delicious fruit when ripe
Yellow or shrubby cinquefoil	6 inches to 4 feet high; pale yellow flower that resembles strawberry blossom in shape; fruit is small, hard achene	Grows from foothills to about 12,500 feet; very adaptable
BUCKWHEAT		
Knotweed, sulfur flower, oval-leaved buckwheat	Small clump of leaves close to the ground, with taller stem bowing slightly under the weight of a white, yellow, or rosy flower, or later in the season, seeds	Found in dry places up to 10,000 feet
MUSTARD		
Lemmon's draba	Yellow blossoms; short, compact, leafy stems	Commonest form of draba; often found growing in a crack in the rock
White mountain draba	White blossoms	Relatively scarce; may be found up to 13,000 feet
MISCELLANEOUS		
Mountain sorrel	Greenish flowers on 8- or 10-inch stem	
Rock flowers	1 or 2 inches high with yellow blooms	
Ivesia	Disc-shaped yellow flower on stem less than 4 inches high	
Gentians	Blue flowers on stem up to 14 inches long	Grows in high, wet meadows, some varieties as high as 12,000 feet
Sierra stonecrop	Up to 6 inches high, with fleshy basal leaves and white or yellow flowers	Likes rocky slopes to 13,000 feet
Alpine saxifrage	Bare stem 12 to 36 inches high; white flower	Grows in wet meadows up to 11,000 feet
Sierra pentstemon	Bluish-purple or bright red blossoms on matted stems; leaves are clustered close to the ground	Called "Pride of the Mountains"; grows in rocky places up to 12,000 feet
Polemonium (sky pilot)	Dense growth of showy blue flowers; stem 2 to 9 inches long, growing from basal leaves	Member of Gilia family; grows above 10,000 feet and is often found where there are no other blooming plants
Also: club moss, cliff brake, rock brake, fruitillary, bitterroot, rockfringe, pipsissewa, dwarf alpine paintbrush, white phlox, and others		

SOME PLANTS OF THE ALPINE BELT (continued)

SPECIES	DESCRIPTION	INTERESTING CHARACTERISTICS
GRASSES		
Small sheep fescue	Grows in dense tufts	Alpine grasses grow short and bear little resemblance to the deep-growing fescues and bluegrasses of wetter, more fertile land
Timberline bluegrass	Tufts have purplish hue	
Suksdorf's bluegrass	Has smooth stems	
SEDGES		
Brewer's	Has a solitary spike	Sedges prefer damp places and grow less than 12 inches high
Heller's	Grows in dense tufts	
Spiked wood rush	Grows very stiff and erect	
RIBES		Members of Saxifrage family; 9 varieties of ribes in Sierra, but only two at alpine elevations; for many years they were systematically uprooted by the U. S. Department of Agriculture because they harbored the fungus white pine blister, which lowered the commercial value of five-needle pine
White squaw currants	Low shrubs with red berries	
Alpine prickly currants		

all: the limber pine, found mostly on the east slope with a few near the South Fork of the Kings River, seeming to be more branches than trunk; and the Foxtail Pine, found around the headwaters of the San Joaquin River, usually with the tip of the trunk sticking up dead and dry from the dense foliage.

Small groves or scattered groups of mountain hemlock stand where there is some protection from the wind, sometimes reaching 90 or 100 feet high but usually no more than half that; often the trunk is quite thick for its height. The slender, flexible branches, thick with short, blue-green needles, grow all along the trunk from the ground up, and the lower tiers often are bent down so that they touch the ones beneath them and afford some shelter. Seeds from narrow cones provide food for small animals and birds. Hemlocks grow slowly, and they grow very old.

So do Sierra junipers—tough, adaptable, picturesque, and a lavish provider of berries to sustain the birds. Along the Lodgepole Belt, the juniper may grow profusely and sometimes 50 or 60 feet high (usually with a conical trunk, which often divides into many parts, part way up). Out on the granite ridges, though, the juniper presses its heavy roots into a crack, or several cracks, with part of the root reaching out across the open rock. It grows away from the wind, putting out only enough foliage to sustain it. Sometimes it aban-

dons its original upward thrust and puts out a long branch or two to leeward instead. The leaning trunk and long down-wind branches are caused not only by the pressure of the wind but also by stunting of the growing tips through drying or bombardment with particles of granite or ice. Too, a thicker and healthier cambium layer grows away from the wind and allows easier passage of water and food between roots and leaves, so that the tree tends to grow best in the direction of the least shock and pressure—not cringing before the blast or evading the elements, but adapting. Without juniper trees, timberline would be much lower.

Willows are trees which sometimes look like shrubs elsewhere, but at the high elevations of the Sierra, the alpine willow is only three or four inches high. Growing in dampish places, it makes a mat with creeping stems and short, erect branches.

The high meadows, some wide open and some with scattered trees growing in or around them, would excite no envy in a farmer who has acres of lush green pasturage—for these are "short-hair" meadows, sparse and often austere, although with a beauty of their own to a hiker coming down from the rocky places. The sight of white heather—also called western mountain heather, or simply Cassiope—prompted John Muir to write: "Here . . . I met Cassiope growing in fringes among the battered rocks. . . . Her blossoms had faded long ago,

Alpine trees stand as dramatic witnesses to the tenacity of living things. The junipers at left and above have found a toehold in the cold granite of some craggy height, where they somehow survive cold and wind, parching and the poverty of soil the rock affords. The shade and shelter and falling needles of the trees help to make the environment a little more inviting for smaller plants that have taken up residence in pockets of soil at their feet. Despite its skeletal appearance, the tree at left is still living.

It is hard to believe that this dwarf pine, rootbound and prostrate on a boulder, is actually a lodgepole, whose brothers stand tall and straight in better soil at lower elevations.

but they were still clinging with happy memories to the evergreen sprays, and still so beautiful as to thrill every fiber of one's being. Winter and summer you may hear her voice, the low sweet melody of her bells. No evangel among all the mountain plants speaks Nature's love more plainly than Cassiope."

The low ground-covering includes grasses, sedges, and rushes, all adapted to the elevation, the lack of rain, and the short growing season. When sheep were indiscriminately herded into the mountains for summer grazing, some of these meadows were set back so far they may never recover. The roots and stems of

plants hold the soil together and help hold moisture, too, so that where the growing covering is eaten or scuffed away by hoofs or feet, erosion starts immediately; once started, there seems no natural way at this elevation to stop it, for new plants cannot take root well in the rocky subsoil, and there is little in the way of organic material floating down from above, as in the forests further down the slope.

Some alpine plants live from year to year, putting out new branches or runners from a "permanent" stem or trunk. Others grow new stems and leaves each year —an almost explosive feat where the growing season is so short. A characteristic of many high-elevation plants is the concentration of foliage close to the ground, and the extension of the flower and the seed on a somewhat longer stem. But some plants never lift any part much more than an inch or two into the wind.

More than one hundred flowering plants grow around 9,000 feet, despite what seem to be inhospitable surroundings. In some places the plants are scattered, even solitary; elsewhere there are rock gardens bright with the color of numerous species so arranged they would appear to have been planted to some mortal plan. The fringes of the streams and lakes may have from six to a dozen or more kinds of plants.

On the rocks grow lichens, a delicate partnership between a fungus and an alga that somehow survives adversity; some of them are centuries old. Some have grown with exquisite slowness, for the lichen cannot prosper unless conditions are exactly right for both partners—what is good for the fungus might not be good for the alga, and vice versa, and only at certain places does exactly the right situation occur. Some lichens use animal excrement for food so grow best where birds or mammals congregate.

In and out of the subalpine meadows and the rocky places where the flowers grow go many birds and a number of animals, but fewer live in the pure alpine environment. There are four or five kinds of mice, busy day and night in search of food, which varies from seeds to insects to green vegetation; these mice are so numerous they make an important part of the food chain. Their smallest enemy is the shrew, but they are also prey for martens, fishers, wolverines, weasels, badgers, red foxes, coyotes, hawks, owls, and eagles—all of which live in the highlands or spend some time there.

Wolverines and red foxes are scarce (rangers and game wardens believe the wolverine may be nonexistent) although seemingly well adapted for the cold heights; the red fox grows its own snowshoes, for example, in the form of dense fur between the toes.

Alpine chipmunks range as high as 12,500 feet, and lodgepole chipmunks perhaps to 11,000, making their living on seeds and fungi; and golden-mantled ground squirrels have been seen almost to 12,500 feet, usually between May and October as they hibernate all the rest of the year. The Aplodontia (miscalled "mountain beaver") lives up through the Subalpine Belt, wherever

he can tunnel into a stream bank to store plenty of green fodder.

Mule deer are usually considered animals of the forest and brushlands, but they are seen in varying numbers all the way to the crest of the Sierra, wherever they can find browse in the summer; as the weather worsens in the fall, they migrate downward, each herd following about the same pattern year after year. Where deer are, there is a mountain lion or two, and the high country is no exception.

Mountain sheep (or bighorns) once were fairly common from the Yosemite back country southward, but now there may be only a few hundred, mostly on the high east side above Owens Valley, moving easily over rocky places on well-established trails from water to meadow feeding grounds to open bedding places on ledges. Hunters and herders of domestic sheep played havoc with the bighorns, but they are now protected.

The cony, pika, or rock-rabbit holds a special place in the affections of those who explore the high country, even though it often takes some careful stalking to see or photograph one. This little relative of the hare inhabits the talus slopes and other rock piles throughout the Subalpine Belt and often higher, in some places seeming to be the only animal around. Conies look more like guinea pigs than rabbits and make a distinctive sound variously interpreted as a high nasal chick-ick or a whistled eenk-eenk. Because the cony does not hibernate but lives out the winter mostly awake, he gathers stems and leaves of plants around his rock domain, piles them up to dry in the sun, and hoards them against the time when snow covers his landscape and the winter winds howl. In summer, with his short legs and hasty gait, he seems to be flowing rather than running over the jagged rocks, leading the observer to wonder how he keeps from wearing out his underbelly.

Bees come and go at the upper elevations, and the bumblebee lives there the year around, hibernating when times are bad. There are many moths and butter-flies—duskywings, skippers, swallowtails, Parnassians, sulfurs, and blues; the banded elfin, lustrous copper, Ivalida arctic, mountain fritillary, and sometimes the prolific tortoise-shell. These are not all seen in one place, however, as each feeds on certain kinds of plants: the checkered skipper must find mallow; the swallow-tails require plants from the parsley family; the Parnas-

sian needs stonecrop.

While most birds do not find the flying or hunting very good above the Yellow Pine Belt, three or four are high country dwellers. The rosy finch chooses to live above timberline, building a thick nest of moss and dried grass on a cliff crevice or under a rock, breathing in winter through a special protective mask of feathers; it raises a family of four or five young on a rich diet of insects, though the adults eat mostly sedge seeds and other plant material. Small flocks of these birds are common, often darting to the edge of the snow to pick up numb bugs. Pine grosbeaks are seen where the trees thin out, eating needle buds, seeds of trees, and berries. A three-toed woodpecker lives a quiet but active life in the timberline conifers year-round, seen by only the most observant. The Clark nutcracker, sometimes called "camp robber," is less reticent—much less—and with numerous mates goes cawing and flapping around the slopes, foraging for pine nuts, plant seeds, carrion, insects, and whenever possible picking up a tidbit dropped or stored by two-legged visitors.

THE HEIGHTS OF THE SIERRA NEVADA and the desert are closely related—not only in cause and effect, but in the mingling of plants and animals. As moist air moves higher up the western slope of the Sierra, it cools, compresses, and drops moisture; then as it spills over the heights and down the eastern wall, it expands, warms, and absorbs moisture—so that it not only does not bring much water, it may take some away.

This effect starts at high elevations along the escarpment, so that sagebrush can be found as high as 10,000 feet. The bold yellow blooms of rabbit brush that line the mountain roads and trails up to 9,000 feet thrive just as well far out in the Great Basin. Whitebark pine, Jeffrey pine and Sierra juniper, which thrive in dry places, go up and over the crest, and the adaptable lodgepole pine goes with them. The piñon pine, once a source of staple food for the Indians, is a desert type tree, but it grows up to 8,000 feet in the mountains on the east side. Quaking aspen and willows grow along the watercourses on both sides. A large shrub called mountain mahogany in some localities and desert mahogany in others grows far up the eastern slope. Some of the typical Sierran animals and birds live at about

their usual elevations on the east side, but their dry-country cousins are there, too. A fragile truce exists along the eastern slope of the Sierra, based on the amount of moisture that spills over the crest—the effect of the "rain shadow" which has profoundly changed the Great Basin since the time when lush plants and large animals grew there in a moist subtropical climate.

The top of the Sierra, then, is a busy place in spite of its seeming austerity. When the sun beats down from a cloudless and smog-free sky, there is intense activity on the ground and in the air, each day of warmth being more precious here than it would be a few miles east or west or a few thousand feet lower. In the winter it is intensely cold, the chill heightened by a wind that must be almost constant—how constant is not known, because there are few weather records for the highest belts. Because of the wind, and because snow falls heaviest farther down the slope, many places up high are not thick with snow. On the lee side of the crest, where the shadows are never dispersed in the winter, snow accumulates in old cirques, just as it did when the big glaciers were there. It does not survive the summer in a volume big enough to provide more than a few score "rock glaciers" which are a mixture of ice and rock fragments and do not move far.

The world at timberline and above is one of intense radiation when the sky is clear; the thin air, which does not itself hold much heat, does not interfere much with the passage of the sun's rays. Microclimates vary almost inch by inch in some places, and plants and creatures have found how to use these small weather zones (or have perished). In the summer a small cleft or crevice provides warmth and protection; in the winter, the layer of snow does the same, for it is never far below freezing just under the snow.

The Sierra Nevada varies from mile to mile. From the foothills to the highest crests, there is infinite variety; from Lassen Peak in the north to Walker or Tehachapi Pass in the south, the Sierra changes its features yet retains its identity; each valley, each meadow, each crag is something like all the others, yet in some way different. No sweeping statement can describe the entire range: it must be explored part by part, latitude by latitude, elevation by elevation, almost mile by mile—in all its anomalies and paradoxes, in its similarities and contrasts, in all its fascinating places.

Whitebark pine is another species that has adapted to the rigors of timberline. These specimens were photographed in Lassen Volcanic National Park, with Bumpass Mountain in the background.

THE TRAILMAKERS

We traveled a few miles every day, still on the top of the mountain, and our course continually obstructed with snow, hills and rocks. Here we began to encounter in our path, many small streams which ... precipitate themselves from one lofty precipice to another until they are exhausted in rain below. Some of these precipices appear to us to be more than a mile high. Some of the men thought that if we could succeed in descending one of these precipices to the bottom, we might thus work our way into the valley below— but on making several attempts we found it utterly impossible for a man to descend, to saying nothing of the horses.

—Zenas Leonard, clerk of the Walker expedition, in the
Narrative of the Adventures of Zenas Leonard, 1839.

The marks of civilized man on the Sierra Nevada were scarcely visible until the the mid-1800s, although for thousands of years native people had traversed the range on trading or food-gathering expeditions. The Spanish who established the famous string of missions along El Camino Real on the coast, and founded Los Angeles and San Francisco, rarely probed the Sierra foothills, and then only by soldiers in pursuit of Indians who had taken themselves or horses, or both, away from the missions.

By 1772, some of Gaspar de Portola's men had followed the discovery of San Francisco Bay by exploring eastward to the delta where the Sacramento and San Joaquin rivers come together. There Fray Juan Crespi recorded that he and Captain Pedro Fages saw "some high mountains very far distant." Later the same year Captain Fages, far to the south, wrote "the range in-

land is very high, and its peaks are perpetually covered with snow."

In 1776, while thirteen small colonies along the Atlantic were declaring themselves independent of England, the Sierra's present name was recorded for the first time. Missionary Pedro Font stood on a hill near the mouth of the Sacramento River and wrote "... about 40 leagues off, we saw un gran sierra nevada ['snowy sawtooth range'] which ... runs from south-southeast to north-northwest." His term, intended to be merely descriptive, was the one that stuck, despite several other names applied by others—some religious, by the missionaries, and some just the opposite, by the immigrants.

About the same time, Francisco Garces, another missionary with whom Font had earlier traveled overland from Mexico, was in the vicinity of Tehachapi,

115

The jouncing, dusty stage ride over old Wawona Road below Yosemite was sheer luxury compared to the emigrants' trek on foot over trackless granite.

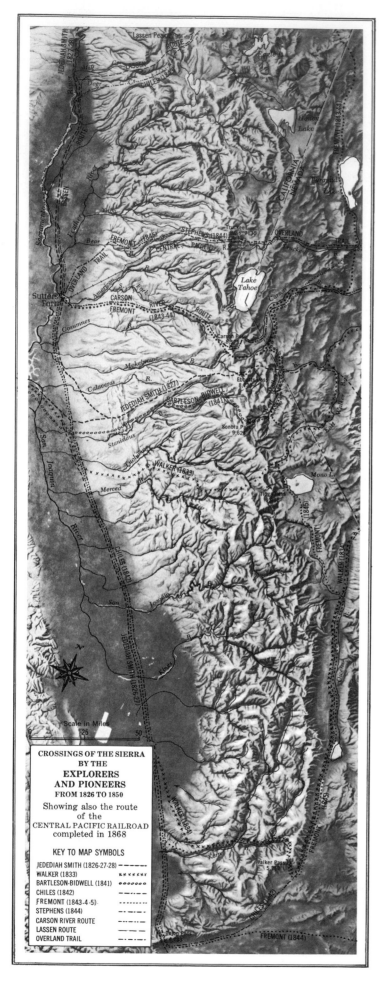

and he named the mountains visible to the north "Sierra de San Marco." Later the two men decided they had been looking at the same range; it is not known whether they discussed a proper name, but by later usage St. Mark lost out to the whiteness of the mountain peaks and by 1817, a later missionary named Narciso Durand referred to "the famous Sierra Nevada" when he saw it from the present site of Sacramento.

The Spanish, having seen it and named it, lost interest in the great range, and it remained for an American fur trapper to make the first recorded crossing of these mountains: Jedediah Strong Smith. Jed Smith may have been the best educated and best informed of all the mountain men who probed the West in search of beaver and other valuable skins.

In early 1826 his probings brought him to southern California, where the Spanish governor summarily ordered him out—out the way he came in, back to the Colorado River by way of the Mojave Desert. This fit neither Smith's plans nor his nature; so instead of retracing his steps all the way, he swung north with his party of trappers into the upper end of the San Joaquin Valley and worked northward along the foot of the Sierra, searching for both good beaver streams and a good way home. There were few beaver, and there seemed no way east. He tried to cross from a camp on what he called the Wimmelche River (now the Kings), but the spring snow was too deep, the canyons too precipitous, the walls too high. He traveled as far as the American River, east of the present state capital, and made a strong attempt at crossing there, but the snow was deep and a storm was making it deeper. His horses were freezing, his men discouraged, and in Smith's own understatement, "utmost exertion was necessary to keep from freezing to death."

The party retraced its path south and set up camp on a river Smith called the Appelamminy, now the Stanislaus. Game seemed more abundant there, and the Indians were friendly enough, but it was essential to get back to Salt Lake in spite of that snow-covered barrier. So on May 20, 1827, Smith set off with two men, seven horses, and two mules, leaving the rest of his party in camp. A week later they were at the top, in the vicinity of Ebbetts Pass, minus two horses and a mule which perished on the snow-drifted trail. In another day—so distinct is the difference between the *terrain of the west and east sides—they were down on the desert near Topaz Lake. A terrible cross-country hike was still between them and Salt Lake (during which they would eat four of their horses and the other mule), but behind them Jedediah Smith, Silas Gobel, and Robert Evans left the first recorded breach in the massive wall of the Sierra Nevada.*

Joseph Reddeford Walker's party, the first known to cross from east to west, picked an even harder way in 1833, one that the road-builders have not tried to follow. The route can only be guessed at by trying to interpret the writing of Zenas Leonard, one of the group. The climb started from Bridgeport, which is only ten or twelve airline miles from the crest but about five thousand feet lower. Even this relatively short climb, which could be done in a day in the summer, was difficult in October after early snows. The party started poorly supplied and probably tired, and when they reached what they thought was the top of the mountains, they were in even worse shape. There was no feed for the horses, which shortly became food for the men as they floundered through deep drifts. At a couple of lakes they found a little exposed grass for the horses, not much and far apart. But they made a few miles westward each day, probably crossing the Tuolumne River between Hetch Hetchy and Tuolumne Meadows. As they crossed smaller streams, scouting parties checked to see if they could follow one out. One day such an exploration took them along a busy stream which ran out to the edge of a chasm. They looked over precipices which "appeared to us to be more than a mile high" and saw, beyond a doubt and for the first recorded time, Yosemite Valley.

Although the waters from the streams could "precipitate themselves from one lofty precipice to another until they are exhausted in rain below," the men and horses could not descend the same way; so the party turned toward the northwest, away from the valley. There was less and less snow to slow them, although the going was sometimes agonizingly hard. A couple of days later they frightened a foraging Indian who dropped a basket of acorns—and in addition to the enjoyment of a meal, they knew they were on the way out of the mountain maze. Deer and bear meat followed as they moved farther down into the foothills. During that stage of the journey, they found some trees

Many early pictures of California were highly imaginative, but this artist caught the mood of the Sierra.

96 to 108 feet around at the height of a man's head— the first recorded sighting of the giant sequoia.

The trip from Bridgeport took the better part of a month. Behind Walker's party lay no usable route across the Sierra, but they had made it against tremendous odds after a tedious crossing of the desert, with almost no food and with equipment so scanty and worn that today's visitor to the marvels of Yosemite and the Big Trees would hesitate to depend on it for a trip to the rest room. In the spring of 1834, Walker started home again. Prudently, he went around the south end of the range, through the low pass which now bears his name. Although the trip was not easy, it was better traveling than the winter before; and when they found the tracks of their westward journey near Bridgeport or east of there, they were well on their way "back to the States."

As the 1840s opened, restless frontiersmen and their families were moving toward Oregon, not to trap but to live. The trail was difficult, they knew, but at least there was a kind of trail and near the end was a river to follow, not a snowy range to cross. But some had heard the call of California, where the climate was benign, the soil rich, the land free. Among these were the Bartleson-Bidwell party of 1841. By mid-October, perilously late in the fall, they were at the eastern base of the Sierra, probably on the West Walker River, low on food and without their abandoned wagons. After some tentative exploration of the mountains that

By the 1860s emigrant trails had become wagon roads, but they were still not for the timid traveler. (One suspects that such a traveler inspired this artist.)

steep eastern side, probably somewhere north of Sonora Pass, and gratefully found a stream that ran westward. It was hard to follow a stream in the narrow and rocky bottom, however, and the party went back on the ridges, which were fortunately still free of snow. They were in the Stanislaus River country, where the long ridges tend westward but are broken by cross ridges and the gulleys of creeks. Part of their frontier lore—wrong in the Sierra—was to follow streams rather than taking to the hilltops, but they made progress each day, struggling along, never comfortable. They came out of the hills at Knights Ferry, and by November 4, 1841, had crossed the San Joaquin Valley and reached the home of Dr. John Marsh on the north side of Mount Diablo, not far from San Francisco Bay. This first crossing of the Sierra by a group of settlers took only about three weeks and was accomplished without casualties. Had there been an early snow, such as occurred a few years later, the tale might have been a different one.

Joseph Chiles was a member of the Bartleson-Bidwell party of 1841, and early the next year he went back to Missouri by way of Walker Pass, avoiding the snow. He organized a large party, loaded the wagons with merchandise and mill machinery, piled in provisions and people including women and children, and by late fall had crossed the plains. The party, by pre-arrangement, split, with veteran Joe Walker guiding the wagons down to his pass on the south end, and Chiles with a faster group taking a vague route around to the north. The plan was to pick up supplies for the wagon train and come back over the top with them. But Chiles did not find the northern route easy or fast; by the time he was ready to cross the range, it had snowed, and he could not do it. The wagon party, with its animals jaded and its stores low, had to abandon the vehicles and the valuable loads, and cross Walker Pass on the tired horses. Another party of settlers had made it, but the first real attempt to move merchandise over the mountains had failed.

John Charles Frémont, who had the best opportunity before 1850 to explore and report on the Sierra Nevada, seems to have had bad luck, ill advice, poor judgment, or a combination of all three, although his expeditions did result in one of the best maps of the early days, done by an unsung cartographer, Charles Preuss. Frémont was an army officer of the Topographical Engi-

lay ahead, the party took a vote and decided to go on.

With great difficulty they reached the summit of the

Overland wagon trains camped in the Carson Valley to rest their animals and prepare for the ordeal of ascending the steep eastern slope of the Sierra Nevada.

neers. In 1844 his urge to explore the West, helped by the fact he was the son-in-law of a powerful U.S. senator, Thomas Hart Benton of Missouri, took him to the eastern foot of the Sierra Nevada near Markleeville. From the cold but almost snow-free upper desert there, Frémont's party floundered westward in snowdrifts which an easterner would find unbelievable. They went up the East Carson River into deeper and deeper snow, determined to reach the Sacramento Valley because they were in such poor shape they could not face the arid trip home. As they left the river and crept up the steep slopes, hampered by the drifts, moving themselves and their sixty-seven animals with difficulty, painfully ascending three thousand feet in a few air miles, they could recognize the bitter truth of an Indian's warning: "Rock upon rock, rock upon rock; snow upon snow, snow upon snow."

When they finally reached the summit, they could see the Great Valley and could pick out Mount Diablo on its western edge, but they were not out of the mountains yet. The temperature was below zero, the men were tired, the food and feed were scant, and the direction to go was unclear because the way to the valley seemed blocked with ridges and cut with canyons—and then it began to snow again. On the thirteenth of that month in 1844, they ate a notable dinner: pea soup, mule, and dog. Cartographer Preuss thought the fare would have been improved if there had been just a little salt. The next day Preuss and Frémont climbed a higher hill for observation, and for the first recorded time Americans saw Lake Tahoe, about fifteen miles to the north.

THE MIGHTY SIERRA

Floundering northwesterly, the party reached Straw-berry Valley on the South Fork of the American, an event which Frémont ceremonialized by falling off a slippery log into the icy stream, out of which he was hauled by Kit Carson. It was not easy from Strawberry to Sutter's Fort, but it was easier than what they had been through; by the first week of March they were safe and had added their party to the roster of the few men who breached the Sierra. Although Frémont crossed the range from east to west once again in 1846, this trip would not match the sheer drama of his first effort —which excelled in flamboyance, if nothing else.

In the spring of 1844, a year after the Chiles party set forth and a few months after Frémont had made it to Sutter's Fort, emigrant parties were forming in Missouri bound for Oregon and California. There was only the vaguest of information to plan on, but a large group of men, eight women, and fifteen children elected Elisha Stephens captain and turned their wagons West. Fortune and good organization prevailed, and the trip across the wasteland, though tedious, went well.

On the Humboldt they were told by a friendly Indian whom they called Truckee to go directly west (instead of southwest as other parties had gone) to a river which rose in the mountains, and perhaps they could cross the Sierra at its head. The river took them to a meadow now occupied by Reno, and from there, with increasing difficulty, to a major fork where a town named Truckee now stands. When snow started falling, a fast party was counted off to head for Sutter's Fort on horseback and bring back supplies and help if the wagons were delayed. The wagons were to go directly west and try to get over the piles of rock and cliffs of granite that could be seen there; not exactly a good route for wagons, but the best that could be found (and, as it turned out, the one that is most used today).

The party on horseback went up the main Truckee River and found Lake Tahoe. On its west side they went up a small stream and over the crest of the range, then down the Rubicon River to the American and to Sutter's Fort. It was November, but the heavy snow was late. Meanwhile, the wagons moved up the smaller branch of the Truckee to Donner Lake. Half of the party decided to cache the wagons at the lake, go ahead

with backpacks, and come back in the spring. The other half pushed against the mountain wall, wagons and all; and by emptying the loads, hooking the oxen to long ropes and chains, and bodily lifting the clumsy vehicles up and over the vertical rocks, they made it.

Or rather, they almost made it. They had crossed the pass, all right, but it was late in November, and the snow began piling up; the wagons so laboriously hoisted up the east face could not go down the west slope. With the wagons as a base, a camp was made a few miles west of the summit, along the upper Yuba River. Two men and all the women and children were made as comfortable as possible, and the other men departed on foot for Sutter's Fort and help. There was enough food and fuel, and by March 1845 relief had come; the camping party got safely out of the mountains—the camping party plus one, for little Elizabeth Yuba Murphy had been born there at the top of the Sierra. In July the Donner Lake wagons were brought down to Sutter's Fort—the Sierra had finally been crossed by wheels.

Several more parties made it over Donner Pass in 1845, each improving to a degree the trail broken before. William Ide found that he and other men could fix up about two miles of the road by removing rocks and trees and making a rough grade, so the wagons would not have to be taken apart as the guide recommended. It was tough on the oxen but made it easier for those who followed.

The year 1846 saw more wagon tongues pointed west than ever before. Most of them got through with only the usual ordeal, but the one that came to be known as the Donner Party combined such bad luck, bad planing, and bad advice with a bad year for snow that it, more than the successful passages, came to epitomize the drama of migration. The wagon trains usually left the frontier on the Mississippi and Missouri rivers in May, as early as travel was possible, and were across the desert and facing the eastern wall of the Sierra by September if all went well; by October if there were delays. It snows some years in October, and for any party that was still along the Truckee by that time, anxiety rode behind each slow-moving ox or mule. So it was for the Donner Party, which arrived at the lake named for them at the end of October 1846. By the time their incredible ordeal was done, only 47 of the 87 who had left Fort Bridger remained alive to tell grisly

For many emigrants gold was the prize that made the hard crossing seem worthwhile. This well-manned placer operation was photographed in 1850 on Sutter Creek near Coloma, where the first color had been found two years earlier.

tales of starvation and cannibalism, in one of the most thoroughly told and ghastly narratives in the frontier experience.

The Sierra Nevada was relatively quiet in 1847, probably because the United States was at war with Mexico, and Mexico had owned California until then. But perhaps ninety wagons made the trip that season; some of them met Jim Bridger and heard about the

Donner tragedy, but none turned back. Each party improved the road over the pass a little; no one was left to face the winter; the wheel tracks were worn a little deeper.

In 1848 the lid came off. At half past seven on the morning of January 24, James W. Marshall picked a fifty-cent flake of gold out of six inches of water in the tailrace of a water-powered sawmill he was building

John Frémont's party crossing the Sierra in midwinter, 1844. This lithograph accompanied the official report

of the expedition, which was published by the Senate in 1846 and by the House the following year.

for Captain John Sutter on the American River at Coloma in the foothills—quiet California was quiet no more.

Much of the gold rush of the next few years came by sea, because from the Atlantic Coast it was easiest to go around Cape Horn or to sail to Panama or Nicaragua, walk across the Isthmus, and embark again for San Francisco. But there were many who came across the plains, and it was inevitable that these would poke and prod at the Sierra in search of an easier way than over Donner Pass—not alone because of that forbidding east wall, but also because of the ridges to cross on the western descent.

A man named Patrick Henness, or Hanness, is generally credited with finding a route to the north of Donner in 1850, but it was mostly used as a foot and horse trail until gold and silver were discovered on the Comstock Lode in Nevada in 1858, when it was widened to take wagons filled with supplies—a reversal of the flow of traffic that usually went over the Sierra. The need for the route diminished with the breaking of the Comstock bubble, and within a few years the wagon road was seldom used, never again to be a major route.

The more northerly Beckwourth Pass was found by explorer Jim Beckwourth (sometimes called Beckwith) in April 1851 and was used by thousands of wagons after being improved by Marysville merchants who saw their town as a terminal. Beckwourth Pass remained a main passageway and now accommodates a state highway and the main line of a railroad.

Neither Henness nor Beckwourth had discovered what was truly an easy route, and the cliffs at Donner Pass, although they had been traversed often in '48, were still not very attractive; it would be the mid-1860s before a real road went over the top there. Much of the tide of travel in 1849 and the early 1850s went painfully up and over Kit Carson Pass, sometimes called Mormon Pass, where the last steep pitch before the summit was known as Devil's Ladder, only a few miles beyond Hope Valley. When this became a U.S. mail route in 1851, it was improved somewhat, and in the 1860s it became a toll road; still later a portion was realigned to an easier grade, and it is now substantially followed by State Route 88.

Although heavily traveled during the gold rush, the Carson Pass road was not good enough. John C. John-son found a more direct way from the Nevada side around the south end of Lake Tahoe and over Echo Summit, then down the South Fork of the American River where he picked up a branch of the Kit Carson route. With the tremendous movement of men and material to and from the Comstock Lode between 1859 and 1866, Johnson's discovery, often called the Placerville Road, was the main artery. Over this road rolled freight wagons, mule trains, men afoot and on horseback, Concord coaches, and the famous but short-lived Pony Express.

For ten years the Placerville Road was the principal breach of the Sierra Nevada, but even as it came into heavy use in 1859, an almost anonymous visionary by the name of Theodore Judah was investigating the possibility of a railroad route across the range. After a determined assault on the mountains, Judah finally calculated that a route very close to that of the old Donner Pass trail would be most suitable; he gained the backing of a group of California merchants and would-be entrepreneurs (forever after known as the Big Four), and after his death they cudgeled the United States Congress out of enough money and land to make construction of the Central Pacific Railroad possible.

This monumental task began in Sacramento in 1863. With the sweat of a small army of Chinese laborers, a twisting, tortuous railroad access was carved into the mountains and up to the summit by early 1868. By the spring of the year, the railroad had been laid into the desert of Nevada near the present site of Reno, and the Central Pacific was well on its way to a rendezvous with the westward-building Union Pacific at Promontory, Utah, an event celebrated on May 10, 1869. The steel bands of the Central Pacific (later Southern Pacific) Railroad were the last major trail across the Sierra Nevada. It is perhaps appropriate that the wagon road that serviced the railroad as it ground its way into the mountains became—with many modifications—the basis for the construction of the major automobile road across the mountains, today's Interstate Highway 80, by which literally hundreds of thousands of pilgrims enter California every year with little or no thought for the emigrants who strained so painfully over the mountains more than a century ago.

In some places along the route, the emigrants faced such formidable walls of granite that they had to dismantle their wagons and haul them to the top with ropes, piece by piece.

PART THREE

SOME

MOUNTAIN

CLOSE-UPS

Sierra river valleys are an important part of both the natural and human history of the range. This is the canyon of the Tuolumne, looking eastward toward the White Mountains on the far horizon.

Chapter 7

AMERICAN RIVER COUNTRY

Route of the emigrants heading west, the railroaders heading east, and modern-day tourists heading everywhere

Down the American river's three main forks comes the water from 1,500 square miles of mountains, draining the central portion of the Sierra Nevada and coming to temporary rest in Folsom Lake. On one of these forks, the south one, the first discovery of gold (there had been other, unnoticed ones) set off the migration known as the gold rush. When James Marshall picked up that small flake in the tailrace of John Sutter's new sawmill in Coloma, the discovery of gold broke the West wide open. In the great triangle of land drained by the American River, man first started changing the Sierra environment, and the process still goes on.

The waters of the American start all the way up at the crest of the range, just west of Lake Tahoe, fed by melt from snow which may have fallen months before. Some of the headwaters and upper tributaries are in wilderness—Desolation Valley, the Rubicon, Granite Chief—and high in the glaciated granite section are many small lakes. Flowing westerly from the ridge, leaving the serene little lakes, the river cuts deeper and deeper gorges, passing rolling uplands between the canyons, until the lesser grades of the foothills slow its pace, and a dam at Folsom finally brings it to a stop; from there, it is doled out to irrigation ditches and hydroelectric turbines. Where it runs deep in a canyon, the river remains nearly in its natural state, crossed only occasionally by a road, flowing and tumbling over ancient bedrock between walls of volcanic and metamorphic rocks, turbulent and forceful in the spring and quieter during the rest of the year.

Along the canyon rims and across the uplands, civilization moves in year by year with paved roads, freeways, new subdivisions, recreation facilities, reservoirs. Like all easily accessible parts of the mountains, the American River country is caught up in the syndrome of general affluence, the gasping of urban people for fresh air, and the demand for winter and summer play areas. The central Sierra also provides a corridor for interstate commerce and main routes for the modern gold rush to the easy money promised by gambling establishments at Reno and Lake Tahoe. Human development appears certain to change the ecology despite attempts of outdoor and conservation groups to slow the pace and efforts of the mountain counties to channel growth with the least destruction; the area still has abundant plant and animal life, much free-flowing water, and extensive forests.

Beneath the surface changes lie the rocks, themselves the product of change and irresistible forces, but changing more slowly as man measures time; even the five or six earthquake faults slicing across the American River provide no surprises. The granite of the area is grayer and less sparkling than it is farther south, and in many places is not as prominent and pervading as it is in the high country. To the north of the American, in the Yuba and Feather River country, the Sierra loses its true identity and eventually disappears under the volcanic overlay of the southern Cascades; to the south of the American, the typical Sierra seems to start.

From the air the terrain appears cut deeply in some places, but gently sloping and marked with high open

The stage route over the Sierra followed the old Placerville Road through the canyon of the American River—a four- or five-day trip for passengers, packages, and mail.

The trestle at Long Ravine—the second stop east of Sacramento—was 1,050 feet in length;
but for the railroad builders, much bigger challenges lay ahead.

meadows elsewhere; from the ground there are vantage points giving a broad sweep for scores of miles, and there are closed-in canyons where visibility is measured in yards. Along the lower elevations people live the year around; above 5,000 or 6,000 feet, heavy snow in the winter limits most activity to the few roads kept plowed, but pressure for more winter play areas is changing this. The geological story of the Sierra is laid bare along Interstate 80, which runs along the northernmost ridges of the American River country, and part of the ancient tale lies far out in the Great Valley, which is a trough filled with sediment from the mountains. Heading northeast from Sacramento (elevation 25 feet) to Newcastle (970 feet), the road unrolls like a carpet, crossing dirt washed down from the Sierra over the ages. Mixed in below the surface may be fragments from as far away as the crest of the range, each perhaps broken off originally by the leverage of ice or frost, washed down from a ridge by the meltwater of snow, tumbled along a rivulet to a creek, then down a river branch

which carried it along year by year until it came to rest on the plain, adding a small bit to the miles-thick deposit which leveled off the Great Valley. The granite that is so prominent at high elevations lies far under the valley floor, probably as much as five miles in some places, beneath the silt and outwash of millennia.

At Newcastle is a volcanic ridge, part of a volcanic layer which reaches many miles north and south at about this elevation. It was formed perhaps two hundred million years ago and later was changed to its present structure by pressure and other forces. Volcanic action is not limited to volcanoes which erupt and scatter material about; in the Sierra it was more often a welling-up of lava rather than an explosion.

It is significant that the Sierra traveler from the coast meets a volcanic ridge at the beginning of the mountains, and skirts another as he goes over the top at Donner Pass.

One of the first major efforts of man to change these mountains was the building of the transcontinental railroad, which enters the Sierra at Newcastle and has been a part of the scene for a hundred years. In its early days great numbers of trees were cut for ties, bridge timbers, and lumber to build miles of snow-sheds which protected the tracks from snow sliding down the cliffs. Soil and rock were blasted from cuts and tunnels, and dragged out into canyons for fills, a topographical change which provided new habitats for small animals among the loose chunks of rock. Wood burning engines occasionally collided with bear or deer, and the diesels still do; but the early trains did not run often enough to make the track kill serious, and the creatures soon learned to avoid the tracks except in winter, when an animal caught between snow-plowed walls ten to thirty feet high had to run until exhausted or hit by a train.

Bear found new foraging around the construction camps and later at section-gang houses. During the dirt-moving stage of construction, small and large streams became heavily silted, disturbing fish spawning gravels and affecting the small organisms which live in and around the water, but this was not taken into consideration in those days of building public works any more than it was considered a few years later in the search for gold. After roadbed and ballast settled, there was little effect on drainage and runoff, since ties and tracks do not channel water as paved roads do.

In the foothills the towns of Auburn and Colfax and other places got an economic uplift from the railroad. There was permanent employment with the railroad company for some, and good transportation made possible a profit in the raising of pears and apples; saw-mills were placed near the tracks, and more changes occurred in the woods. The pastoral environment close to the towns changed to the urban one of the times. Oaks and pines came down, imported nut and fruit trees and ornamentals were planted. Deer, black bear, coyotes, mice, rats, and some birds learned quickly to live near people and, in fact, prospered—but other animals shifted their locality or disappeared, among them the grizzly. Fish in the streams dwindled and so did the streams themselves.

Crossing of the range by the railroad provided bonuses for scientists and others: the first consecutive record of the weather in the Sierra and the exposure of geology in cuts and tunnels. Although there are more

weather stations now than ever, daily temperatures and precipitation, wind direction and force, cloud cover and other factors are still unknown for many parts of the Sierra, and the records along the railroad are used for deducing meteorological facts.

The interstate highway has made more drastic changes than the railroad, by its nature and by its route. Vast amounts of rock have been blasted and moved; the streams have been forever altered and forced into new channels; migration routes of deer blocked, and natural drainage of surface and spring water changed substantially. But deep cuts give a glimpse into the Sierran past. Between Bowman and Clipper Gap, and near Applegate are rocks formed in an ancient ocean 200 million years ago, long before there was a hint of the Sierra; and from near Applegate to just east of Colfax, there are newer sea deposits—if 135 to 180 million years can be considered new. As geologists think of time, the hill against which Colfax is built is a newcomer, being capped with volcanic material which welled up just before the Ice Age, only a couple of million years ago, long after the seas which deposited the surrounding material had receded.

The route over Donner Pass in the central Sierra is not as heavily forested as most other areas, but the thinness of the forest garment here lets the anatomy show through and reveals the many marks of time. This part was not tilted as high as the southern part in the last great uplift ten or twelve million years ago, and in some ways lacks the impact of the true High Sierra. Most of the canyons are not as deep, the granite not as white, the overall topography more rolling, the peaks less challenging.

The lower elevation of the crest is only one reason for the difference; the other is the volcanic action during an earlier uplifting which poured cinders, ash, and mud from craters near the crest, the layers accumulating until they were a thousand feet thick or more. The western slope here may have once been a nearly featureless slope of ash, mudflow, and light material which filled the former stream canyons and slopped over the divides, leaving only the highest peaks exposed. Before the fireworks the streams probably tended toward the northwest, but as layers of pyroclastic material and mud churned by suddenly heated snowpacks thickened (and as the Sierra was bowed up from below), the waters

*Interstate 80, looking toward Donner Pass, out of view at upper right. Emigrants
who managed to breach the crest came down through the wooded area at right into Bear Valley, left.
Famed Emigrant Gap lies just beyond the highway bend in the center of the picture.*

Looking westward along the same stretch of highway, one can see the roadbed of the Southern Pacific, which follows the survey of the original transcontinental. The ridge along which both road and rail lie is a watershed, with drainage on the north (right) into the Yuba River and on the south (left) into the American.

Heavy snows in the high country presented a serious problem for the railroad builders. They solved it with snow-

were redirected more nearly westward, cutting their way in new channels down to the deeply buried hard rocks that are now the stream beds—rocks which were once lake or sea bottoms, compressed and heated to form slates (fine grained) or schists (coarse grained) —down through the new deposits to the very old, the bedrock. Great quantities of water from melting of the big glaciers at the crest added to this cutting action farther down the slope, while the glaciers themselves removed much material as they slid along, grinding to the granite.

The glacial ice came after the greatest volcanic flows. The bare rocks and domes visible eastward from Emigrant Gap (and all the way down the Sierra to the south) are evidence of the size and power of the glaciers, which came and went three or four times, with periods of mild weather for thousands of years between ice periods. In the American River country there probably was a sea of ice 250 miles square, in its greatest stages covering Donner Pass and inching slowly down both sides of the divide, with tongues two to fifteen miles long, widening the canyons and forming

sheds such as these, still in use at Donner Pass. Under cliffs, sheds had sloping roofs to let avalanches slide past.

the typical bowls, many with lakes in them, visible from any vantage point.

The thickness and power of the moving ice field is hard to imagine, but at Cisco Butte is a very good hint. This bare rocky mountain (easily identified from below by its airway beacon at the summit and two microwave stations in its saddle) helps choke the South Yuba River into a narrow canyon. (The South Yuba and the North American are just a stone's throw apart here.) The Butte is made of resistant rock, and when an arm of the Donner glacier pressed against it, it held

firm. The ice thickened and flowed upward until it overrode the peak, perhaps by several hundred feet, the chunks of granite in the plastic mass grinding and pushing away all that was loose of the blackish native rock. As the last ice period ebbed, the glacier slowed to a stop, then melted away, dropping boulders, rocks, and small stones wherever they might land.

On top of Cisco Butte, 6,639 feet above sea level and 1,000 feet above the adjacent river, are huge chunks of light-colored granite setting on the darker base rock, the chunks identical in structure to granite found seven

Laying enormous fills, as here at Sailor's Spur, called for a fleet of dump carts and the unflagging industry of an army of Chinese workers.

to ten miles farther east. Each boulder had to have been left there by the glacier. Long before that, each was part of a flow of magma (molten rock) which welled up beneath the ancestral Sierra, cooling and hardening below the surface; each then became part of the visible surface when the overlying material was eroded or scoured off; each was plucked from its position by the power of plastic ice working against cracks of weakness which were imposed in the process of cooling from magma to granite; each was carried along in the downhill crawl of the ice mass; each was lifted a thousand feet up to this mountaintop, finally being gently set down in its present resting place.

The portion of the glacier which squeezed through the narrow gap to the north of Cisco Butte laid bare some ancient Sierra bones, as did the cuts for the railroad, and for the highway later. Just east of Yuba Gap is pyroclastic material showered down from volcanoes in the Pliocene age, maybe 10 million years ago; a short distance farther east at the highway level is granite forced upward in a hot mass in Mesozoic times, perhaps 130 million years ago. Around the curve is a short zone of ultrabasic intrusive rock also welled up in

Mesozoic times but a few years older—perhaps one to three million years older—and containing material different from the granite; then a narrow strip of basic intrusive, also formed from magma, but at a still different time and of different minerals.

Next to these *igneous* rocks (formed by heat) to the east is a finely grained *sedimentary* rock, laid down when this was the bottom of the sea in Jurassic times, likely 155 million years ago, long before the early Sierra was crumpled and uplifted. In the midst of this ancient stuff lies a strip of alluvial soil washed there by water in the past few thousand years. To the east of that is a quarter mile or so of rock which flowed from a volcanic fissure perhaps 160 million years ago and then was altered by heat and pressure to its present form. The traveler's car becomes a time machine, speeding through rock which records mountain-building activity that took place (in well-rounded figures) 10 million, 130 million, 133 million, 155 million, a few thousand, and 160 million years ago, and there hasn't been even a bump to mark the transition.

The years are only approximate. In thinking about those multi-million-year-old rocks, it helps to remember that California was settled by United States emigrants just over 100 years ago, and that 150 years ago none of the cities of California existed as more than small outposts of Spain. About 200 years ago the United States was ready to become an independent nation, and it has been less than 2,000 years since the birth of Christ. Man probably began his present kind of existence (cutting forests, killing wild animals, domesticating other animals) 11,000 to 25,000 years ago, but as a caveman he probably goes back two million years; the rocks along here are eighty times older than that. While some of these great stone masses were just grains of silt settling in a sea bed, large reptiles swam in the water and others flew through the air, and there were dinosaurs along the beaches; the first birds were appearing. The weather was warm, and tropical vegetation grew on the land (although there was less land then), and among the strange plants was a tree very much like the present pine.

There is evidence that water once flowed from the Great Basin of Nevada and Utah to the Pacific (Fremont thought there was a river as late as the 1840s), but the mountain-forming sequences in ancient times blocked off this westward stream; the new mountains did not make it any easier for people, either, when they wanted to go west. The great trek of 1846 and the overland gold rush a few years later came through the central Sierra and found it rough; most made it, but some did not, and it takes only a little imagination, when the wind is driving a heavy snowfall through the trees and against those granite cliffs, to see a thin file of gaunt men doggedly tramping a sinuous trail, and behind them desperate women stumbling along with quilt-wrapped children in the arms—or, on a night when the snow is twenty feet deep and the temperature far below freezing, to see a little campfire of wet wood flicker and then go out, leaving nothing but silence and the cold dark.

CALIFORNIA'S HISTORY is intimately linked with the American River and the ridges just to the north and south. This where Jed Smith tried to cross the mountains from west to east in 1828, but deep snow and difficult terrain turned him back. Where the American meets the Sacramento, far from other settlements of the day, John Sutter built a fort in 1839 and started an empire of his own—a dream shattered less than ten years later by the gold discovery on the South Fork about thirty miles into the foothills. The Stephens Party, coming across the desert in 1844, split on the east side of the Sierra, horsemen crossing the crest just west of Lake Tahoe and following the general route of the Rubicon down to its junction with the American, and the wagons going directly up and over in the vicinity of Donner Pass.

The South Fork of the American touches two other historical passes: Echo, where Johnson's Placerville Road crossed, and Carson, where much of the 1849 and 1850 traffic went up and over. Both of these are used today, and each illustrates significant aspects of the Sierra.

Echo Summit is no narrow defile through bare rock, but a nearly level plateau heavily wooded with red fir and lodgepole pine. The present road crosses in a dense woods at 7,377 feet. Westerly from the high point the grade is only about fifty to a hundred feet to the mile; southerly along the crest the rise is gentle for two or three miles; northerly it is about two miles to Echo Lake, which is only about thirty-seven feet higher in elevation. The terrain in these three directions would look familiar to an easterner accustomed to the rolling of old hills, although the immense red firs would seem strange. But a few yards eastward from the trees on the plateau is one of the Sierra's awesome sights: a step away the granite escarpment drops almost straight down to a pile of broken rock at its foot.

From here northward to the Cascades, the Sierra becomes less distinct, and in fact the crest splits around the sides of Lake Tahoe. The main series of peaks to the west of that incredibly beautiful lake mark the watershed, separating the streams which flow westerly to the Pacific from those which flow easterly, with no outlet to the sea, into the sinks of the Great Basin. Storms beat heavily on these peaks, and the snow is caught in Desolation Valley and Rockbound Valley, along Chipmunk Ridge, in the Granite Chief country, in glacier-scoured canyons and basins where the creeks are named Powderhorn, Long John, Buckskin, Whisky, Squaw, Grizzly, and Hell Hole; and where ice and snow cover high lakes so plentiful some of them have numbers instead of names. The peaks are 9,000 feet or

more high, and 63,600 acres around them has been declared primitive and is closed to roads and motor vehicles, although inundated in the summer by hikers.

Desolation Valley is a granite basin, glacier-gouged, dotted with lakes, and defined roughly by Ralston Peak, 9,235 feet; Mount Tallac, 9,735 feet; Dick's Peak, 9,856 feet; Mount Price, 9,974 feet; and Pyramid Peak, 9,983 feet. The lakes drain into the South Fork of the American, taking a roundabout course around the end of the jagged Crystal Range, a fifteen-mile-long subcrest. Just to the north of Desolation is Rockbound Valley, similar in its glacial origin but drained by the Rubicon River, a tributary of the Middle Fork of the American, which here flows toward the north. The glaciers seem to have split on Mount Price and Jacks Peak, and on a wedge between them at Mosquito Pass (8,400 feet), dividing the plastic lower mass so some went northerly to Rockbound and some went southerly to form Desolation, with part of the latter glacier edging over and gouging down to Lake Tahoe and the Echo Lakes. While granite, a product of the Mesozoic times, is the dominant rock, there are ridges here of earlier undersea sediments side by side with three kinds of volcanic material— an occurrence not unusual along the Sierra crest.

In Carson Pass, like Echo, the approach from the west is gradual for several miles and the descent to the east is abrupt; but Carson Pass is more picturesque, going through a cleft in the rocks, with gnarled and twisted high-country trees on both sides and substantial peaks to the north and south, the terrain broken and not easy on feet or lungs. The pass is 8,573 feet above sea level; Elephant's Back, a mile south, humps up to 9,603; Red Lake Peak, from which Fremont and Preuss made the first recorded sighting of Lake Tahoe, is a little over a mile to the north and just over 10,000 feet. A step or two to the east is the typical rocky pitch up which pioneers had to pull their wagons with chains and ropes—oxen or mules double and triple-teamed to make the lift. A sharp search reveals dulled marks of this ordeal on the rock face.

Now two generations of roads take a less abrupt route, an abandoned one on the steep southern ridge and a more gentle new grade around the north side of Red Lake, which occupies a bowl about seven hundred feet below the pass. Easterly flow the various branches of the Carson River; westerly flows the South Fork of the American. Most of the rock at road level is granite, but a few feet higher a change in color marks the change to rock blown out of a volcanic vent in the last one to two million years.

West of the pass, Caples Lake and Silver Lake have granite at the shoreline and a high backdrop of volcanic rock at the sides or upper end. Most of the ridges for thirty or forty miles westward alternate between these two materials; the road from the pass to Jackson goes down such a ridge, and another divides the waters of the American from the Mokelumne River. From time to time there is an outcropping of a basic intrusive rock or a glacial deposit of the past million years and near it an accumulation of sand, gravel, and soil of recent times; but the mountains here are mostly gray granite, exposed as humps and bosses, and darker volcanic rocks, not as smoothly formed and often with talus slopes of broken boulders at the foot of the cliffs.

About halfway between Caples and Silver lakes, just west of Carson Spur, one hundred yards north of the road, is an ancient juniper, growing among younger trees but still holding its own—many-trunked, thick at the bottom, spread wide at the top; no giant like a sequoia, no symmetrical beauty like a white fir, no spectacular patriarch like a storm-blasted sugar pine—just a tough and tenacious veteran of the Sierra. It was already old when the remnants of the Mormon Battalion went by, picking a new trail eastward to join the other Saints at Salt Lake after playing a part in the California drama of the 1840s. Some of the Mormon soldiers are still nearby—a few miles farther west, at Tragedy Springs, where, in June 1848, an advance party of three men, trying to find a route for sixteen wagons and the rest of the battalion, were found a month later in shallow graves, badly mutilated. (At the time, the massacre was blamed on Indians, but more recent investigation suggests the murderers may have been whites who wanted the gold the Mormon party was carrying.) As in thousands of other trailside deaths in those days, the bodies were reburied with as much dignity as possible, a crude marker erected, and the rest of the party moved on. The spot is marked now, and tourists stop there for a drink of spring water and a moment of wonder at the perils of traveling not much more than four generations ago.

Before the completion of the transcontinental railroad, all travelers and supplies had to cross the mountains over a wagon road that wound precariously among boulders and along dizzying ridges.

Chapter 8

YUBA RIVER COUNTRY

Land of the Northern Mines, where the Yuba washed a fortune
in gold through pan and sluice and hydraulic diggins

A LOG BRIDGE crosses the North Fork of the Yuba River at about 5,400 feet above sea level. In winter the river here runs swift and deep; in summer it is just wadeable. The canyon walls are steep and high, although at this point a confluence of side streams and the work of ice have widened the valley somewhat; to the southwest three or four miles, the crags of the Sierra Buttes jab into the skyline, about 3,000 feet higher.

The bridge across the North Fork is not much to see, and it could go out in the next heavy winter— but it marks a point in the stream above which live eastern brook trout, and below which live rainbow trout. There might be a little intermingling for a short distance, but there is something right here which tells the trout it is a territorial boundary; not the bridge, certainly, but perhaps the cascades just a little farther downstream. There seems to be no noticeable difference in the small aquatic life on which the trout feed. To a human being, the boundary lines of nature are a mystery, but to insects, fish, birds, and larger animals, their multitude of territorial limits must seem simple. A casual walk along the stream here shows no apparent differences, but obviously there are some, and to trout they are significant enough to establish this as the edge of the world—the top edge for the rainbow, the lower edge for the brookies.

Above, the North Yuba flows through a great spread of granite, its sources at about 7,000 feet; right here and for a few miles downstream, to about Sierra City, it is in glacial debris up against volcanic hills; then for miles in its course to a dam in the foothills, it cuts through uplifted sea beds, volcanic rocks, and pockets of granite. Above, the canyon is narrow, the stream shaded and cool; below, the canyon opens out, and the water temperature goes up, becoming warmer and warmer, and eventually becoming so warm that the rainbow in turn gives way to lesser breeds of fish. Above, the granite offers little to inspire miners to dig; right here, there has been extensive hydraulic mining; below, the hills have been honeycombed with shafts and tunnels, and blasted by jets of water, clear back to the days of '49.

The Yuba River (named after either wild grapes or Indians, depending on the version) has three main forks—the North, most easily accessible and possibly most scenic, starting near Yuba Pass and fed by streams draining out of spectacular glacial lakes; the Middle, less distinctive but with a high-elevation reservoir which attracts recreationists and makes the stream more familiar to fishermen; and the South, starting just below Donner Summit, fed by dozens of glacial lakes, running through deep and sometimes inaccessible canyons, distinguished near the top by the oldest still-used dam (French Lake, 1850), and near the bottom by the oldest still-existing covered bridge (Bridgeport, 1865).

From the ridges between these forks and their uncountable tributaries has come a great pile of gold— panned from gravel in the creek bottoms at first, or picked with a knife from crevices in bedrock; later dug from old streambeds on the hillsides and separated from the sand and gravel by flowing water; still later,

On the north fork of the Yuba, below Downieville, an old bridge connects State
Highway 49 with the almost deserted mining town of Goodyear's Bar.

*Many towns built on gold prosperity quietly crumbled when the bonanza
faded, but Nevada City in the Northern Mines remains active and busy while
preserving evidence of an earlier way of life.*

This old covered bridge over Oregon Creek, a tributary of the Yuba, floated away in the 1880s when a dam upstream broke. It was hauled back into place by teams of oxen; later it was found to be reversed, end for end, and so it remains today.

Gold, which for millenia had been washing down from the Sierra into the Great Valley, was recovered in the nineteenth century by giant dredges, such as this one at Natomas, east of Sacramento.

washed down by high pressure jets which left new kinds of canyons; and in some places, dug out of quartz rock from shafts and tunnels reaching far into the earth.

For almost a century—until the early 1940s—the fortunes of Grass Valley and Nevada City, where the foothills meet the Sierra, were tied to gold mining of the hardrock kind, where miners blasted and picked along

146

and smashed into fragments by stampmills which shook the earth around the clock. The gold was separated from the dust and debris, and kept; the rest was run out into tailing piles, which are still there.

The hardrock miners, mostly from Cornwall in England, worked deep in the underground darkness, moving a yard or two of rock at a time; but a few miles away, in the Yuba country, a different kind of miner was at work in a different kind of way—using the force of water to move thousands of yards of earth at a time, slamming his jet at the hillside and washing it down through the long rows of riffles which let the heavy gold sink to the bottom and the lighter silt and gravel go out the lower end. Called "hydraulicking," the method was efficient for its purpose but devastating to the mountains, where it left huge scars, and to the Sacramento Valley, where the debris flowed out and stopped, burying farms and causing floods. After court actions, legislative battles, and gun fights, the farmers finally stopped the big nozzles, but the scars are still visible all through the Yuba Country. The Malakoff Diggins State Historic Park contains one of the largest of these great pits.

Life in the streams was significantly altered by the hydraulic mining, not only at the time but probably "forever." While the hydraulickers were working, tremendous amounts of water were diverted far upstream and run through ditches to the head of the workings, leaving the streambed almost dry for miles in the summertime. Below the workings, the channels were filled with boulders, tree trunks, root clumps, millions of tons of fine silt, and millions of yards of gravel.

All things living in such a stream were snuffed out, and fish trying to return for spawning were unsuccessful; if they made it to the former spawning bed, there was no chance for eggs to hatch, for silt was everywhere and the essential gravel beds nowhere. The narrow creek canyons and even entire riverbeds rapidly filled with debris, causing the streams to meander over open, baking-hot beds of gravel instead of running briskly down shaded, narrow channels; heat went up, and oxygen content went down. There was no permanence to these shallow channels, for each spring the high runoff from melting snow tore through the choked canyons and rearranged them all over again; to some degree this still goes on in those canyons.

veins in which the gold was locked, going thousands of feet down and outward from the main tunnels. Each shovelful of ore was hauled to a lift in little cars on miniature railroad tracks, then taken up to daylight

There are fish in the Yuba forks and tributaries now —some of them planted in current years from hatchery stock trucked in and placed in pools, and some of them wild descendants of old plantings or fish which migrated after the mining havoc abated.

But impressive though it is, man's demolition of stream life in this part of the Sierra and elsewhere cannot compare in scope and power with nature's own destruction in the great cycles of change which occurred here. Salt-water fossils and the structure of some of the rocks show that there once was sea here instead of streams; the great tilts changed for all time the type of life that could survive. Deeply buried petrified trees, with all the wood replaced by minerals which percolated in with water and then solidified, show where forests stood, later to be buried by mud and lava flows from volcanoes. The streams were buried along with the trees.

Bare granite, scraped clean and deeply scratched, marks the paths of immense glaciers which for thousands of years filled the upper ends of the streams from the Yuba to the Kern, caused heavy seasonal flows in the lower portions, and created stepped ledges in the granite up which fish could not climb to the streams and lakes above. After the last glacier receded, there were no fish at all in the high waters; man has restocked them all, hoping that the lesser forms of life on which fish depend had somehow found their way into the sterile environment. In most places they had, thanks to the wind which lifted seeds and spores upward and wings which briefly gave movement to aquatic insects at the reproductive end of their life cycle. There are still some lakes, however, which are fine for photographers but frustratingly empty for fishermen —cold, clear, sparkling, but unable to support the web of life.

The jagged pinnacles of the Sierra Buttes dominate the Yuba country, higher at 8,587 feet than the pass eight or nine miles farther east. Snow sticks in a small patch or two all year, most years, high on the northeast side in old glacial cirques. To the north there is a series of major and minor lakes in glacial bowls; along the western side an earthquake fault runs for ten or fifteen miles; the little town of Sierra City nestles at its southern base, and on top is a Forest Service lookout stuck tight against the topmost crag. From here

In the Mother Lode country quiet
back roads wind over grassy foothills dotted with
blue oaks and digger pines.

Lassen Peak is visible about seventy miles to the northwest, and the lights of Reno, about forty-five miles to the east, make a colored glow in the sky. There was a time when this peak afforded a hundred-mile view, but smog now obscures the Great Valley, and a smoggy haze has crept up into the mountains.

The sun comes up early here, and day arrives long before the deep canyons below are touched by the sun. No one knows how hard the wind blows at the summit in winter storms, but even in the fall it gets up to forty or fifty miles an hour. During some autumn electrical storms the lookout is wrapped within a thunderhead, and the fire-spotters who man it turn off their radios, sit on insulated stools, cross their fingers, and wait. Cables tied into the volcanic rock hold the building in place in the storm and (the people inside hope) conduct lightning strikes safely to the ground. Visibility is as close to zero as it is from the bridge of a ship in the fog, and when the storm lifts or the clouds move on, there is a sense of relief that the world is still there below—streams, valleys, lesser mountains, lakes, and all.

The Sierra Buttes are used to storms, perhaps 200 million years of them, for one side of the mountain is made up of Paleozoic marine deposits laid down originally under the sea, and the other side is volcanic rock (much changed by time) which must have boiled up through the same sea while it was receding, or just after. Fifty million years later more volcanic material either surged up or flowed here from elsewhere, for some of the cliffs around Sardine Lake are dated thus. The glaciers bulldozed through all of these, leaving debris and moraines spread seven or eight miles to the north, past Salmon, Snag, Goose, and Gold lakes—all of them in glacial basins dammed by moraines.

The Melones earthquake fault zone runs through all the Yuba country, marked on the geologic map as a line running almost due north and south, in some cases clearly established and in others dotted where lava flows have obscured the evidence. (The same fault line runs far to the south through the American River country and far to the north across the Feather River.) Between the South Yuba and North Yuba many lesser fault lines appear, all along the edges of intrusions of Mesozoic ultrabasic rock going back 100 to 185 million years; the ultrabasics did not cause the earthquakes, but took advantage of weaknesses in the earth's crust to push up and outward. The ultrabasics occur in small and large patches in the Sierra, mostly in the north, and have been described for the layman as "just the opposite of granite." Both were once molten, but the ultrabasics have less silica and hardly any quartz or feldspar, being mostly metallic oxides and sulfides and native metals.

DOWNIEVILLE, one of California's smaller county seats, sits on the Melones Fault; the Downie River, which joins the North Yuba there, flows through a canyon that follows the fault. The first earthquake ever recorded in the northern Sierra was at Downieville in 1851, not long after the first gold rush miners arrived; how many there had been before pencils and paper arrived with the picks and pans is nature's secret.

Perched at the junction of the two rivers, hemmed in by steep sides of the canyons, Downieville has also been hard hit by floods several times. Within the last generation several homes were floated away bodily, and the community was cut off for days; supplies finally were delivered on a cable strung across the torrent where the bridges had gone out. The descent of the North Yuba to the foothill reservoir at Bullards Bar is gradual for this kind of a river—even though the overall drop of the Yuba is almost 100 feet to the mile compared with the Missouri's 17 feet and the Hudson's 14.

Goodyear's Bar, a few miles below Downieville, is another old mining town, at a spot where the river passes through a cut in the ultrabasic rock that follows a branch fault of the Melones. Here, too, the two prominent creeks to the north and south follow the fault-line canyons. The hundred or more square miles north of Goodyear's Bar and Downieville, all the way up to Port Wine Ridge, which divides the Feather from the Yuba, is pockmarked with small mines with names like Clippership, Deacon, Golden Sceptre, Mountain Boy, Magnolia, Brown Bear, Bunker Hill, and Wideawake; and there are long-abandoned townsites like Bee Tree and Red Ant.

Richer mines with longer lives were between the North and Middle Forks of the Yuba, along Pliocene and Lafayette ridges, where the town of Alleghany waits for the price of gold to go up. Those two ridges are mostly lava flows which came from the east, cover-

Steam from this old boiler once drove a small sawmill near Sonora. It was replaced with more powerful equipment when improved transportation made larger mills practical.

ing up the gold-bearing streams where the riches lay until the miners found—rather quickly—that they could dig under the volcanic overlay and get into the ancient free-gold gravel beds. The old Henness Pass Road, traveled heavily by miners going to get rich on the Comstock in Nevada or on their way back to more familiar diggins, picks its way along such a volcanic ridge. It is now used only by four-wheel-drive vehicles.

The Middle Yuba is a lonesome place, not easy to get to, although the Bedbug Smith Trail crosses it north of Graniteville, and an occasional switchback dirt road dips down almost to the stream edge. There is one bridge in thirty miles. Up around 6,000 feet elevation, however, the Middle Yuba, like many other Sierran streams, is less precipitous and in broader basins; one of these, Jackson Meadow, has been flooded by a man-made dam, thus returning it to a lake as it probably was before naturally eroded silt made it a meadow.

The South Yuba travels farther than the other two forks, both in distance and in history, and has spawned one of the world's largest electric power companies, the Pacific Gas and Electric Company. The upper South Yuba was familiar to many emigrants and gold miners who came across the plains and surmounted Donner Pass; on its initial twenty miles were acted out the tragic Donner Party story and many other dramas of the great emigration. The wagon trail parted company with the stony South Yuba where both twisted around Cisco Butte, never to meet again. The river then cascades down a thousand feet in five miles, tumbling over granite ledges to the glacial basin which is now Lake Spaulding, then runs out through a 1,200-foot deep gorge to the northwest, picking up the drainage from more than a dozen lakes high above the rim and reaching civilization of a sort at the town of Washington, where a mining road crosses—the first crossing in fifteen or twenty miles. From Washington, more canyon for another fifteen miles or so to Edwards Crossing, then Purdon's Crossing (hardly used now because of one of the West's worst roads), then on to the Highway 49 bridge at 1,200 feet above the sea. Some of the bedrock over which the South Yuba runs is granite, but most of it is hardened old seabed, greatly altered by many forces through 200 million years, usually tipped so the layers make jagged riffles where loose

gold collected; for this gold, early miners lugged huge packs up and down these canyon walls.

The same kind of loose gold, liberated when new streams cut across old channels and then washed the fragments down until they lodged in gravel or crevices, provided the incentive for waterworks so extensive they were later the basis for a power company. The Yuba Canal went thirty airline miles back and three thousand feet higher to tap the high country lakes and streams, dug by hand and black powder in a 450-mile network. Where gullies had to be crossed, flumes were built, and whole rivers transported to hillsides where no water had been since the Eocene. This water, sometimes fought over but more often peacefully distributed on elaborate schedules, washed the heavy gold from the light sand, bringing riches to some men and ruin to some streams.

As the mining petered out, the demand for electrical power increased, and so did the need for agricultural irrigation water. Small hydroelectric plants were built, most of them using a type of waterwheel invented originally for mining by a Yuba country man, Lester A. Pelton, and the mining towns of Nevada City and Grass Valley were among the first in the world to be lighted by electricity. The first long-distance telephone lines were in the Yuba country, installed to achieve quicker control of mining water; and some kind of a record for delivery of fish was made when ditch tenders high in the Sierra nailed the morning's catch of salmon to boards, put them face down in the icy ditch, and let them float to the powerhouse twenty miles below, where a screen above the penstock held them until the camp cook picked them up and prepared them for dinner—nearly as fresh as the moment they were caught that morning. Salmon no longer get upstream on the Yuba, because of the numerous dams—if they ever did; the fish in the story may have been large rainbow, commonly called salmon trout in the early days.

From the Yuba watershed, 40 or 50 miles long and up to 36 miles wide, has come more gold than from any another river in the United States—more than has ever been accurately counted—but to get it the miners and their giant monitor nozzles, their picks and shovels, their black powder and mulepower had to move two-thirds of a billion yards of earth; and still, millions of dollars of gold remains.

Near its headwaters the North Yuba River races over a boulder-strewn bed, churned by rocks carried down from the east face of Sierra Buttes. The hillside at left is a good example of natural reforestation; young oaks are thriving on a slope where the original conifers have been destroyed by fire.

*At the 2,500- to 4,000-foot elevation,
the North Yuba slackens its pace somewhat,
alternating between rapids and quiet
pools. Overhanging vegetation helps provide
food for the plentiful trout.*

155

Cliffs six hundred feet high mark the point where giant monitors stopped blasting down the hillsides to wash out gold in what is now Malakoff Diggins State Historic Park—a reminder of the destructiveness of hydraulic mining. Various colors mark the beds of ancient streams where the gold was concentrated.

The contours of the northern Sierra in the upper Feather River country are more rounded than farther south. Where the slopes are not heavily forested, manzanita flourishes among scattered red fir trees, as on this hillside in Plumas-Eureka State Park.

Sand Pond, at the eastern base of Sierra Buttes, is actually man-made, dammed by waste rock from a gold mine; but with the passing of years it has taken on many of the characteristics of a natural lake.

159

Chapter 9

FEATHER RIVER COUNTRY

*The spectacular canyon where man has ensnared a
rushing river and bent it to his will*

THE SIERRA NEVADA merges with the Cascades
and the Modoc Plateau about forty degrees
north of the equator, the basic Sierra giving
way to a volcanic overlay from Cascade volcanoes. The
Sierra divides into two crests just below the parallel,
and loses its granitic character there. (At this same latitude between the Sierra and the Atlantic, lie Denver,
St. Joseph, Indianapolis, Columbus, and Philadelphia.
The latitude of the south end of the Sierra is about the
same as Albuquerque, Charlotte, and Cape Hatteras.)
Geologists say that Lassen Peak is part of the Cascades,
not the Sierra; but it makes a convenient northern
terminus, and the water from the heavy snow on its
southeastern face flows into the Feather River and may
eventually reach Southern California through aqueducts.

The Feather drains about two million acres of mountains, none of them as high as the high peaks far to the
south. The elevation, climate, accessibility and geo-
graphical arrangement make year-round activity possible, and there are many permanent communities in
addition to the usual seasonal resorts. Except for the
Tahoe Basin, this is the most heavily settled part of the
range. Even so, there are not many people per square
mile, because the settlements are spaced along the
travel routes, and the travel routes follow the easiest
terrain; the back country, though not distant on the
map, is often wild and rugged.

Early-day mining gave way to extensive lumbering;
hydroelectric development grew fast; and the tourist
trade is now edging in as the leading industry. The
mines made little change in the ecology here except to
bring in humans and their funny ways; the lumbering
had a more measurable effect, in places almost a catas-
trophic one; the tourist business, including hunting,
fishing, and winter sports, will not help to restore the
Feather country to the way it was before the Fourth
of July, 1848, when John Bidwell thought the lower
reaches much resembled the gold-discovery site at Coloma, and made a major similar discovery himself. The
name Feather was bestowed by the Spanish (Río de
las Plumas), either because of many wild-fowl feathers
floating down the stream, or because the many cascades gave a feathery appearance, or perhaps because
the floss from upstream willows gave the impression
of feathers all three versions are favored locally.

The Feather has the usual three forks common to
Sierra rivers: north, middle, south, and one extra—the
West Branch, on which was discovered one of the
largest gold nuggets ever seen, more than fifty-four
pounds of pure gold. The character of both the north
and south forks is changed forever by elaborate hydroelectric and irrigation works, but the Middle Feather
is mostly its own master. Tame at the top, trapped in
a reservoir at the bottom, the Middle Feather neverthe-
less runs wild for forty miles, deep in a trout-filled
canyon, scarcely touched by roads. It is just over a
ridge from the county seat, Quincy, but far distant
in time and uncompromising in ruggedness: each year
rescue teams must struggle into the canyon to find lost
or injured persons who misgauged their ability to cope
with this kind of land.

*A complex and imposing geological feature, Sierra Buttes dominate
the watershed between the Yuba and Feather rivers.*

Lassen Peak

Lake Almanor

North Fork Feather River

Lake
Oroville

A dozen stages of the building of the Sierra can be identified along the route of the Middle Feather, and it crosses about a dozen earthquake traces. The tame part is in Sierra and Mohawk Valleys, both filled-in former lakes, where the visible ground was laid down in recent times, say the past half million years, having been eroded from the ancient surrounding ridges and washed into the basin by rain and snow runoff. Below Mohawk, the stream, constantly gaining in size from tributaries, snakes between hills of loose volcanic material, still flowing leisurely although capable of great force in the spring. The casual meandering has warmed the water, and there are more non-game fish than trout, although brown trout and an occasional rainbow are taken. Before the building of the Oroville Dam, eels came upstream this far.

A few miles below Sloat, the wild part of the river begins, cutting through the belt of ancient seabed which extends all along the northern Sierra at about this 3,000- to 6,000-foot elevation. Colder side streams come in. Aquatic insects thrive. Rainbow trout prosper because of the abundance of food and the relative absence of fishermen, most of whom do not want to make the 2,000-foot climb back out of the canyon.

The heights above the canyon are the typical volcanic flows, some with flat tops which look level enough to land an airplane on, and the uplands between the main canyons give the same rolling and slightly tilted appearance of most of the Sierra. No one seems to know where those volcanic flows really originated. They are not the remains of lava pouring down the sides of some pointed mountain in spectacular fashion, but are mixtures of boulders, pebbles, clay, mud, gravel, and sand which spread out, perhaps as far as fifty miles or more from the source, when volcanic action occurred. Melting snow and ice, with some condensed vapor vented with the other material, could have provided the water which transported it all and helped cement it together in its present place. In the Feather country, and clear out to the edge of the Sacramento Valley, these flows occurred at intervals, usually laying down a record of their activity in various strata which indicate

This artist's-eye view of the Feather River shows how thoroughly dams and hydroelectric plants (⚡) use and reuse the water.

that the Sierra here was not more than 2,000 feet high at the time. Much of the material in many of the layers, here and elsewhere, came from ash and other particles ejected from the vents.

The tilting that came after the volcanism made the streams run faster, and they cut down through the flow to the harder rock below, leaving volcanic material only on the ridges. The eroded material went on down to the Great Valley and some of it went on out to sea. On the north side of the Middle Feather, visible from Nelson Point on the gravel county road to LaPorte, is "Little Volcano," which is not a volcano at all but a limestone outcrop sticking up out of the Paleozoic sea bed. It has a vertical cave in it from the top of which blows a cool draft of air on the hottest summer day, but no one can find any opening at the base.

The Middle Feather, at its lower end, hits a great dome of granite and changes direction from westerly at more than a right angle to southeasterly, twisting through Bald Rock Canyon, a 1,000-foot deep cleft with nearly vertical walls in some places. The water alternately splashes over cascades and runs under boulders as big as a house, which came down from the precipices at each side. In flood, this is a formidable river, and there is reason to believe the great granite boulders are sometimes moved downstream by its force. Since even that kind of flow could not have cut a groove like this one in solid granite, it is surmised that the channel runs between two separate masses that welled up separately while molten.

A tributary stream flows into the side of Bald Rock Canyon from the east, at one point dropping 640 feet in one of the highest falls in the United States. A little farther down, the Middle Feather merges its wild waters with the tamer flows from the North and South Forks in the Oroville reservoir at 900 feet above sea level. The reservoir is backed up behind the highest earth-filled dam in the world and has a shoreline of 167 miles, holding water which will travel to the southern end of the state in a thousand-mile complex of conduits, pumps, and tunnels—surely an ignominious end for a river which for forty miles was wild and free.

Pilot Peak at 7,457 feet is not the highest mountain in the Feather country, but it is one of the best known, its distinctive pointed shape making it a landmark for early miners traversing the twisted trails of the day and an easily climbed vantage point for looking over the terrain. It is still used for a fire lookout. This peak is a cloud-splitter and a watershed-splitter, for five streams originate within a quarter mile of its summit, leading to three rivers: the North Yuba, Middle Feather, and South Feather. The rock at the top is volcanic, very old like many of the ridges and mountaintops all down the northern range. The South Yuba flows westerly for twenty miles or more through this material before it gets into granite; this is a "project" river, dammed at intervals for hydroelectric and irrigation purposes.

No great glaciers passed through these canyons, although snow falls heavily in the winter. The little town of La Porte on Rabbit Creek, once a tremendously busy mining center, was for many years cut off for months each winter by heavy snowdrifts, but better roads and power plows now keep it open. The buildings are often nearly buried by snow, and movement by the few residents is in narrow paths dug here and there to doorways. Mining was in old gravel beds, mostly by hydraulicking. The town saloon is perched on the edge of a hydraulic pit, as if the miners stopped digging abruptly, perhaps to protect their source of whiskey. The legendary Lotta Crabtree danced for the miners here, and one of the West's major breweries got its start in a wooden building across the main street from the major store. Now the town is the summer gateway to a recreational lake in Little Grass Valley, and the winter peace is shattered every weekend by snowmobiles taking off for the cabins there.

Plenty of rugged and lonely land is left around La Porte, though—on Slate Creek and Canyon Creek, and on the little flats and gulleys with names right out of the story books: Poverty Hill, Poker Flat, Tennessee. A road made up of equal parts of gravel, dust, and chuckholes twists from Gibsonville, a few miles above La Porte, to Johnsville (where there is a state park more easily reached on a paved state highway), following the route of one of the emigrant and mining trails from the East to Marysville. A slow trip along this road, with plenty of stops, is an exposure to a lesson on the formation of mountains, the cutting power of water, the weathering of rock by minute amounts of chemicals, the fracturing of cliffs by freezing, the spread of chaparral plants into difficult places, the growth of

Lake Almanor, the largest reservoir on the Feather, was formed in 1914 and is maintained today as a recreation area. Lassen Peak (center) and Mount Shasta punctuate the horizon.

forest trees with species at their assigned elevations—and the persistence of man in getting where he wants to go in spite of hills and high mountains.

The North Fork of the Feather has been housebroken in a process which started just after the turn of the century, and it now turns a series of turbines to generate electricity. Step by step from Mountain Meadows through Lake Almanor and down the canyon are reservoirs and their dams, tunnels through mountain spurs, steeply pitched penstocks to direct the falling water downward against the generators—repeated over and over. This fork runs through the gorge which has been widely advertised as the "Feather River Canyon" by the railroad which snakes through it and more recently by boosters of the state highway which leapfrogs the railroad. Adjectives about the beauty of the spectacular canyon are true, but there are also many other canyons of the Feather.

In this one, man's needs have taken priority over nature's. In two or three generations, native rainbow trout have virtually disappeared from the river, and those planted from state trucks usually must be caught or perish, for the temperature of the water is too high for their survival. Suckers, whitefish, and squawfish, however, tolerate the warmth and find food in the algae and along the bottom, and frogs and snakes are as plentiful as ever. Animals which either ignore, tolerate, or prosper from humans are still there—mice, squirrels, skunks, raccoons, porcupines, a fox or two, a few deer. There are occasional reports of bear, bobcats, and mountain lions—probably visitors from the uplands on each side, for up there one or two thousand feet vertically and a mile horizontally is a different world, primitive in spots. There are small lakes, streams with more cascades than pools, forests, and almost impenetrable thickets of manzanita and other brush.

Much of the brush is there because of wildfires, and there is an argument that the huge brushfields are fairly recent and the result of overmanagement. According to this theory, before the past hundred years, small ground fires regularly swept through the foothills and mountains, burning for weeks or months but only consuming small bushes and the low groundcover. Because heavy fuel close to the ground thus never got a chance to grow thickly, the fires did not get intense enough to ignite the crowns of the trees, or even seri-

ously damage the trunks close to the ground. When man started to fight these fires and put them out to protect his livestock or his buildings, or just on general principles, the heavier groundcover got a good chance to grow; if a fire did get started, it was hot enough and high enough to destroy the trees along with the brush —then the brush grew back but the trees did not. In recent years, vast acreages of brush have been bulldozed into windrows and commercially valuable conifers planted between so that in another hundred years there will be forests there.

These brush fields are not part of the foothill chaparral—the unique "elfin forest" of the lower elevations —but extend up and over many of the highest ridges in the Feather River country. Growing head-high in some spots, they provide shelter for small and large animals, innumerable insects, and a dozen kinds of birds, some year-round and some seasonally. Their roots hold the soil and prevent erosion, and the soil holds the rainfall; much moisture is returned to the air by respiration of the plants. The seeds and leaves nourish the wild vegetarians, and the vegetarians nourish the carnivores. In this system there are tiny, almost invisible creatures: mites which live on the leaves, and lice which live on birds' wings. And there are imposing creatures: the mountain lion, six or seven feet from nose to tail-tip, eating mostly deer; it is second in size only to the black bear, which eats almost anything and grunts happily over ants, rodents, or the great crops of berries the brushfields produce. There are no grizzlies anymore.

The Feather country is heavily hunted over in the fall for deer and through the early winter for bear. Not all hunters are successful, but enough are so that others follow. During summer the deer browse on shrubs and other vegetation at the higher elevations; in late fall they move slowly down the slopes to wintering grounds on the Nevada side or to the canyons of the western slope, usually descending just far enough to avoid the heaviest snow. The mule deer is the most common deer throughout the Sierra, even more common than most people suspect, as they have become experts at hiding, and have adapted to living near human beings even though usually wary of too close contact. The upward migration follows the availability of green food (spring comes late at high elevations),

and the downward trip usually starts when there are a few inches of snow on the ground. The deer will go as high as they can find enough to eat, and usually go low enough to avoid all but a foot or so of snow. Some herds spend all their time in the foothills, moving only a little, but most prefer the mountains. The Feather country affords the right conditions in a rather short trip, making it excellent for the deer and handy for the hunter. The size of the herd is regulated, not by the hunter, however, but by the availability of winter feed and the ability of the animals to get to it; there is reason to believe that several mild winters in a row get deer in the habit of not moving so far downhill, and then a severe snow season comes along and takes a heavy toll because they cannot move around readily or find food.

Between La Porte and Mountain House, a little dirt road leaves the pavement and runs a short way to the north, into the upper end of Valley Creek. Huge pines and firs grow there, and in the moister places are dogwoods, which gleam green and white in the springtime and flaming red in the fall. There are lesser plants as well, each growing in its favorite kind of place in unchurned soil, a layer of disintegrating duff making a natural mulch. The sunlight in summer reaches the ground in slowly moving patches, never glaring in one spot very long. A gentle uphill movement of air in the afternoon and slow downhill movement at night keeps the grove ventilated but never takes away an indefinable aroma not found in cities. If there are deer nearby, they are standing motionless back on the edge where no one will see them. Small animals wait silently for intruders to leave. Insects keep steadily at their busywork while they wait to be eaten, and birds fly through to oblige them. The evidence of squirrels and their relatives is plain, because pinecones are plentiful here. Surely skunk families and raccoons cross this glade, and just as surely, a fox and a coyote make regular visits.

What sound there is comes from the movement of millions of pine and fir needles, from a bee flying by, from a woodpecker. Although the storms of winter strike here as fiercely as anywhere, and at the beginning and end of the summer there are smashing electrical storms, usually the aspect is gentle, the surroundings serene. This is the way the woods used to be.

Bucks Lake, near Almanor, stores Feather River water behind the dam visible on the far side of the lake. From here penstocks carry water nearly half a mile vertically to the power house.

Chapter 10

RIVERS THAT RUN TO NOWHERE

*Streams of the eastern scarp that lend water to a thirsty
Southland disappear in the desert sun*

MOST RIVERS FLOW to the sea, but not those of the eastern side of the Sierra Nevada; their fate is to run out into the desert, briefly irrigating fields and gardens along the way, or to be penned into an aqueduct and led to Los Angeles. There are four such rivers: the Truckee, Carson, Walker and Owens, listed from north to south. All but the Owens start up near the crest of the range and drop swiftly down the steep slopes, at peak flows carrying with them fragments of silt from a prehistoric sea bed or ash from some ancient volcano, slowing at the foot of the escarpment, meandering across the alkali flats, and ending in a porous sink or in a lake with no outlet except the evaporating air.

The Truckee runs the most eventful course. It starts between Echo Summit and Carson Pass, high above Lake Tahoe, and flows into that lake at the southern end through a flat, wooded plain that is mostly outwash from the glaciers. In the lake it mixes with tributary water from many creeks coursing down the high ridges, getting more from the Mount Tallac and Granite Chief side toward the west, where the precipitation is about 50 inches a year, and not so much from the Carson Range side, where about 20 inches of rain a year falls. Translated into snow, which is ten or twelve times as deep as the water it contains, that would be about 40 feet if it all piled up at once. However, some is in the form of rain, and not all the snow sticks, so the average snow depth is only 8 or 10 feet, mounting to 25 or 30 where the wind swirls it into drifts.

At Tahoe City on the northwest end of the lake, a regulated flow runs out, cold and so clear that the awesomely large trout in a protected pool between the dam and the highway bridge can be seen distinctly. (Locally, the structure over the pool is called "Fanny Bridge" in honor of the tourists lined up and leaning over the railing.) Large streams come in from place to place below the lake outlet, flowing down high granite past old lava flows and draining the winter sports area including Squaw Valley, where the winter Olympics were once held.

On its thirty-two-mile northward arc, the Truckee picks up more water from the Donner Lake basin, runs through the town of Truckee, collects the flow from the Little Truckee (one of the most beautiful minor streams of the Sierra), and twists down through a canyon so rugged that in the early days emigrants made a detour to avoid it. Much of the rock along that canyon is volcanic; the river flows past six or seven cinder cones a million or more years old. This stream marks the northern end of the Carson Range—the offshoot of the Sierra which cradles Lake Tahoe—and is at the southern end of the Diamond Mountains, another branch of the Sierra where the great range begins to lose its identity and starts to merge with the Cascades and the Modoc Plateau.

Christopher ("Kit") Carson's name is stamped indelibly on landmarks along the eastern side of the Sierra Nevada, including a river and the desert sink in which it ends. There are two forks of his river in the Sierra, starting many miles apart, coming together in the Carson Valley, and then running eastward into the desert.

*At Twin Lakes, halfway up the eastern slope, one sees a mixing of vegetation
—trees from the Yellow Pine Belt and sagebrush from the desert.*

At the eastern foot of the Sierra lies Mono Lake. These salt columns testify to the brackishness of the water and

This river was picked up by explorers and followed with difficulty into the mountains. The west branch was found to afford the best going, for it climbs at an easy grade through Diamond Valley, ascends about 1,500 feet in five or six miles of exceedingly tough terrain, then traverses gentle Hope Valley. Above this valley, most wagons left the river and went over Carson Pass, the earliest using ropes and chains to surmount the cliffs. Some followed through Faith and Charity valleys on a long route which took them over an indis-

record earlier water levels of the dying lake.

tinct crest into Hermit Valley, then down along what is now the Ebbetts Pass road to the promised land.

The West Carson is not very long, more like a creek than a river, but it has a substantial place in western history. On a cold January evening, at the 8,000-foot divide between Faith and Charity, it is not hard to imagine that a flicker of light out there at the edge of the trees comes from the fires of Fremont, Carson, and their men, who camped hereabouts in eight or ten feet of snow—their second or third camp in nine or ten

miles; that tomorrow they will resume their floundering course toward Elephant's Back, 9,600-foot guardian of Carson Pass, four agonizing miles away— a walk of an hour or two in summer on the level, but here where the drifts are fifteen or twenty feet deep, a tremendous test of the will and muscle of men. The willows along the West Carson and its tributaries grow more than head high, but they are invisible for a third of the year, the snow is so deep.

In the summer, a great variety of wild flowers grows on the volcanic slopes about the three pleasantly named valleys, blooming well into the fall. The visible rock is either granite or volcanics from the Pliocene time, with some glacial results visible, and there are many traces of earthquake faults.

The East Fork of the Carson rises just north of Sonora Pass, below Sonora Peak and Stanislaus Peak, both higher than 11,000 feet. It runs northward down a granite channel, dropping three thousand feet in seven or eight miles, then cascading over a falls to a series of small alluvial valleys, where it slows and in the spring drops some of its sand to add a slight amount to the leveling there. Through these valleys it flows at reduced speed, sometimes winding between the cliffs of old volcanic flows, passing near Markleeville, and finally running out to the pastureland of the Carson Valley, and then to the desert sink. If this were a westward-flowing river at the same latitude, it would have sixty to eighty miles to run through the Sierra and another hundred or more to reach San Francisco Bay and the sea; but on the east side, the active Sierra portion of this stream is only about twenty miles long, and most of its life is spent, literally, in the desert.

The Walker River was named for another early trail blazer: Joseph Reddeford Walker. Like the Carson, it has two forks that rise just below the Sierra crest and flow northeastward into Nevada. The West Fork can be identified all the way up to its origin above 10,000 feet, where Forsyth, Tower, and Hawksbeak peaks stand against the sky on the northernmost boundary of Yosemite National Park. This is glacier-hewn granite

Tremendous amounts of eroded material have washed down the eastern escarpment into the Owens Valley. The road in the foreground leads to Onion Valley and Kearsarge Pass.

173

174

country, mostly, and the small lakes in the rocky hollows were named Bonnie, Harriet, Stella, Helen, Cora, Ruth, Anna, and Millie by someone with fond recollections.

From the high granite, the West Walker pours down through wild country where federal rules prohibit any motor vehicles. Earthquake faults abound below Pickel Meadow, and the West Walker finds one of these to follow out into Antelope Valley and Topaz Lake. Then what is left after irrigation demands goes by a roundabout course into Walker Lake, far out in Nevada.

The East Walker starts inauspiciously a few miles above Bridgeport Reservoir, where a great outpouring of glacial debris meets the alluvial valley floor; but in the reservoir it gathers together the waters of dozens of large and small streams before flowing out to Mason Valley and joining the West Fork in its winding trip to Walker Lake. Most of the tributary streams rise in the Hoover Wilderness along the east side of Sawtooth Ridge, more than half with a small tarn or lake pocketed in a glacial cirque. Buckeye Creek is in a glacial canyon, floored with enough outwash to form Big Meadow. The high ridges on both sides are granite, rising almost 3,000 feet in a mile or so. Robinson Creek comes from Peeler Lake, situated right on the crest, so close to the divide that only a few feet makes the difference between draining to the Pacific or to the desert. Midway down Robinson Creek are the Twin Lakes, obviously glacial in origin and at most half a mile wide, their three-mile length divided near the center so that the upper lake is a dozen feet higher than the lower one.

The ridges on each side of Twin Lakes 3,000 to 4,000 feet higher, are of at least two volcanic periods—the newest, created just a million or two years ago; the oldest, metavolcanic rocks 130 million to 185 million years old. On Crater Ridge and near Tamarack Lake are even older formations: 200-million-year-old metasediments which can be tied to similar places in the Sierra Nevada to support the theory that the range was

Most of the moisture has been wrung from clouds by the time they have crossed the crest, so the eastern slope, as here near Markleeville, looks arid with a sprinkling of cactus and sparse groves of junipers, pines, and aspens.

once lower and milder, and before that, was submerged.

Virginia Creek, another main tributary to the East Walker River, has only a brief contact with granite, for it starts in lakes dug out of volcanic formations which sheltered powerful glaciers, and it flows through the volcanic debris near Conway Summit for most of its brief length. Virginia Creek is at the southern end of the complex of watersheds which drain out into Nevada; from here south, the drainage pattern and the appearance of the terrain is different.

To the north, the Sierra Nevada scarp is less of a wall, and more of a crest with ridged extensions branching out over the state line to meet the mountains of the desert; to the south, the Sierra stands high and dominant, overwhelming in the grandeur of its cliffs, furrowed on its face and whittled intricately at its crest, the distance from ridge to valley so short that no rivers can form—only brief turbulent streams cascading from snowline to the Owens River.

Near this dividing point is Mono Lake—big, bare, and brackish—not in the Sierra but deriving most of its water from the great range. There is evidence that it once was deeper and its water flowed directly to the Owens Valley farther south; but now it has no outlet, and the surface stands at a normal level of 6,409 feet above sea level. Technically, the Owens River rises where three creeks come together about midway between Mono Lake and Crowley Lake, flowing southward from there. But actually these headwaters are greatly supplemented by water from the great mountains along the eastern line of Yosemite Park—Dana, Gibbs, Conness. It flows steeply down toward Mono Lake, then pours through a long tunnel and aqueduct to the Owens River. Many of these streams pause briefly in scenic little cirque or glacial basin lakes.

Small existing glaciers in the shadows of Mount McClure, Rodgers Peak, and Mount Davis contribute their melt, the water running into Rush Creek. It is joined by Reverse Creek, where the usual direction was switched by a whimsical glacier. At Grant Lake, the flow is picked up and disappears into a tunnel headed, not for its natural destination in Mono Lake, but for Los Angeles by way of Crowley Lake. To the hydrologist and the public works administrator, Crowley is a gathering place for the water of many streams, but to the fisherman and the awestruck spectator, it is the lake which, during the opening days of trout season, is almost solidly covered with boats. So much string is dangled in the water it would go around the world seventeen times and, if braided together into a net (which it sometimes is), would strain the patience of a thousand anglers.

Into Lake Crowley run the streams which drain Mammoth Mountain and its several small lakes. (Only three miles west of Mammoth is Devil's Postpile, where the main stream is the upper San Joaquin, which eventually flows to San Francisco Bay.)

Convict Creek and Convict Lake, where glacial moraines are clearly visible, contribute to Crowley Lake. Mount Morrison, almost a mile higher than Convict Lake but very near it, has rock in it that is much older than the granite on which the Sierra rests—the 400-million-year-old mixture going back to the early Ordovician age, which even to geologists was a long time ago. These pre-granitic rocks are estimated to be 32,000 feet thick. Since Mount Morrison is 12,268 feet above sea level, those ancient slates, marbles, hornfels, metacherts, and thick-bedded calcareous orthoquartzite reach almost four miles into the earth. Such a formation is called a "roof pendant"; when the molten magma which later hardened into granite welled upward, it divided here and left the old "roof rocks" (now gone from much of the Sierra) protruding downward into the granite pool. Because of the heat and pressure, some of the old rock was absorbed into the granite, or changed its form, but under Mount Morrison it preserved almost all of its original identity.

Owens Valley is a trough, dropped down almost in a piece when the Sierra was settling itself after the series of uplifts. It is filled with debris from the mountains and is drained along its length by the Owens River —not a Sierra stream, but one that gathers the outflow from all the short creeks and torrents which cascade from the nearby crest. Mount Whitney, the highest point in the contiguous forty-eight states, makes its contribution by way of Lone Pine Creek. Farther down the Owens, almost all the collected water is picked up by an aqueduct to satisfy thirsty Los Angeles, leaving a dry valley with one of the world's most spectacular views.

When the mining boom ended in Bodie, only a ghost town remained. The miners went back to California or tried their luck in Virginia City.

Chapter 11

THE GRANITE PEAKS

*Mount Whitney and its majestic neighbors—some of
the highest high country on the continent*

THERE IS AN OLD JOKE about the hillbilly who tells an interviewer, "Yessir, Sonny, my folks was livin' here when these mountains was just little hills." No one has been living near Mount Whitney that long, but the highest peak in the contiguous forty-eight states actually did grow from a little hill into its present mountain eminence, and so did its great neighbors along the Muir Crest—ten of them over 14,000 feet above sea level, almost two miles higher than the valley at their eastern foot.

The peaks along this great crest have been uplifted, changing from low, round hills a few miles inland from a great sea, and in the same process, or as a result of it, losing great portions of themselves so that only traces of the roundness remain. Along the scarp there are great, fluted cliffs. About two horizontal miles of Whitney are gone; if they were still there, the granite top would probably arch a little higher and then slope down to the east where there are now small lakes in glacial pockets. Great thicknesses of the original rock have been stripped off, too, leaving as the main surface granite which once was buried deeply—and even now frost wedging is at work to break that up.

When the Sierra was first built, perhaps 120 to 130 million years ago, the material lying on the surface and below it for many hundreds—in some places, thousands—of feet was vulnerable to erosion, and eroded it was, clear down to the most resistant rock. The most resistant rock in most cases was the granitoid batholith now so visible, but in some places the older rock had extended downward farther into the cooling granite

and now provides a way of dating and comparing for geologists, and a pleasant variety of appearance for the nonscientific visitor.

After 50 to 60 million years of erosion, there were left just rows of low-lying hills running northwesterly and southeasterly, with a gentle slope westward to the ocean and eastward to who-knows-where. Then came the uplifts of the Sierra block, and as this section of the earth's crust tilted it lifted those eroded low hills almost as a unit—thus accounting for the parallel crests now so obvious on a relief map or from a high-flying airplane. Some of these crests, such as the Ritter Range along the eastern boundary of Yosemite National Park, LeConte Divide, and the upper canyon of the Middle Fork of the San Joaquin River, are carved from some of the faulted and folded early rock, but most of the high ridges are worn away to the granite. Still they run parallel and tend a little off the north-south line.

Mount Whitney is part of one of these crests—the one named for John Muir—and stands in the distinguished company of Mounts Tyndall, Williamson, Barnard, Russell, Muir, and Langley (all over 14,000 feet) , and a host of only slightly lesser peaks. Geologists think that 40 or 50 million years ago, Whitney was a dome-like hill rising about 1,500 feet above the nearest valley and about 2,000 feet above the sea. A later uplift probably added about 2,000 feet, so that Whitney was perhaps 2,000 feet above the valley and 4,000 feet above the sea. In the late Miocene and early Pliocene, there was a second deformation of the Sierra, and when it was over Whitney stood 7,000 feet above

*The Minarets, in the Ritter Range, are a familiar landmark to hikers and climbers. Sedentary
types may see them from the road between Mammoth Lakes and Devil's Postpile.*

sea level, but still about 2,000 feet above the valley to the west. A short time later on the geological clock, there was still more tilting, and the whole locality lifted another 2,000 feet. Just before the Pleistocene epoch it went up some more to about the present height, and while there is a tendency to call that uplifting the "final" one, nobody really knows about that.

The "front" of Whitney—the side visible from the Lone Pine vicinity—is steep and jagged, but the back side is a remnant of the slope of a gentle hill, a pattern repeated many times along the top of the Sierra. The glaciers did not reach this high, and so these topmost peaks retain their broad surfaces; constant wind kept the snow from collecting, and what snow did stick often avalanched down the slopes, making the notable chutes which start about a half mile west of the top point of the peak and about 500 feet lower in elevation. The chutes run out into a gentle grade almost 2,000 feet lower and about half a mile farther west, and from there to the canyon of the Kern River (about five miles), the terrain is a rolling plateau.

The top of Mount Whitney, despite its immense height and the ruggedness of its appearance and surroundings, is accessible in the summer and early fall to anyone who can walk uphill for a few hours—and thousands do, including very small children and a scattering of oldsters—after driving to the foot of the trail west of Lone Pine. Enjoyment of the hike and the view is often greatly impaired by the sudden change of elevation, which makes most persons dizzy if not sick, so a few days in the vicinity before the climb is recommended, and the earliest hours of daylight are best to avoid intense radiation. Many parties camp part way up, so that they can get an early start up the switchback trail, and Forest Service officers are worried about their numbers in relation to the facilities.

There are some extraordinary vistas from breathing-stops along the trail, and the views and the breath-catching increase in number nearest the top. As the trail winds upward along the rocky sawtooth main ridge for the last mile of distance and the last thousand

Mount Whitney, at 14,494 feet, was the highest point in the nation until Alaska became a state. The trail to the top winds behind Day Needle and Keeler Needle (at left).

181

The Palisade Glacier, resting on the shoulder of 14,162-foot Mount Sill, is one of the largest remaining in the

feet of elevation, there are glimpses to the east through openings in the peak, giving a foretaste of the thrill of looking downward and outward from the very top, across the Owens Valley, over the dry mountain ranges which lie in parallel ridges far out into the Great Basin. For many, the feeling of great accomplishment ("My gosh—did I climb all the way up from down there?") gives way to a feeling of man's insignificance in such immensity.

The valleys and arid mountain ranges of Nevada are to the east. To the south, the mountains diminish in size, and there are forests on the slopes. Although the peaks for five or six miles are more than 13,000 feet high, beyond them the mountains decrease in height, so that twenty-five miles south, only one or two are over 10,000 feet.

The grandeur and the reality of the Sierra Nevada stand out starkly in the quadrant from west to north in the view from Mount Whitney. Westward, the slope tapers down to the edge of Kern Canyon. Beyond the canyon, there is another matching plateau (remnant of that ancient broad valley) and then a sweep upward

Sierra. This photo was taken from the moraine.

to the jagged skyline of the Kaweah Peaks Ridge and, beyond, the Great Western Divide. Northward to the end of vision stand spired peak after peak, so high and so bold in relief that their ancestry as low hills seems incredible.

Mount Whitney is 14,495 feet, give or take a foot or so depending on the map or authority. There are ten other peaks over 14,000 feet in the Sierra, and in the close neighborhood are about a dozen over 13,000, plus the highest lake in the country, Lake Tulainyo at 12,802 feet.

Mount Williamson, five or six miles north, is almost as high as Whitney at 14,375, and its partner, Mount Tyndall, reaches 14,018. Near them is Lake Helen of Troy at 12,515; since the legendary "thousand ships" will never be launched at that elevation, the lake must be named for its great beauty, or perhaps for the trouble in getting to it, or perhaps because it lies in the arms of Trojan Peak, 13,950.

Northward from Williamson for about forty miles, the mountains along the crest fall just short of the magic 14,000-foot mark, although they are tremendous; but then, cradling a row of glaciers which are the southernmost in the United States, is the Palisade Crest: striped Split Mountain, or South Palisade, at 14,058; Middle Palisade at 14,040; Mount Sill at 14,162; and North Palisade at 14,242. All of these look like mountains should look; the climb up North Palisade and the view from its summit are spectacular.

AT THE PALISADES, the main crest bends from a north-south direction to northwest-southeast—exactly the right orientation to shelter glaciers away from the brightest sunlight and just where the snow stands without rapid melting, protected from the prevailing wind but collecting snow blown over the summits. The largest glacier is a combination of two—one heading in a cirque between Mount Winchell and a spur of Thunderbolt Peak, the other between Thunderbolt and Mount Sill, with the North Palisade at the top. Like other existing Sierra glaciers, this one is probably not left over from the Ice Age but is of more recent origin. It covers perhaps a square mile. Time was when the ice extended for hundreds of miles along both sides of the crest; all of the high country except the topmost peaks bears its marks.

This high country is protected against much exploitation. Sequoia National Park reaches from the main crest westward to the foothills and from Coyote Peak on the Great Western Divide at the south to Junction Peak and the Kings-Kern Divide on the north, including the Mount Whitney country. Kings Canyon National Park starts at the north boundary of Sequoia Park and continues northerly to Glacier Divide, Muriel Peak, and Pavilion Dome, including the Palisades country. The eastern side of the crest, between the

Mount Muir (left center), only a mile south of Mount Whitney, is a 14,015-foot giant in its own right. The trail to Whitney, out of sight at left, meets the John Muir Trail on the other side of Mount Muir.

peaks and Owens Valley in the Inyo National Forest, has been set aside as the John Muir Wilderness. North and west of Kings Canyon Park in the Sierra National Forest is the High Sierra Wilderness.

The peaks bear a profusion of names, some classical, some topical, some humorous, some confusing, some descriptive. Many features are named for persons who were there: Dusy, LeConte, Colby, Crabtree, Clarence King, and many others. Some are named for persons who never were there: Darwin, Ruskin, Shakespeare, Pinchot, Izaak Walton, Stanford, Huxley, and Julius Caesar. Some describe the terrain: Split Mountain, Round Mountain, Indian Head, The Miter, Diamond Peak, Striped Mountain, Pincushion Peak, Black Mountain, The Thumb, Red Mountain, Seven Gables, Red and White Mountain, and so on.

Animals from gnats and mosquitos (of which there are many) to moose (of which there are none) are honored with lakes, passes, meadows, and canyons; emeralds, pearls, diamonds, crowns, castles, and sceptres add an air of value and majesty—and Homer's Nose is a suitable distance from Garlic Spur. Catastrophes are noted: landslides, avalanches, rockslides, cyclones, tornadoes, and thunder and lightning all lend their names.

Indians are recognized, not always appropriately: Piute, Comanche, Kaweah, Tehipite, Tokopah, Tunemah, Chagoopa, and Indian this-and-that. There are many places named for girls, including Lucy's Foot Pass and Painted Lady Peak. And for sheer poetry, who can top Roaring River, Sky Parlor Meadow, and Lake of the Fallen Moon?

THE HIGH COUNTRY does not slope up smoothly to one main crest but is broken by parallel crests and by lateral ridges. The Muir Crest, with Whitney as its topmost peak, is the highest, but across the Kern Canyon, swinging in a great arc for some thirty or forty miles, is the Great Western Divide; between them the Kern River flows southward in its deep cleft. The Kings-Kern Divide connects these two crests at the north end with a six- or eight-mile link, which is also the boundary between the two national parks; the drainage to the north feeds the Kings River. Everywhere on both sides of the Kings-Kern divide are hundreds of lakes, 11,000 or 12,000 feet above sea level.

The upper Kings River Drainage is bounded on the east by the continuing main crest and on the west by interrupted crests, including Sphinx Crest and the LeConte Divide, with Glacier Divide crossing at the north. Then the main range continues northwestward to the Mammoth Crest, the Ritter Range and to the boundary of Yosemite National Park, the streams running into the San Joaquin River. On a road map of California, this entire wild country can be covered with one hand, but in it is some of the finest remaining wilderness in the world. Roads penetrate it part way from east and west, true, but none goes through—yet.

The most modest acquaintance with the Sierra—even a trip to Yosemite—demonstrates the sculpting power of the glaciers and the wearing action of flowing

Testifying to problems along the trail are Hell-for-Sure Pass, Poopout Pass, Lousy Spring, Poison Meadow, Siberian Outpost and Hungry Packer Lake. On the morbid side are The Tombstone, Disappointment Lake, Graveyard Meadow, Gorge of Despair, Inconsolable Range, Spook Canyon, Hell Hole Meadow, and various devilish places including Devil's Crags and Devil's Punchbowl.

water. But it takes a trip to the high country to see the best examples of two other forces: the splitting of rocks by frost and the gouging of immense smooth chutes by avalanches. These are at their best above the glacier-ground valleys and canyons, and the avalanche paths in particular seem to end where the surfaces of the larger ice masses were.

On a small scale, the cracking of granite into blocks and slabs can be seen wherever there is granite. But on the gently sloping old erosion surfaces of Whitney and other extremely high summits, the rock cracks apart and remains almost in place because there is nothing to move it; in these highest places, there are no streams. If the rock is wedged apart by ice on or near a cliff, however, it falls downward, causing the talus slopes which are so common below canyon walls.

This is intensified when a cornice of snow breaks loose, sweeping down the cliff with rock fragments mixed in it—plunging hundreds of feet and grinding a smooth chute in the process. While this action is still going on today, it was most prevalent during the glacial periods, as the glaciers undercut the mountainsides and made them steeper and perhaps also because there was more snow. The chutes are most commonly wider at the top than the bottom, possibly because some of the falling snow flies outward into the air, and often the path is split near the top. They can be very steep and, at their climax of development or where they are close together, cause a fluted appearance on the whole mountainside, with many chutes separated by thin and almost vertical ridges.

The peaks, spires, ridges, divides, canyons, valleys, rock piles, and crests of the High Sierra present a bewildering appearance from a distance or from the air and appear to make up such a formidable landscape that it would seem to be uncomfortable if not hazardous to be on foot in the midst of it. However, this is not the case. Trails wind in and out, skirting the most rugged spots, linking together the lakes and meadows, and reaching out to vista points. Some of the trails go back to Indian times, and others were pioneered by sheep and cattle men. They are often well marked with

Castle Rocks are a huge granite ridge towering above the wooded Kaweah River Canyon in Sequoia National Park. Timber reaches almost to the 9,180-foot crest.

187

The Sawtooth Ridge, with Matterhorn Peak at left, runs along the northeastern boundary of Yosemite. Cars can approach to within a few miles of it, by way of Twin Lakes. Dense pockets of snow in the shadow of the ridge are glaciers.

signs and most are on suitable maps.

Throughout the summer and into the early fall there are hundreds of hikers on these trails—in some places, thousands. Every age is there; scout troops and outing-club groups are herded up and down the paths like the once-prevalent sheep. When a club's high camp moves from site to site, the participants are scattered for miles along the trail. Solitary hikers, or one or two couples, are common. Foot travelers step aside, preferably on the downhill side, for horses, mules, or burros. At some of the more popular lakes, the shoreline may be rimmed with campers; but in the out-of-the-way places, it is possible to go for days without a human encounter.

Portions of the California Riding and Hiking Trail wind along at 7,000 or 8,000 feet, and the John Muir section of the Pacific Crest Trail runs approximately north and south from Yosemite to Whitney. There are many places to which trails do not go—but this does

habits of sea level. Each item of food and equipment is carefully thought out and its advantages and ounces weighed: so much for comfort, convenience, or a full stomach in camp, so much less in the pack for those uphill miles; after the first trip, the pack usually wins the decision. But this is not self-punishment—it is just the small price one pays for the joys of the high country.

THE NEVADA-CALIFORNIA line angles sharply at Lake Tahoe, leaving the entire Sierra south of the lake in California, although Nevadans say the crest of the range should have been the boundary. Three California counties lie on the east side of the Sierra, their county seats far distant from the capital at Sacramento especially in the winter. In this region are situated some of the Sierra Nevada's finest collection of peaks.

The Carson Range joins the main range near Carson Pass, and from there the Sierra divide extends southeasterly, the peaks getting higher and more sharply etched against the skyline. Around Markleeville the Sierra dominates the scene, with many peaks over 9,000 feet forming the skyline. Carson Pass is less than a dozen miles due west of Markleeville in a direct line, but by road the distance is doubled. Ebbetts Pass, which to the traveler seems west of Markleeville, actually is about ten miles south. Both passes are more than 3,000 feet higher than Markleeville. The volcanic hills around Markleeville run out northeastward to meet Nevada's Pine Nut Mountains, and have a pass of their own: Monitor Pass, at about 8,300 feet, which is considered a secondary pass because it is several miles east of the main crest.

Below Monitor Pass to the South is Antelope Valley, squeezed between the Sweetwater Mountains of Nevada and the Sierra, in the midst of a geological hodgepodge of granite, alluvium, volcanics, marine deposits, and lake deposits—all laced with earthquake fault lines. The unmistakable marks of the glaciers are visible upstream from Antelope Valley, and in a pocket of the valley is Topaz Lake. South of the Sweetwater Mountains is Bridgeport Valley, a lake bottom filled by the outwash from the high peaks which mark the boundary of Yosemite Park, just over the ridges to the west. Along those ridges were some mighty glaciers, for there are two narrow canyons and one broad one with thick

not deter the experienced mountain people, for it is possible, and not uncommon, to pick a way, strolling along an easy contour here and rock-hopping there, or scrambling up an unmarked slope. For the fittest and those with resolve and a nylon rope, there is rock-climbing, making it to the top the hard way.

Switchback trails up to some distant pass tend to focus attention on muscles not known to city walkers; and a certain shortness of breath points up the shallow

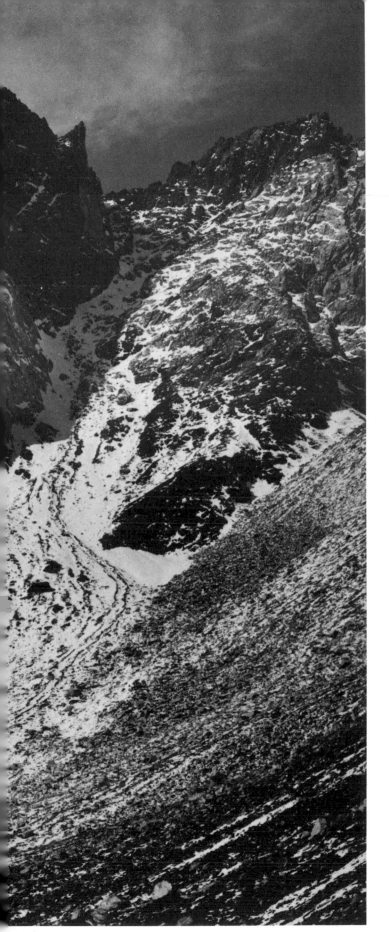

deposits of material left when the ice masses melted, and west of Bridgeport Valley there is bare granite worked over by the ice. Great jagged peaks with glacial cirques are visible to the west from the grade between Bridgeport and Conway Summit, earning the name of Sawtooth Ridge; almost all are above 11,000 feet. The glaciers from that ridge, which ran eastward into this valley, must have been short and powerful, for the basin between Conway Summit and Bridgeport is filled with their debris. Out of that basin the Hunewill Hills rise like islands. These hills, part of the volcanics which extend out into Nevada, are probably nine or ten million years old; but up on top of the Sawtooth Ridge, surmounting the granite, are older volcanics, much changed in the millions of centuries of their existence.

Around the Bridgeport area are hot springs, and there is surmise that a great deal of the volcanic "river" on the far side of the Sierra may have originated in this vicinity before the great uplift.

Conway Summit is a saddle in a ridge which dips eastward from the Yosemite Park boundary about seven miles away. The ground halfway to the crest was washed there by glaciers, accounting for the rolling and almost gentle appearance compared to the sharp and rugged heights. Up where the hard rock starts are forty or fifty lakes, some so small as to be only ponds, only half large enough to bear names. Collectively called Virginia Lakes, they drain by many creeks into the Walker River and thence out to a sink in the desert.

The lakes and a long strip northward are in the 42,800-acre Hoover Wilderness, "an area where the earth and its community of life are untrammeled by man, where man himself is a visitor who does not remain." There are no roads, no motorcycles on the trails, no landing aircraft, and no outboard motors on the lakes. During most summers, pockets of snow remain in the shaded cirques. In the deep canyons are patches of meadow, with quail around the higher ones, sage grouse around the lower ones, and luxuriant plant life in all. Bears, bobcats, and coyotes live here, and the lakes, especially those beyond the roadheads, are

Chunks of granite, broken from the peaks, have rolled down to form huge talus slopes in the Humphreys Basin, east of the Sierran crest and north of Kings Canyon National Park.

191

stocked with rainbow and eastern brook trout; up high there are golden trout.

Against the skyline are Excelsior Mountain, 12,446 feet, and Dunderberg Peak, 12,347 feet, only a little higher than their companions: Cleaver, Sawblade, Three Teeth, Doodad, Gray Tooth, Blacksmith, and Matterhorn.

Part of the glacier which helped carve the east side of these jagged spires and provided the basins for their many lakes split at Conway Summit and left a tongue of debris down toward Mono Lake; a separate glacier came down Lundy Canyon toward the northern end of that alkaline lake, which has one side in the desert and the other snuggled up under the great scarp of the Sierra Nevada. Less than a dozen miles away is the top of the range—6,000 feet higher.

From Mounts Conness, Dana, and Gibbs, and other great peaks came a huge volume of mixed debris, carried down by ice toward Mono Lake and left in a huge morainal belt from Leevining Canyon to June Lake. The glaciers played a strange trick near June Lake, for the stream which runs from the lake flows *toward* the Sierra, not away from it, and then makes a horseshoe loop through Grant Lake and thence toward Mono Lake. An arm of the glacier which ground down past Grant Lake was shorter and thicker (about 1,800 feet thick) and met weaker rock, so it dug deeper than the 1,300-foot-thick, two-mile-long June Lake branch. When the ice was gone, the water just flowed down the deeper channel and earned its name of Reversed Creek.

Civilization and wilderness are side by side around Mammoth Mountain, where there are summer cabins and resorts around numerous glacial lakes, and winter sports facilities. West of this complex, between the Mammoth Crest and the Ritter Range is the Devil's Postpile, where nearly a million years ago a basaltic lava flow from Mammoth Pass ran down the middle fork of the San Joaquin River (far, far from the same river's tame extremity in the Great Valley) about six miles to Rainbow Falls. As the flow cooled, it cracked into spectacular columns, and then a thousand-foot-thick glacier came along and quarried much of it away. The Postpile was left, scratched and ground at the top and cut away at the side.

On the road to the Postpile is the Mammoth Earthquake Fault, a cleft as deep as fifty-five feet in places,

possibly connected with the earthquakes of the 1700s which are part of the legendry of the Indians of the area. Mammoth Mountain is a greatly worn old volcano; the Postpile is part of a younger laval flow; glacial evidence is everywhere in the vicinity; and the earth is cracked open—telling in a few square miles the story of the forming of the Sierra from seabed and rolling plain by ice, fire, and convulsion.

The Owens Valley lies below the great Sierra Nevada escarpment, the 14,000-foot peaks and spires seeming very close, although actually four to twelve miles away. Owens Valley is a trough with a full length of over a hundred miles, nearly as long as the San Joaquin portion of the Great Valley of California. At one time, the valley floor was higher, rising with the rest of the Sierra, but then it subsided to a point much lower than it is now. A great lake formed, with the ancient beaches still etched in the alkaline soil, fed by glacial runoff in the ice age and by the many short streams coursing down from the Sierra Crest—which brought with them sand and silt that filled the sink with sediment a thousand feet thick. In the late 1800s, ranching was started and remained productive until the city of Los Angeles acquired the water rights and built an aqueduct to take it all to town.

Mount Whitney—at 14,495 feet the highest point in the United States until Alaska joined the Union—dominates the Sierra Crest, but from the Owens Valley other peaks seem higher because they are closer. Whitney stands in some upright company; along this part of the crest from Mount Darwin on the north to Olancha on the south, the highest peaks are all above 13,000 feet, and the most used pass over that ridge, Kearsarge, crosses at 11,896. Over the crest to the west is the south-running Kern River, and the gorgeous wilderness country of Kings Canyon and Sequoia National Parks. Near at hand, the marks of earthquakes during the past few hundred years are visible; in 1870 the town of Lone Pine was almost wiped out by tremors as the earth beneath it continued adjusting to the pressures which tilted the Sierra long ago.

That tilting produced the uplifted raw edge of the eastern escarpment, where Mount Whitney is almost 11,000 feet higher than Owens Lake below it—and where the plants and animals live on a thin border between alpine heights and the dryness of the desert.

The east face of Mount Whitney is fluted and craggy, but one need not be a daring mountaineer to climb it—there is a relatively easy trail that climbs up to the broad, sloping top, remnant of some ancient plateau.

Overleaf: Seen from the Owens Valley, the rough Alabama Hills are silhouetted against the much higher, snow-capped Sierra beyond. Mount Langley is at right.

The last rays of a winter sun cast a rosy glow over the granite crags of Mounts Ritter and Banner.

The clear glacial lakes in the Ionian Basin are fed throughout the year by residual snow. Since the area is above timberline, only hardy alpine plants survive.

Enchanted Gorge, between Black Divide and Ragged Spur, is one of the loneliest spots in the Sierra—remote, austere, and often choked with snow.

Thompson Ridge, reflected in Blue Lake.

THE INDUSTRIALISTS

Tornado, flood, earthquake and volcano combined could hardly make greater havoc, spread wider ruin and wreck, than are to be seen everywhere in the track of the larger gold-washing operations . . . Many of the streams are turned out of their original channels, either directly for mining purposes, or in consequence of the great masses of soil and gravel that come down from the gold-washing above. Thousands of acres of land along their banks are ruined forever by the deposits of this character. A farmer may have his whole estate turned into a barren waste. . . . Then the tornout, dug-out, washed to pieces and then washed over sidehills, masses that have been or are being subjected to the hydraulics of the miners, are the very devil's chaos indeed. The country is full of them among the mining districts of the Sierra Nevada, and they are truly a terrible blot upon the face of Nature.

—Samuel Bowles in *Across the Continent*, 1865.

Man has tinkered with these mountains and in many ways changed them. It may seem impossible that a force a foot thick, two feet wide, and five or six feet high could compete with the forces of pressure, heat, and ice that gave the Sierra its shape, but in only a little more than a century man has tunneled under, cut across, washed away, blown into the air, and hauled to distant points an uncalculated but large portion of the rock and soil; has diverted, dammed, and sometimes destroyed running rivers, lesser streams, and some lakes; has filled canyons with trash or piled it helter-skelter on the surface; has stripped grass and giant trees from the landscape and let fire run loose at unnatural times. When viewed against the geological backdrop of eons, man's efforts may seem puny and short-lived, but it is obvious that they have altered the environment of the mountains in ways that will last

for as long as man may expect to remain a tenant on the earth.

On a more positive note, those efforts also have contributed substantially to the economic growth of California, first lifting her from the status of a semi-wilderness to a full-fledged American state in less than two years, then helping to develop her into one of the financial citadels of the nation. However damaging all of this has been—and continues to be—to the ecological quality of the Sierra Nevada, its importance to the historical life of California cannot be denied.

The first, and in many ways the most traumatic manifestation of man's using the Sierra Nevada as a tool for his enrichment came with the California gold rush of 1848–1852. When James Marshall stumbled across flecks of gold in the tailrace of Sutter's Mill in January 1848, he set off a chain of detonations that would alter his-

201

Flumes vastly speeded up the transport of logs from slope to sawmill. But the occasional passenger—and there actually were some—found it a harrowing trip.

Second-growth timber from the mountains above Sonora is dumped into a millpond, then fed to saws through jets of water to clean the bark. Part of cut is usually stacked in "cold decks" for sawing later.

tory. By the spring of the year, there were four thousand miners scuttling around in the foothill country; by the end of the year, there were at least ten thousand; and by the late summer of 1849, when most of the hundred thousand forty-niners had arrived from points east, west, north, and south, the foothills crawled with some forty thousand—in a region that less than two years before had been populated mainly by transient bands of Indians.

The immediate effect of all this activity was not particularly damaging; the miners dirtied some streams, littered with abandon, and erected camps and towns where they had no business being, but they altered nothing substantially—at least until the early months of 1850. By then, however, things began to change. The free placer gold that had inspired the rush in the first place had been so thoroughly picked over that efforts on a more ambitious scale were necessary for a profit to be made. From an adventure, mining rapidly evolved into an industry dominated by companies that were little more than gold-finding factories. Enormous networks of flumes and sluices were constructed all over the foothills to bring water in great quantities down to "dry diggins" of one gulch or another. Rivers were dammed and diverted for mile after mile of their length, so that small armies of miners—most of them in the employ of companies—could get at the gold in their gravel bottoms.

By 1852, the year that the rush itself came to an end, such industrial enterprises thoroughly dominated mining in the mountains—which by then had produced some $224 million in gold. They were abetted the following year by the development of hydraulic mining, by which water brought down from the high places of the mountains through a system of ditches, flumes, and pipes was directed with immense force through nozzled hoses against entire hillsides, moving thousands of yards of earth at a time, washing it down through long rows of riffles which let the heavy gold sink to the bottom and the lighter silt and gravel go out the lower end —and ultimately into a convenient river or creek. By the 1880s this highly efficient method of getting at gold mixed thinly in vast amounts of dirt had become an enormous industry, with a capital investment of $100 million and more than 8,000 miles of flumes, ditches, and pipelines carrying 72 million gallons of water every day. It also was incredibly destructive, creating such man-made badlands as those now memorialized in Malakoff Diggins State Historic Park. Even more significantly, it dumped millions of cubic yards of debris

A sawmill on the American River, circa 1890. In the early years of the transcontinental railroad, wood from this area fed the fireboxes of little locomotives for the steep climb up the Sierra grade.

on the river plains of the Sacramento Valley, raising stream beds, creating flood danger, silting up the Sacramento River, and destroying farms. The damage was so great that the industry was outlawed in 1884—in spite of the fact that it had by then contributed more than $200 million to the gold output of California's mines.

Dredging, which utilized flat-bottomed boats that crawled over water covered gravel, was a longer-lived, more productive, and much less damaging method of industrial mining, although windrows of tailings left behind by these curious vessels can still be seen throughout much of the foothill country. The first California dredge began operations on the Yuba River above Marysville in 1850, and the last dredge shut down on the same river in 1968. In between, dredging produced an estimated $400 million in gold.

Deep mining was the ultimate expression of industrial mining in the Sierra Nevada. It produced most of the $2.5 billion eventually pried out of the mountains, and implanted industrial towns from Alleghany in Sierra County to Jacksonville in Tuolumne County, and numerous points in between: Nevada City, Grass Valley, Plymouth, Amador City, Jackson, Jamestown. . . . It, too, was long-lived, beginning as early as 1851

with operations of the Quartz Mining Company in Grass Valley, and ending as late as 1964, when the Sixteen-to-One Mine of Alleghany closed its shafts and allowed water to start creeping into its depths. Aside from the tailings from its mills and the dumps from its shafts and tunnels—many of which can still be seen as mute, weed-grown lumps—the main effect deep mining had on the physical character of the Sierra Nevada was beneath its surface. Many went to incredible depths as they traced the course of the golden veins that laced the mountains; the Kennedy Mine of Jackson, Amador County, reached a maximum depth of 5,912 feet before it closed in 1942—at the time, the deepest mine in North America.

With the closing of the Sixteen-to-One Mine in 1964 and the cessation of the last gold dredge in 1968, the era of mining in the mountains ended. It was the first great industry in the Sierra Nevada, but it is interesting to note that the total productivity of its mines in the 124 years since James Marshall noticed "something shining in the bottom of the ditch" amounted to only a little more than one-half of California's annual agricultural production today. In the long view, perhaps, gold mining seems less significant than all the fuss might have warranted; but it was the spark that set off

Hydraulic mining was a massive enterprise—in terms of investment, effort, and reward. Riffles were removed while workers cleaned the sluice boxes of this mine above Brownsville, Butte County.

a chain of events, founded the economy of the West, helped save the Union in the War Between the States, and changed forever the direction of California.

There have been other ores extracted, including tungsten and manganese, and much gravel and rock to grind into cement; but in the minds of most people, mining means gold, and the search for gold has left a great mark on the mountains.

T*he timber resources of the Sierra Nevada, dormant and untapped until the gold rush, then leaped to take an important part in the economic life of the state—a position they hold today. The abundance of yellow and sugar pine on the western slopes of the mountains, in fact, was a major contribution to the development of the mining industry, according to W. H. Hutchinson: "Lumber became the first natural resource to be exploited after gold, although it also can be said that it was exploited concurrently with gold. It can be said further that, without the extravagant supply of timber in close proximity to the gold belt, the production of gold would have been far smaller. . . . The availability of these species in quantity*

throughout the Mother Lode provided the raw materials for cradles and sluice boxes, for water flumes and diversion dams, and for the timbers and planks so vital to both the shaft- and hydraulic-mining processes. For building and for fuel as well, the Mother Lode's timber resources were indispensable."

Until the advent of the railroad in the latter 1860s, however, the difficulties of transportation made Sierra Nevada lumbering a singularly localized industry, one that satisfied only the needs of the immediate area. San Francisco and the other growing cities of the coastal region obtained the bulk of their building materials from the stands of coastal redwoods to the north and south. After 1860, the emergence of the Comstock Lode in timber-poor Nevada inspired further development, and the land of the Tahoe Basin was systematically wiped clean of huge stands of its timber, as logs were towed across the lake and sent screaming down the Valley of the Truckee in great flumes (remnants of which can still be seen by the motorist).

When the Central Pacific Railroad sliced into the mountains and the Southern Pacific later began sending shoots out into the Great Valley, Sierra Nevada lumbering came into its own, spreading its produce

This picture was taken shortly after the Central Pacific rails reached Cisco in November, 1866. Wells Fargo's stage and express business continued to thrive long after the completion of the transcontinental railroad.

into the growing agricultural communities of the valley and on to the coastal cities. By the turn of the century, the lumber industry—like the mining that had inspired it—had shaken down from a collection of numerous small companies into one dominated by a few large corporations, complete with company towns.

The impact of all this activity on the Sierra Nevada was predictably brutal—in a manner characteristic of all exploitive industries in the nineteenth century. The supply seemed inexhaustible, and the resultant waste and misuse of the land was incredible. Only the prime cuts of timber were hauled out of the woods, the rest left to rot on the forest floor; clear-cutting was the order of the day, and entire mountainsides were literally stripped of their cover; reseeding as such was almost unknown, although foresightful companies did leave "seed trees" standing amidst the ruin in order to perpetuate the forest; watersheds were wiped out, erosion encouraged, streams polluted with mill wastes, and man-caused forest fires allowed to burn unchecked.

Even as all this was going on, however, there was a movement afoot that recognized the value of preserving, as well as utilizing, the forestlands of the Sierra Nevada. Under the prodding of local conservation

groups appalled by the destruction in the Tahoe Basin, a State Board of Forestry was created in 1883 to regulate timber resources, and while it was dissolved in 1893, the concept was kept alive and was re-instituted in 1903. Two years later, the United States Forest Service was created under the leadership of Gifford Pinchot; the bulk of the timber lands in the Sierra Nevada fell under federal control, and over the years a decent system of management was developed to replace the uninhibited procedures of the nineteenth century.

Today, the business of logging remains a major ecological factor in the mountains. Huge trucks, thousands of them, roll from dawn until long after dark hauling trees to mills for lumber. The extensive federal lands have been on a sustained-yield basis for many years, with selective cutting supposed to match the amount of wood fiber (not always the same species) which can be grown in a given area either from natural regeneration or by planting new seeds or seedlings. To the nature-lovers' protest against cutting of trees, the lumber man answers that people must have building material. For each person in the United States, thirteen acres of woodland are required to supply essential fiber in paper, fuel, and lumber used by the individual and

Donnells Dam, on the North Fork of the Stanislaus River, spans a granite gorge to impound water for generating

in industry—an acre and a half for paper products, about two acres for fuel, and most of the remainder for boards and beams. Not much paper is made from Sierra trees, but a great deal of lumber is—and large numbers of foothill trees such as oak are cut down for fuel.

During World War II, thousands of small sawmills sprang up all over the mountains cutting boards, often wastefully; these have been consolidated now into larger and more efficient factory-type operations, many of which use more of the tree without as much waste; the "peckerwood mills" are gone or are slowly disintegrating into sometimes picturesque ruins which artists and photographers seek out. Their sawdust piles, accidentally or purposely ignited, may burn and smolder for months. The sawmills are now on the edges of towns and are even trying to control the smoke from their dust and bark burners, but out in the woods where

the logs are cut, disruption of the natural setting is the rule.

Behind the obvious changes (new roads with loose cuts and fills, churning of the surface by tractors, slash discarded everywhere) are some more subtle ones: the habitats of many small animals either altered or eliminated, nesting places for birds and tree-climbers changed, insect cycles which are the basis of the food chain shifted or destroyed; streams diverted or silted. But logging seems to help the deer to feed and multiply, especially in the summer months, because they feed along the edges of the woods, and logging provides more edges; and new roads let more people get into more places, a blessing which conservationists seem dubious about.

Millions of people make use of the Sierra without leaving home and without knowing their dependence. The collection, storage, and distribution of water is the

206

electricity. Unlike many such reservoirs, Donnells Lake has no public access road and no recreational development.

most important task to which the mountains have been harnessed. As early as the mining days of the 1850s, small and medium-size natural lakes, quite often those left over from glacial action or the streams below them, were tapped by crude ditches to convey the water elsewhere to wash gold from gravel. If a gulley had to be crossed (and there were many of them), a crude flume was constructed. Gradually the ditches and flumes became longer and better built, and rough rock dams which raised natural levels a few feet gave way to engineered dams. When the need for mining water diminished, the need for domestic and industrial water had already increased, and so had the need to irrigate growing acreages of crops. Later, electric power, first generated as a sort of luxury by-product of falling water, became of overwhelming importance; so the old dams were built higher still and great new works constructed, often using the same water over and over again as it

stair-stepped from level to level—dam to powerhouse to dam and powerhouse again.

Floods which once contributed to the wealth of the Sacramento and San Joaquin Valleys by contributing topsoil and essential minerals were found to be disasters after civilization moved in; flood protection became an essential factor in damming the streams and doling out the water which previously ran untamed to the sea. Water demands took precedence over everything else and altered forever some parts of the Sierra. In 1913 the great economic leverage of Los Angeles put Owens Valley on the east side of the range almost out of business and dried it up so that water could flow through a 230-mile aqueduct around the end of the mountains and all the way to the San Fernando Valley. A deep gorge at Hetch Hetchy, which almost equalled

in beauty and grandeur Yosemite Valley a few miles away, was dammed and filled with water for the taps of San Francisco in 1934.

In the 1930s, the Central Valley Project was launched, and all of its waterworks projects (except for the enormous Shasta Dam on the headwaters of the Sacramento) were added to the Sierra Nevada's collection—principally Friant Dam and Folsom Dam. Another Central Valley Project enterprise is under construction at Auburn on the North Fork of the American River, where Auburn Dam will ultimately impound some 2.3 million acre-feet of water. In 1961, construction began on Oroville Dam on the Feather River, the central feature of the Feather River Project, which was the central feature of the California Water Project—which was the central feature of the California Water Plan of 1959; construction was completed in 1965, and today the Feather is a captured river.

Water is almost everywhere in the Sierra. Natural lakes sparkle all the way to the top, and they, with the large and small streams flowing from them, are one of the glories of the mountains. Where glacial action has been strongest, the lakes step down from terrace to terrace, pocket to pocket, the stream of which they are a part gradually increasing in size and strength and beauty as it pours over a waterfall here, splashes down in a cascade there, or flows through a deep clear pool. The sound of running water is one of the distinct pleasures of the Sierra Nevada, and the constantly changing reflection of light from a still lake or foaming fall one of its greatest joys. At the highest elevations, the austerity of bare rock is softened by a stream or tarn; in the lower canyons, the flow of a creek or river enhances and is enhanced by the thickets of brush and the grace of overhanging trees and shrubs; everywhere life is most active where the water is.

Business and pleasure are intertwined, though, and the pleasant sounds of cascading water in the mountains are matched by the ringing of the cash registers in the cities, made possible by the dams, ditches, and powerhouses. The era of dam building is not over, although it may be waning. Agriculturalists sometimes see the possibility of building dams and canals at a low cost to themselves for irrigation water, by charging construction and operating expenses to the sale of electricity. In some instances, this has been accomplished,

but a straw in the wind is the fact that on the Middle Fork of the Feather River an alliance of sportsmen's groups, mountain county supervisors, state and federal agencies, conservationists, and private citizens lined up in bitter and expensive battle against rice growers of the Sacramento Valley and won: the Middle Feather has become an officially designated "wild river," protected against any encroachment.

Minerals, timber, and water—these have been the principal resources of the Sierra Nevada that man has used to his immediate benefit, if not to the benefit of the mountains. Another has been its grasslands, for many years used as summer feed for California's livestock population. In the mid-1860s, the state's cattlemen, driven out of the Great Valley by drought, turned to migratory grazing, moving their herds up into the mountain prairies. The pattern was followed by the sheep industry from 1870 until about 1890, when enormous herds (perhaps five million head a year during the 1870s) were driven from the valley up the east side of the Sierra Nevada in the spring, ate their way over the mountain passes in summer, and moved back down into the Great Valley through the mountain meadows. The devastation to the native grasses was profound. In many places, the grazing capacity of the grasslands was halved by overgrazing and erosion, and while today grazing is stringently regulated by federal agencies, those original grasslands have never returned to their original form.

The final legacy of man's enthusiastic tinkering with the resources of the Sierra Nevada is hard to determine. Certainly, the mountains eventually will triumph over all his efforts: the eons to come will see the great reservoirs filled with mud, the scars of hydraulic mining obliterated by erosion and vegetation, the trees again growing to maturity and a natural pattern, and the grasses and small plants returning to hold the earth, perhaps even to break up and conceal the pavements. But what of the time on which man himself can count? Has he altered the quality of life so that the resources he has taken and continues to take may never equal in value the life that he and his descendants might have had if these treasures had been left in the Sierra Nevada?

209

Tourism is the newest major industry in the Sierra. This complex at Squaw Valley, site of the 1960 Winter Olympics, includes ski lifts, ice rink, parking lots, hotels, and a subdivision for private homes.

PART FOUR

WONDERS
AND
CURIOSITIES

Mount Whitney (breaking the horizon in the center of the picture) and its majestic companions in the southern Sierra look like a choppy sea of granite when viewed from the air. Moose Lake is in the foreground.

Chapter 12

JEWEL IN THE SKY

*Lake Tahoe—whose cold blue waters and peak-rimmed shoreline
fight for survival against encroaching man*

TEN MILES WIDE, 20 miles long, 1,600 feet deep, more than a mile above sea level, and harboring 50 million crayfish; holding enough water to cover the states of California and Nevada to a depth of eight inches, or to supply the domestic and industrial needs of the entire population of the United States for over five years; about 71 miles around, covering 193 square miles; water so clear that light penetrates over 400 feet and a dinner plate can be seen more than 100 feet down...

There are more statistics—but statistics alone cannot describe Lake Tahoe: part wilderness, part suburb; part residential, part recreational; part park and part neon jungle; with mountain cabin hideaways barely out of sight of gambling casinos which run twenty-four hours a day regardless of sun or storm; row upon row of motels crowding the car-packed pavement here, serene mansions set in groves of sugar pine there; the scantiest of bikinis in July, padded ski clothes in January; crowded, brightly lit restaurants beside the lake, and thousands of feet higher among the peaks a handful of hikers cooking a lightweight meal on a small fire; great clumps of artificial illumination of every type the designers can devise and, over the screening ridges, the glitter of the stars, very close in the clear air, and the soft reflection of the moon.

Lake Tahoe lies exactly on the California-Nevada state line, so the paradoxes and problems of the Tahoe Basin are being studied, argued, and perhaps solved by many agencies working together and separately (and sometimes against one another). The unique charac-

teristics of the place have produced some unique situations, mostly caused by large numbers of people, for Lake Tahoe was doing quite well all by itself until the twentieth century. The cataclysms that occurred before people arrived in such great numbers were natural—and though some were tremendous in their effects, each seemed to add to the splendor, not spoil it.

When the Sierra Nevada was lifting, not all the land affected could stand the strain, and there had to be a boundary to the tilt somewhere. North of Tahoe, the break was not clean but irregular; far south of Tahoe, the line could have been cut with a knife; but at Lake Tahoe, a chunk of the land about the size of the lake failed to rise with the surrounding area and in fact dropped lower along cracks caused by the tension. The result was a double crest for the Sierra, one in the main range and the other along the Carson Range, almost equally high. Between the two was a basin, with its bottom just about the same 4,700-foot elevation as the Carson Valley, on the desert side of the double crest, and about a mile lower than the crests themselves.

Into the new basin poured the runoff from five hundred square miles, and the lake began to form. As it rose, volcanic action around Martis Peak at the northerly end sent a flow of lava and mud across the gap through which the Truckee River flows, and behind the new dam the water continued to rise. Glaciers spilled over from the west and south; as they thawed, more water was produced. For a long time, the level of the lake was seven or eight hundred feet higher, before it washed away part of the volcanic dam; at several

*The hand of man is clearly seen on the southeast shore of Lake Tahoe,
a boisterous collection of resorts, casinos, and summer homes.*

Long ago a great block of granite sank, forming the bowl that Lake Tahoe now occupies, contained on the west by the main range of the Sierra and on the east by the Carson Range. Majestic sugar pines fringe the shores.

points on the mountainside there are old beach benches. The level may have been lower, too, for a hundred years or so during a dry period in the late eighteenth and early nineteenth century, because there are tree stumps below the present surface, now held at about 6,229 feet above sea level by gates in a small dam at the north end.

The Truckee River flows out of that end, making a big loop to the northward, then running eastward past Reno and north again to lose itself in Pyramid Lake—if it survives a gantlet of irrigation diversions. The Truckee is a brisk river except in the driest of summers, and in winter it can be a terror. In recorded times it has caused some damage and destruction, but during the early part of the Ice Age it really rampaged, probably several times.

Great tongues of ice extended eastward from Squaw Peak and Granite Chief, pressing down to form Squaw Valley and the canyon of Pole Creek, moving inexorably toward and across the Truckee River two or three miles below the outlet of Lake Tahoe. Probably all the streams which fed the lake were frozen, and the lake's

the lake behind it rose to 90 percent of the height of the dam, the blockade simply lifted and floated, and down the canyon of the Truckee River went a great torrent—Lake Tahoe unleashed—carrying Squaw Valley rocks clear out onto the flat east of Reno, fifty or sixty miles away down a twisting channel. The water, rocks, and chunks of ice, traveling at great velocity, must have made an awesome sight from a safe vantage point; but this was almost a million years ago, and there was no one there to record it.

The Carson Range—the spur of the Sierra on the Nevada side of Tahoe—gets less than half the annual precipitation of the main crest, although almost the same height and only about twenty miles farther from the ocean; so glaciation was less on that side. On the western wall of the Tahoe Basin, however, great masses of ice carved out distinctive bowls and formed sawtoothed ridges, pushing down into the lake and leaving great moraines along the edges.

One such glacial path formed the setting for Fallen Leaf Lake, a fine body of water in its own right although dwarfed by Lake Tahoe a quarter mile north and 150 feet lower; another glacier gouged out Emerald Bay, one of the world's most scenic (and seen) spots. On a skinny ridge, formed by a lateral moraine southeast of Fallen Leaf, Angora Lookout commands an even more impressive view, and unlike most Forest Service lookouts, it has a paved, though narrow, approach road. Up higher in the same canyon as Fallen Leaf are other lakes, and beyond them is the wilderness country of Rockbound and Desolation Valleys. All around Tahoe, woods alternate with resorts and homesites, and there are state parks on both sides.

On the Nevada side of the state line at both north and south ends are clusters of gambling casinos, garish buildings surrounded by acres of parked cars, and at the south end a ski complex has cut a great slash up the side of the mountain. On the western side, a subdivider's bulldozer apparently went berserk, building zigzag roads up a steep slope, and at the northeast corner another large development has altered the terrain in odd ways. But these defacements are lost in the hugeness and overwhelming beauty of the lake and its setting; almost every vista, in any of the four distinct seasons, is extraordinary.

From the lake's edge, the nearest mountains loom

outflow was slight; the ice stream moved across the river canyon and formed a huge dam seven hundred feet high, which grew thicker and thicker. During the thawing season, water from the liberated tributaries backed up against this dam to the level of the lake; then the lake itself began to rise, becoming over many seasons about six hundred feet deeper.

But this was no ordinary dam, securely anchored and packed; it was mostly ice, with some rock and gravel mixed in, just lying there across the canyon. Ice is only nine-tenths as heavy as water. Inevitably, when

Emerald Bay, on the west shore of Lake Tahoe, is one of the most photographed spots in the Sierra. Much of the land around the bay is reserved for public enjoyment in a state park.

almost overhead, but those on the opposite shore are so far away they seem low and unremarkable. The water can be placid and smooth, or churn up waves suitable for a small ocean, and the change from one to the other can occur suddenly. In some seasons, great dark clouds come down almost to the surface, turning the water a leaden gray; in other seasons, the clouds are high, white, and immensely fluffy. Most of the time, there are no clouds at all.

In summer the sun warms everything with the radiance peculiar to high elevations, making the shade of the many groves especially attractive; at dusk it disappears so there is a distinct and welcome chill. In winter snow drives in over the peaks from the west and southwest, and the temperature stays below freezing, although the many clear days provide the Sierra paradox of cold feet and sunburned nose.

The lake never freezes over. The volume of water and the shortness of winter seem to prevent deep ice from forming; the entire lake turns over and completely mixes once a year. Numerous predictions have been made as to the fate of Tahoe if the present man-caused

action (though it is not a volcano) 150 million to 200 million years ago, and now is much changed by time and the forces which work on the earth. It is thick; the peak is 9,735 feet above sea level, and the metavolcanic layer is about 7,500 feet deep; below that layer lies another 7,500 feet of ancient sediments, hardened mudstone, sandstone, siltsone, and shale. Beside this are the dark old granites and the lighter, younger granites typical of the Sierra. Where the molten granite pressed upward, it altered the ancient rocks, absorbing some and modifying others; some of the granite has been dated at 106 million years. Erosion and the glaciers have worn away the less resistant rock, and what remains is Mount Tallac and its companion peaks —high, rough, and austere.

The marks of volcanic activity are all around Lake Tahoe, and some of these probably led to the early erroneous idea that the lake fills an old crater. South of the lake, Stevens Peak is a volcanic pile 2,000 feet thick; on the north shore are Mount Watson and Mount Pluto, both centers of eruption, and there are cinder cones dating back one to two million years.

Great volumes of silt and sediment have washed into the lake over the millennia and formed the valley meadows at the south end. Some of this material has been pushed around by the glaciers or transported by them from above; some is recent, the result of human activities; much has come off the ridges and peaks with rainwater, snowmelt, and avalanches. Streams in the spring carry heavy burdens of disintegrated granite in the form of silt, for some varieties of the rock which makes up the great Sierra Nevada batholith (and which seems so hard and durable) are weaker than others. Around Tahoe the rocks disintegrate along the boundaries between separate mineral grains, so that the grains can be washed away by water or blown by the wind— sometimes traveling long distances, but more often accumulating in little piles below boulders or along road cuts. If there is a layer of forest litter or other protective material, the grains stay loosely fitted together and appear to be real rock; take the protection away, and it all goes to pieces.

During volcanic action the molten lava, steam from vents, melted snow, and diverted streams all combine into extensive mudflows. The volcanic glass in the mudflow breaks down into clay as it weathers, and this

pollution and siltation continue, including one that if the clarity of the water dims, the heat budget might be altered and the lake might freeze, for in winter the water temperature dips to within half a degree centigrade of freezing.

MOUNT TALLAC REARS UP as a spectacular eminence southwest of the lake, three miles from the shore but seeming much closer. It is old; the visible rock of the upper part probably was formed by volcanic

A low-lying fan of alluvium, washed down from the heights over the centuries, may account for the greater development along South Shore. At Tahoe Keys, a developer has dredged channels to divert the lake to boat owners' doorsteps.

permits extensive erosion. Only the solid lava flows and the ancient sediments which have been metamorphosed into hard rock resist the weather, and these are constantly being attacked along joint planes in which ice presses outward, so that there are extensive talus piles under the cliffs, deposits of broken rock that provide homes for rodents and other small animals.

The Tahoe basin supports a large assortment of plant and animal life—in the air, on the ground, under the ground, along the wet places of the shoreline, in the streams, and in the lake itself—almost all typical of the Sierra's 6,000- to 9,000-foot elevation. Deep in the cold water of Tahoe are big lake or Mackinaw trout,

a cannibal of careless spawning habits, which has prospered after being introduced from Michigan around the turn of the century. There used to be huge cutthroat trout, with twin red slashes under the jaw (sometimes they were called black-spotted trout), but these became virtually extinct during the 1940s, done in by predation of the Mackinaw and rainbow, heavy market fishing, or interference with spawning by irrigation dams on the Truckee River. Another introduced fish, the Kokanee salmon, feeds on minute life in the open water, competing with small trout for this food, but itself providing forage for the Mackinaw. Kokanee are red in the fall when ready to spawn (which they do once and then die) and in a typical spawning stream appear to be packed from bank to bank.

The Forest Service has a visitor information center at Taylor Creek near South Tahoe which includes along with displays and a nature trail, an underwater chamber showing a typical profile or cross-section of a stream with aquatic insects and fish, affording in a brief visit information which would require many hours of study and observation in the wilds.

LAKE TAHOE WAS ONLY A ROMANTIC RUMOR in the middle of the nineteenth century, "an enchanted lake and wood hidden in the Sierran crest," poorly located on the maps of the day. Indians had been using its shores as a summer camping ground, and a few settlers tried their luck there in the 1850s with some cattle and a few trading posts offering overnight accommodations. There was little business, the wagon trains preferring easier grades, until 1859 when the Comstock commotion a few miles to the east reversed the usual tide of traffic. Miners on their way to the silver bonanza found shortcuts around the south end of the lake and over the Carson Range; in the next few years there would be an incredible burden of wagons, stages, pack trains, and people, not headed for Lake Tahoe's beauty but just passing the lake incidental to getting rich—or going back to California broke, a pattern which can be duplicated even today.

The alluvial soil of the valley at the south end of the lake and in a few other places began producing food for the mines. But more important were the trees growing thickly on the slopes, which could provide lumber and fuel for homes and mills, and timbers to shore up the mine tunnels. The lumbering period around Tahoe lasted from about 1873 to about 1890. Whole forests were felled on the east side, cut into lumber, and hauled to the Comstock. As the best trees disappeared, the fallers moved all around the lake; sometimes logs were rafted to the mills, but soon there were logging railroads to move the wood faster and cheaper. Inclined railways went up to the top of the Carson Range, and from there steep chutes with water flowing down them carried the boards at high speed to the Carson Valley, where they were loaded onto another train and rushed to Virginia City.

All this activity made roads necessary. With the roads came visitors to see what was going on; many of the visitors returned again and again, and then acquired land and built summer retreats. In spite of the logging, Lake Tahoe was a beautiful place; because of the logging (which required vast landholdings), the shore was not broken up entirely into tiny parcels, so much of it remained "undeveloped."

From the turn of the century until the 1950s, resort areas were developed and large summer estates built—all separated by woods and cliffs, and reached most easily by boat. Steamers ran on the lake and delivered mail along with groceries and visitors. The federal government established "forest reserves," which are now the national forests. As automobiles became more prevalent and people of ordinary means were able to drive to the lake, the luxury hotels declined, and more camps and motels were opened. As this demand increased, less and less of the shoreline remained unused, although the large estates with wide beaches remained fenced off and so preserved much of the natural appearance. The towns at the north and south ends of the lake were lived in all year at first, but there was not much winter activity, so the local populace remained small, and the residents were isolated much of the year.

But in the 1950s, with good all-year roads kept open in the winter by great effort, two shifts occurred: the Reno casinos set up branch shops at the state lines, and year-round use of summer homes became common. In the years since, the first casinos have multiplied, and their neon splendor has attracted a parasitic growth of motels, eating places, souvenir shops, gas stations, pavement, traffic signals, and supermarkets. Large subdivisions, reminiscent of those around the major cities, have been laid out and partly built, each taking on the socioeconomic characteristics which provde for instant status recognition; no one need feel lost in the wilderness here, nor out of his peer group.

And yet, here is a place of incredible beauty and diversity, still a jewel in the sky; high, clear, cold, sparkling, whipped by the wind, serene in the sun, the granite sand of the beaches sun-warmed in summer, rimmed with rime in winter; as busy as a racetrack at the highway intersections, but serene and quiet in the shade of the woods; all phony glitter at the ends, but across the broad expanse of clear water reflecting the peace and distant quiet of the stars.

Chapter 13

THE INCOMPARABLE VALLEY

*Yosemite—wondrous Ice Age masterpiece that has awed
and delighted visitors ever since John Muir*

LIKE THE REST OF THE SIERRA, the Yosemite country was tipped up in the great block movements which gave the range its characteristic profile: a long western slope and a sharp eastern escarpment. Long before that uplift, much of the ancient marine sediment which had been folded up out of the sea had been worn down and carried away by water, exposing masses of granite but leaving layers of sedimentary rock on some of the higher places. The Merced River wound westward through rolling country no different then from other broad valleys being eroded by other westbound rivers along the early Sierra. It would have been an easy walk from the Merced River bank to the top of El Capitan, then just a rounded hill about 900 feet above the stream (now it is about 3,000 feet to the brow of the nearly vertical cliff and another 500 to the very top).

The first tilting speeded the flow of the Merced, and the Valley became more pronounced as the river gave up meandering and tried to cut straighter and deeper; the final tilting of the Sierra turned the stream into a torrent, and it cut a deeper and straighter gorge in the floor of the former gentle valley (which was itself a channel in the older, broader valley). If the action had slowed or stopped there, Yosemite Valley would be a good example of a Sierran canyon, with side streams cascading down steep walls into a gorge. El Capitan would have been quite a climb, though, for it had been cut away at the bottom and the soil eroded at the top so the woods were gone—and it was 2,400 feet above the river. But the action did not stop there,

for Yosemite lay due east of the break in the Coast Range at the Golden Gate—and through this funnel and over the low-lying hills near it came the Pacific storms, loaded with moisture, breaking against the 14,000-foot barrier of the Sierra. For one or two million years the average temperature all over the world was so low that the winter snow could not fully melt in summer.

Snow piled upon snow, year after year. The weight of the pile compressed the lower part into ice, and still greater weight made the ice plastic instead of rigid. The plastic ice, much denser than mud or putty but able to flow when forced, could move reluctantly around obstructions or over them, or could pick up anything loose which got in its way. The plastic lower mass carried within itself pieces of rock, from grains of sand to boulders bigger than a house; on its back was layer after layer of brittle ice, and on top was the softer snow of the current winter.

This was the basic structure of the Yosemite glacier. The first pressure against the mountains was straight down where the ice and snow mass was greatest; great bowls or cirques were stripped out, the ice forcing its way into cracks, pushing down and sideways, splitting off chunks of all sizes; the tremendous pressure became greater or less depending on the weight of the accumulating pack above. The movement outward from the points of heaviest pressure pushed against other rocks, crumbling them, and the fragments of the mountain crest became part of the creeping downhill movement, themselves forming the cutting edge of the almost irre-

221

*Melting snow makes a lacy cascade between El Capitan and its east buttress as a spring
storm moves in. Full-size pines look like seedlings atop the great monolith.*

Yosemite Valley, the most magnificent gorge in the Sierra Nevada—some would say, in the world—sits amid the snows for its classical portrait, taken looking east from Inspiration Point.

sistible ice engine as it moved toward lower elevations.

Almost irresistible—but where the resistance was great, the glacier accommodated itself, squeezing around an obstruction here or over one there; most often the obstruction was invisible from outside the mass, but sometimes its presence was indicated by bulges or cracks in the brittle surface of the ice. Where the obstructions were the sides of a preexisting canyon or valley, as at Yosemite, the glacier moved along the same route as the stream which had been there,

sometimes overtopping the ridges on each side, but more often being directed by the valley walls while at the same time chewing and grinding at them and at the valley floor. As in a water stream, side flows came into the larger main ice stream, each keeping its identity for miles by a border of debris displayed at its edges. Eventually, the front of the ice flow had to halt, because of more level valley floors, diminishing pressure from above, and melting at lower elevations, where there was rain instead of snow and the air was

222

the seasons. A lake in the center then filled with sediments to form a meadow. Wind, water, and the winter freeze continued to etch into even greater variety the varied features of the canyon walls.

The walls, though so steep as to seem vertical, are not just blank slabs of rock but great cliffs, monumental rounded masses, and spires alone and in groups. The sides are not parallel but display a variety of bosses and embayments; the valley is squeezed narrow at El Capitan, widens out at the central meadow, and forms a sort of a T at the upper end near Half Dome, where glaciers came together from canyons on both sides. At its widest, the valley is not much more than a mile; at its deepest, it is over a half-mile, so that often the only way to look is up.

T HREE ROCK FEATURES are most memorable to casual visitors, framing other recollections of waterfalls and meadows: Half Dome, Glacier Point and El Capitan. Half Dome is one of nature's great compromises: the weaker part toward the valley is gone, sacrificed to gravity and the glacier which came down Tenaya Canyon, but the other half resisted the cracking of slabs, plucking, pressure, and grinding. Before the Ice Age it was probably a crescent-shaped rounded hill, sloping down westerly in the form of a fairly gentle ridge. Under a layer of old sediments was the rounded dome of granite which had welled up, molten, from below. Eons of erosion wore away much of the overlay, probably leaving the top bare, but the ancestral Half Dome was still only a sizable mountain among many other mountains, and none of the neighboring granite cliffs across the valley were even visible.

Then came the glaciers a great one grinding down through Tenaya Canyon, another down Little Yosemite. Only the top few hundred feet of Half Dome showed above the great moving ice sheets; even the high saddle toward Cloud's Rest was covered. The two masses came together below Half Dome and then continued their way westward, plucking out boulders wherever there were weak joints. When the ice finally receded, there was a lake perhaps 2,000 feet deep where the present meadows are, and reflected in that lake was Half Dome—nearly a mile wide, a quarter mile thick, and 4,800 feet high, almost half that height a vertical

warmer. Such was the icy chisel that carved out Yosemite, coming and going two or three or four times, in a sequence not yet fully determined—an insensate sculptor working with gigantic materials in a vast studio through tens of thousands of years.

When the last of the glaciers was gone, something less than twenty thousand years ago, there remained a U-shaped valley with sheer walls of great height from which dropped many waterfalls varying in appearance according to the new terrain and changing flow with wall of granite. Then as the deep lake filled with debris to become a flat meadow, chunks of wall broke off into great talus slopes of rubble—and Yosemite was much as it is today.

Mirror Lake, not a remnant of the old lake but a fairly new one dammed, geologists think, by a rockslide from an earthquake, provides a faint reminder of that earlier one, but it too is filling and will soon be a meadow, and Half Dome will have no pool to be reflected in.

Glacier Point rises sheer above a rubble slope, about two and a half miles southwest of Half Dome as the eagle flies, cut away from it by a chasm of the Merced River near Vernal and Nevada Falls. The glaciers went over the top of Glacier Point, as much as 700 feet deep at times, and scraped it clean. The Point is easily accessible by road, so millions of persons have peered over its precipice at Yosemite Valley, which seems to be directly below, and from this lofty platform have tried to visualize the scope and energy of the glaciers.

Some of the great falls are visible from this perch: Yosemite Falls, full in the spring, slim and wispy in midsummer, dry or nearly dry in the autumn, flinging a torrent of snowmelt down 1,430 feet (nine times the height of Niagara) in the top leap, surging through 675 feet of cataracts, then dropping another 300 feet to the valley floor; Vernal Fall, which the Indians called "Cloud of Water," about 320 feet; and Nevada Fall, where the water pours over a glacial step and breaks spectacularly at the bottom after falling almost 600 feet.

The immense height of the valley rim makes the water in the falls appear to drop very slowly, and the wind and air resistance breaks the flow into spray, ribbons, and clumps, causing rainbows and a special long-remembered booming during peak flows. The wavering column of Yosemite Falls, its deep boom in the spring, and the ice formations around it during the winter, all are unique.

The Valley floor is 4,000 feet above sea level, and the animals and plants typical of this elevation thrive. But since elevation is not the only factor involved, there is a greater variety than usual packed into the relatively small space. The sun heats the cliffs on the north side of the meadows while the southern cliffs stay cool and shaded; the Merced River wanders slowly along; spray and splash from waterfalls makes moist spots; a light breeze moves up-valley in the day and down at night. On the cliffs themselves, vertical streaks mark where water has dripped down, and lichens have taken advantage of the extra bit of moisture to get a foothold.

There are immense incense cedars and ponderosa pines, and countless smaller conifers; willows, cottonwoods, and alders grow along the stream bottoms. Giant sequoias grow on the uplands, but not in the valley. Shrubs range from the lovely and fragrant western azalea in moist places to the typical chaparral plants from the foothills. Throughout the park are about 60 kinds of mammals, some 200 kinds of birds, and 1,300 kinds of flowering plants; while many of these are at the higher elevations, most are in the valley. The National Park Service provides talks, movies, and guided hikes; and there is a museum and information center where questions are answered and books and pamphlets sold.

THE FIELDS OF GRASS AND FLOWERS, the shrubs and towering trees, the flow and splash of water, the soft winds and changes of light—not to mention the amenities and luxuries for visitors—soften the dominant feature of Yosemite, which is rock.

Nowhere else in the Sierra are there so many types of granitic rock visible, for "granite" is not always the same from place to place and may not be granite at all from a strict geological analysis. There are differences in age and in mineral make-up, in hardness and brightness, in ability to hold together or likeliness to fall apart; but it does the non-geologist little good to know that granodiorite contains at least twice as much plagioclase as orthoclase.

The oldest of Yosemite's rocks are the granodiorites at Gateway and Arch Rock. The second oldest are the diorites of the rock slides west of El Capitan, where weakness and closely spaced joints let the front of the mountain fall down under attacks by ground water, frost, heavy rain, and snowslides, so long ago that the great sloping pile of broken boulders was stable enough to provide a base for one of the main roads into the valley in the early days. The rock there had prominent master joints, cut by numerous cross joints, and must

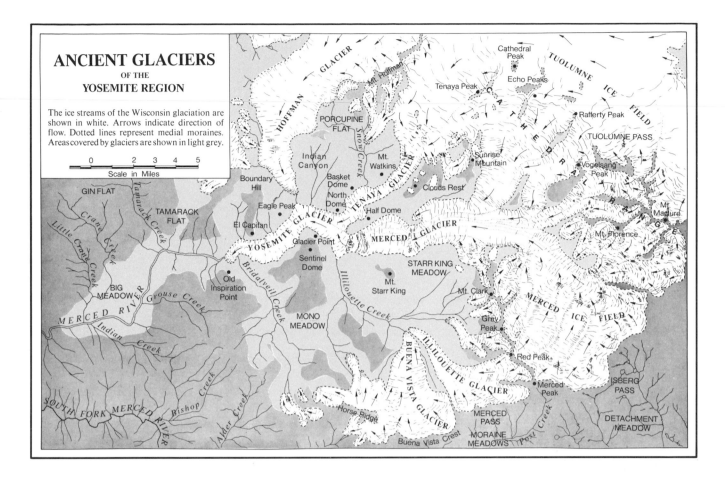

ANCIENT GLACIERS
OF THE
YOSEMITE REGION

The ice streams of the Wisconsin glaciation are shown in white. Arrows indicate direction of flow. Dotted lines represent medial moraines. Areas covered by glaciers are shown in light grey.

0   2   3   4   5
Scale in Miles

have been formed at a different time and under different stresses than neighboring El Capitan, only a little younger but much, much stronger.

The Taft Point granite arrived next, with a somewhat different composition and with sloping joints along with vertical ones, so that the up-and-down sculpture of El Capitan becomes asymmetric here. Profile Cliff, nearby, became especially open to weathering and erosion because of slivering which occurred just after the granite solidified from its original molten condition. Taft and Profile are across a wide part of the valley, about three miles from El Capitan. Just across from El Capitan, and somewhat closer, are two successively younger rocks—the quartz monzonite of the Leaning Tower and the Bridalveil granite—with oblique master joints so well matched that Bridalveil Creek runs down to the fall in a symmetrical V-shaped canyon. Just east of these, Cathedral Rocks stand high

and firm, while next to them, in great contrast, the valley wall is cut and chiseled into a mass of slivered spurs, with only the Spires surviving the dismantling of the cliffs around them.

The Sentinel Rock granodiorite is younger still, but is the second hardest of the Yosemite granites and is unusual in being jointed in only one direction so that it seems to be formed in sheets, giving it a distinctive sheer, smooth cliff.

Half Dome is the toughest of them all—lighter in color, younger in age, flaking off in onion peels but essentially a great monolith with a curving humped back and a sheer face. Before the Ice Age, the "missing half" must have been a furrowed or craggy hillside underlain by splintered rock different from the surviving eminence.

The cliffs, domes, and spires of Yosemite Valley are not neatly divided into areas of these granites—the up-

225

welling of the molten magma that formed the rocks went where it could, and each of the types is found in several places.

Domes are a distinguishing feature of the Sierra Nevada, not found in most other mountain ranges, and they reach their greatest profusion and perfection in Yosemite Park. While a few Sierra domes seem evenly rounded like half an orange with the cut side down, most are irregular—whaleback spurs, rounded ridges, buttresses, and arches, not round but rounded. They were not carved that way by the glaciers, as a first guess might indicate, although many have been polished or scratched by the passing of the ice sheet, and most are not now in their "permanent" form, because large chunks keep breaking loose and sliding down the sides; many, if not most, of the domes are getting smaller year by year.

When the molten granite welled up from below, with great pressure and heat, it could take many shapes; in the Yosemite region and much of the Sierra, it tended to be in large masses, somewhat rounded. The outside cooled faster than the inside, and lines of strain developed along curves which roughly paralleled the outside shape (other lines of weakness occurred, too, depending on the situation). The Sierran granite was deep below the old sediments, of which a layer totaling about fourteen miles thick may have been eroded away over the eons. As the burden of the old rock was removed, pressures within the granite were released; the energy was enough to separate the outermost granite into layers like an onion peel. After exposure to the weather, these layers started to peel off, one by one, sometimes in huge slabs and sometimes in smaller squares and rectangles, depending on how other fractures occurred. The process continues today throughout the Sierra and can be seen in many places around Yosemite.

A peculiarity of granite is the freckled effect often, but not always, seen—some of the freckles being of dinner-plate size or larger. These darker spots are of two kinds: concentrations of minerals which clumped together as the rock was being formed, and "xenoliths," which are much-altered chunks of older rock incorporated into the granite as it moved upward, for the walls against which the magma pressed could not withstand the heat and to some extent merged with the new material. Oddly, these darker spots tend to be of the same strength and texture as the surrounding granite and break with it along the same lines. The same uniform breakage occurs across the light lines which show where later solvent material squeezed into cracks caused by cooling; in a crumpled wall of granite such lines can be traced from broken boulder to boulder, a clue to how the jigsaw puzzle of broken rock once was a seemingly solid cliff.

THIS INCOMPARABLE VALLEY was unknown except to Indians until three years after the discovery of gold in California, although only twenty-five or thirty miles from some of the diggings. True, Joseph Walker's party, struggling over the Sierra from the desert in winter, traveled along the ridges to the north, and some of his scouts peered over the brink; but they were desperate to get out of the snow and out of the mountain maze—half-mile high cliffs held no attraction. James D. Savage established a trading post where the south fork of the Merced joins the main river, only about fifteen miles west of El Capitan, but he knew of the valley only by Indian hearsay, and there was an impassable canyon along the river above his place. Two of his visitors, however (William Abrams and U. N. Reamer), were looking for a millsite in September or October of 1849 and while chasing a bear somehow wandered into Yosemite. Abrams recorded in his diary: ". . . A waterfall dropped from a cliff below three jagged peaks into the valley, while farther beyond a rounded mountain stood, the valley side of which looked as though it had been sliced with a knife as one would slice a loaf of bread. . . ." They had seen Yosemite Falls and Half Dome, all right, but Abrams' diary did not come to public notice until 1947, almost a hundred years later, and the two mill men have had no acclaim as the forerunners of the hordes of visitors to Yosemite.

The first public record puts the "discovery" in March 1851, when a militia company chased some Indians over the high ridges from the south side. They came out of the hills at about Inspiration Point, and one of the company wrote: "The grandeur of the scene was softened by the haze that hung over the valley— light as gossamer—and by the clouds which partially dimmed the higher cliffs and mountains. This obscur-

227

This unusual aerial view, looking west, helps to put Yosemite Valley and the wooded uplands that surround it into perspective. In imagination one can almost see the glaciers.

ity of vision but increased the awe with which I beheld it, and as I looked, a peculiar exalted sensation seemed to fill my whole being, and I found my eyes in tears with emotion." The Indian fighters had not only found and recorded Yosemite, they had first seen it from its finest vantage point.

Yosemite Valley, despite the overwhelming size of its cliffs, the immense plunges of its falling water, the splendid, solid monoliths and fragile, sculptured pinnacles, is only a small part of the Sierra Nevada—a great and wondrous gorge to a person standing in a Merced meadow but really just another gulley in the furrowed western slope of the great mountain range. Yosemite Park covers about 1,200 square miles, and the valley and adjacent cliffs only about twelve of them, so that even in its own region it is relatively small. The uplands which roll away from the top of the cliffs of the valley wall are filled with the riches of nature; a few miles to the north is another great gorge, Hetch Hetchy, now a tame lake; a few miles to the south is a great grove of giant sequoia trees near Wawona; and to the east, tier upon tier, lies the Yosemite high country, a part of the legendary High Sierra—magnificent.

The boundary of Yosemite National Park swings in a wiggly arc, first north and then northwest to take in the high streams which drain into the Tuolumne River, and from Lyell south and then west to the big trees near Wawona. The boundary line hops from peak to pass and then to peak again, two miles or more above sea level.

Within that arc is an area about the size of Rhode Island, rimmed with 12,000- and 13,000-foot peaks along the east edge. Almost all of the park is above 4,000 feet, although it does dip as low as 2,100 feet in the Merced Canyon at the west entrance. There are more than three hundred lakes, most of them the legacy of the glaciers, and an intricate network of streams. Forests march up through the elevations in their usual order of species—the foothill oak and digger pine, then incense cedar and yellow pine and sugar pine, then red fir, and lodgepole—and up in the rarer air grow the silver pine, sierra juniper, and mountain hemlock.

At timberline, above which are almost no trees at all, is the whitebark pine, which has given up the soaring, shapely pine characteristics in order to live along the Sierra crest. In some sheltered places it may straighten up and grow as high as forty feet, but out on the rocky summits wherever a crack or pocket of soil makes a foothold, the whitebark inches up to three or four feet high during a lifetime of centuries; it can spend a decade or two growing a branch six inches long. Against the light-colored granite, the dark green mat of needled branches, small purplish or chocolate-colored cones, and reddish catkins make a welcome, relieving sight. The seeds from the occasional ripe cones are eaten by nutcrackers and squirrels, and the dense branches make a shelter for white-tailed jackrabbits and sometimes for hikers caught in a storm.

THIS IS HIKING COUNTRY. A glance at a map of Yosemite Park shows three highways winding in from the flatlands to the concentration of tourists and facilities on the valley floor, with a side road to Glacier Point and another to Hetch Hetchy—but only one road goes into the high country and out toward Nevada, so that the best of Yosemite must be seen from a standing position on one's own feet or from the back of a horse. The great sweeping panoramas visible from well-marked vista points on the road are tremendous and awesome, and may be overwhelming to the flatlander—but out there among those rounded domes and jagged peaks is a network of trails through country usually friendly and, at close range, strikingly beautiful.

Between the ridges, spurs, and peaks are the little garden meadows, where it is just becoming spring long after the Fourth of July; and unseen from roadside vista points are the lakes and ponds, large and small, often with a ring of green around them or at least a patch of vegetation near the outlet. Below the outlet of each lake, the Yosemite waters that so impressed John Muir sing and sparkle; where the lake is cradled in the northeast bowl of a mountain, perennial snow or a residual glacier may provide the backdrop.

Walking, there is time to savor this glorious panorama. With each step the hiker moves only twenty-four to thirty inches, two to three miles in a steady hour and less, much less, on a steep switchback trail. In the Yosemite back country, as in the rest of the High Sierra, on any summer day there are hundreds of persons threading the trails, each footfall taking them past or over some natural facet wondrously wrought.

Distance or speed is usually not the object; experience is. The same kind of experience can be found without a long hike, by walking to the edge of a small meadow a few feet off the road. There is the padded ground under the lodgepole or red fir trees, with needles thickening the mat each year and dry cones rolling at random. The red firs usually stand together in whole forests with the characteristic fir litter all over the floor where branches and whole trees have come down with the wind and the snow, for in spite of its giant size and appearance of great strength, this tree is brittle and depends on its neighbors to help keep it intact when high winds blow. The denseness of the red fir woods keeps other plants from growing below, so only birds which can forage on the trunk, leaves, and cones of the tree live here; small animals like chipmunks and chickarees make homes in cavities of damaged trees and burrow down under trunks or among the twisted roots of blow-downs.

If the grove is mostly lodgepole pine, there is a sense of light and airiness, for this most adaptable tree has a light bark and slender trunk, and does not grow much over fifty or sixty feet. It can thrive in the dry soil of rocky hillsides or in the wetness of a meadow; standing alone, it becomes thick of trunk and heavy of branch; locked into a crevice on a granite dome, it twists and squirms for survival and sometimes wraps around a boulder as if defying the elements to tear it loose. The lodgepole seems able to adapt its growing season to the amount of moisture available and, as a species, to thrive on catastrophe. A special insect mines out the inside of its needles, killing whole forests; wildfire prospers on its resinous trunk and low crown; windstorms uproot the taller trees or blow down lone individuals—but the lodgepole manages to keep spreading, growing lush on the glacial moraines, singly on the mountainsides, and in successive generations out into the high meadows, step by step.

The Yosemite meadows, then, are often ringed with lodgepole pine and, farther back, with red fir. Around the edges may be visible deer or a nearly invisible coyote, and within the trees perhaps a porcupine and some grouse—and almost certainly some chickarees. This little "red squirrel" gallops up and down the trees gathering green cones, some of which it puts in cold storage for the winter, and some of which it stops to

cut open and eat while keeping an alert eye out for hawks and weasels. Beneath the soil the pocket gopher burrows, and in the trees, unseen, are flying squirrels. They come out at night, still unseen, and the only evidence of their presence is an occasional quiet thump as they land on a tree trunk after gliding down from the heights.

Whisking around the edges of the meadow are one or two kinds of chipmunks, very busy in the summer with the sure knowledge of winter ahead, stopping to eat occasionally but usually burying little caches of seeds here and there, chasing each other over log and rock either in rivalry or play, running for an almost invisible burrow when danger threatens from human, owl, hawk, snake, weasel, or coyote. Shyer are the mice—white-footed deer mice, jumping mice, and meadow mice—some leaving no more trace than the wind, some clipping runways through the grass, some able to bound two or three feet at a jump, all of them eating enormously but selectively according to their species: green vegetation for the meadow mice; grass seeds or small fruits and insects for the jumpers; seeds, fungi, and insect larvae for the white-foots. They bear young in large litters; though they provide abundant food for the meat-eating mammals, birds, and reptiles, large numbers still survive.

Such a meadow is a filled-in lake and may still have a pond or a wet spot in the middle of it or down at one end. Some of the soil is disintegrated granite, but most of it is organic material, perhaps 50 to 80 percent. Some of this material was produced in the lake or pond, and much of it washed down from up higher—leaves, rotting wood, loose dirt mixed with needles and twiglets—and within it are algae and fungi busy at work. In the dappled sunlight around the perimeter may grow Mertensia, also called mountain bluebell or languid lady, knee to shoulder high, light blue; or mountain gooseberry, with bright berries in the fall; or western bog blueberry, low and compact with small elliptical edible fruit; mountain brome, and many kinds of small plants.

Farther out in the open may be corn lilies, looking like a cornstalk, tall and with large leaves and long, wooly flowers; shooting stars, with pink or crimson petals turned backward; little white or blue violets; blue Sierra gentians; blue camas, with an edible bulb

Stage 1: While the great mass of the Sierra was still rising—perhaps twelve million years ago—Yosemite was a broad valley lying between gentle slopes.

Stage 2: After the final uplift of the Sierra, about three million years ago, Yosemite presented a more rugged profile, as a deep canyon of the Merced River.

Stage 3: During the last Ice Age the bed of the river lay buried beneath Yosemite Glacier, which gradually carved the canyon into a deep, U-shaped valley.

Stage 4: As the climate warmed and the ice cover melted, a lake filled the valley. At its west end a moraine marked the lowest reach of the glacier.

Yosemite today: Gradually the great lake has filled and become a meadow, leaving only small Mirror Lake as a remnant. But the work of the glacier remains to delight the latest phenomenon in Yosemite Valley—man. Some prominent features of the area are:

(1) Merced River,
(2) Bridalveil Fall,
(3) Yosemite Falls,
(4) Mirror Lake,
(5) Indian Creek,
(6) Ribbon Fall,
(7) Bunnell Point,
(8) Glacier Point,
(9) Taft Point,
(10) Dewey Point,
(11) Sentinel Rock,
(12) Cathedral Rock,
(13) El Capitan,
(14) Royal Arches,
(15) Washington Column,
(16) Cathedral Spires,
(17) Leaning Tower,
(18) Liberty Cap,
(19) Half Dome,
(20) North Dome,
(21) Quarter Dome,
(22) Basket Dome,
(23) Sentinel Dome,
(24) Clouds Rest,
(25) Mount Maclure,
(26) Mount Lyell,
(27) Mount Florence,
(28) Mount Watkins,
(29) Mount Broderick,
(30) Sunrise Mountain,
(31) Eagle Peak,
(32) Echo Peak,
(33) Cascade Cliffs,
(34) Tenaya Canyon,
(35) Little Yosemite,
(36) Yosemite Village.

231

that looks like an onion but has a poisonous cousin; pink or scarlet or yellow monkeyflowers; tiger lilies or leopard lilies; and some of the sixty or more sedges which grow in Yosemite Park, providing copious harvests of seeds for the small creatures of the meadows.

The meadow is a busy but fragile place, not to be treated roughly. Most trails go around, not through, the meadows, but indiscriminate walking, riding, or grazing has injured many and destroyed some. Those in Yosemite can best be enjoyed from a quiet spot along the edge.

At dawn, the sun first touches the trees on the western side of the clearing, brightening the red fir cones that cluster near the high tops; in the shadows in early spring or late fall, frost edges the sedge and grass blades, and thin ice rims the water. As the sun rises over the peaks, it shines more directly into the meadow, and where the warmth touches, life starts moving. Through the day, part of the meadow is in the light, part in shadow; then at dusk, the work of the plants slows, and the night feeders start to move about. In summer, the sun fills the glade with its light and energy, and these plants are organized to utilize it quickly and efficiently; in winter, snow has sifted down all over the meadow—even covering the stream if it is slow-moving enough to let ice form a crust—slowly and quietly piling up to great depths. As in all the Sierra, the snow is soft at first, but soon develops a hard top, and on this crust are left the criss-crossing tracks of small animals and the larger ones which pursue them, for life and death go on even in the winter. Spring comes late, the sunny side of the meadow feeling it first; by the time the tame flowers of the suburbs and cities have bloomed and dried, the wild flowers of the mountain meadows are starting to be at their best. The hidden activities of mites and spiders and fungus are well under way, and the larger animals move in and out around the edges. In the brief late autumn, the dogwoods flame red, willows and quaking aspen turn yellow—colors made more brilliant by the somberness of the dark green conifers all around.

There are other kinds of meadows in the Yosemite country, at the higher elevations. The best known is Tuolumne Meadows, large, accessible, used by thousands through the summer as a camping place or as a jump-off to more remote attractions. It is at about 8,600 feet above the sea, slowing down the upper Tuolumne River in its course from Lyell and McClure glaciers to the spectacular falls above Hetch Hetchy. This is a "short-hair" meadow, different from the lusher spots around 6,000 and 7,000 feet, covered with shorthair and beaked sedges; tufted hairgrass, Sierra ricegrass, and both bluejoint and shorthair reedgrass—and brightened with Lemmon's Indian paintbrush. The sedges provide hard little achene fruits, and the grasses have small seeds, feeding a large population of insects and rodents, who in turn feed the meat-eaters.

In John Muir's time, the principal plant in Tuolumne Meadows was the reedgrass, slender and delicate, covering the ground with a faint purple mist when in bloom. He also tells of "gentians, dwarf daisies, potentillas, and the pink bells of dwarf vaccinium . . . Cassiope and bryanthus may be found where the sod curls over stream banks and around boulders . . . broad velvet lawns . . ."

Higher goes the Yosemite country, to Mounts Conness, Dana, Gibbs, and Lyell in a loop around Tuolumne Meadows; Matterhorn, Hawksbeak, Tower, Bigelow, and Wheeler along the north boundary. Between Tuolumne Meadows and the valley floor are Mount Hoffman, Cathedral and Unicorn peaks, and others above 10,000 feet; to the southwest between the meadows and Wawona stand peaks like Foerster, Ishberg, Triple Divide, and Gale, and two great piles which are mountain ranges in themselves—the Cathedral and Clark ranges.

Yosemite Park, especially the valley itself and to some extent Tuolumne Meadows, is being loved to death. Some say the hordes of visitors are as bad as the "hoofed locusts," the sheep which injured so badly vast areas of the Sierra. From Memorial Day to Labor Day, the seven square miles of the Yosemite Valley floor may seem to be wall-to-wall humanity. But up on the rim and in the high country beyond, there is space and quiet and distance; there is the chill of early mornings; the baking radiance of sunlight through clear air on bright granite; the flaming descent of the sun behind great piles of cumulus clouds, the highest peaks touched with the changing light; the coolness and serenity of night, when familiar groups of stars slide upward from behind the bare Sierra crest, drift slowly over the high meadows, and slip down beyond the treeline to the west.

Devil's Postpile is a monumental bundle of five-sided basalt crystals, each as large as an architectural column. A similar formation may be seen on the Sonora Pass road not far from Dardanelles.

At Vernal Falls the Merced River drops over one of two great granite ledges that separate Yosemite Valley from Little Yosemite. Hikers at right are on Mist Trail.

Preceding page: Sunrise over Emerald Bay, Lake Tahoe.

El Capitan stands serene behind coloring trees along
the Merced River. Autumn is a delightful time to visit
Yosemite, after the tourist season has passed.

237

Mist Falls in Kings Canyon National Park play out the varying moods
of Sierra streams—flowing quietly over granite, plunging down a precipice,
then lying tranquilly in a deep pool.

Down among the grasses and wildflowers of a Sierra meadow thrives a whole community of creatures, mostly unseen by the human visitor intent on his own pursuits.

Chapter 14

THE TWIN PARKS

*Kings Canyon and Sequoia—where giant redwoods and miles
of spectacular wilderness are held in trust*

TWO GREAT NATIONAL PARKS—Kings Canyon and Sequoia—reach up and across the spectacular southern part of the Sierra, and within them and in adjacent national forests are the largest groves of massive Big Trees, *Sequoia gigantea*. Sequoia Park was established in 1890, fortunately in time to stop the devastation of lumbering in the Big Tree country before it demolished all of the giants, though not in time to prevent the loss of many of them. In 1926 portions of the High Sierra wild country were added, including Mount Whitney. Kings Canyon National Park was created in 1940, primarily because of its great canyons and mountains. At the time of reorganization, a small tract, the General Grant Grove, was taken out of the "monument" class and added to Kings Canyon Park.

Both present parks, administered together, reach from the foothills to the Sierra crest—1,300 square miles of glory. Roads penetrate only the western third, leaving vast areas of wilderness or near wilderness. In the tourist part, the Generals Highway is one of the world's most interesting roads, climbing from about 1,700 feet at the Ash Mountain park entrance through flourishing wild flowers and shrubs, hanging above Marble Gorge, and running through sugar pine and cedar until the first of the sequoias appear, climaxed by the Giant Forest.

This is a true forest covering hundreds of acres from 5,500 to 7,500 feet above sea level, a "magnificent growth of giants grouped in pure temple groves, ranged in colonnades along the sides of meadows, or scattered among the other trees, from the granite headlands overlooking the hot foothills and plain of the San Joaquin back to within a few miles of the old glacier fountains," in John Muir's description after his first visit. To Muir, it "seemed impossible that any other forest picture in the world could rival it."

A long-time superintendent of the park, John White, said the Big Trees of the Giant Forest are so numerous, individually and in groves, that many other well-known groves outside the park might be dropped into this forest without being noted except by experts. One giant in this company of giants is the most massive in the hemisphere, ten times the size of the average lumber tree—not in height, but in sheer bulk. That is the General Sherman tree, which if milled would produce 57,336 board feet of lumber. (Big Trees make such poor lumber that many of those felled before the turn of the century—and since—have ended up as grape stakes and fence posts.) The tree is as tall as a sixteen-story building and four feet higher than the national capitol in Washington. Its trunk, 32 feet through at the base, would fill the width of most city streets and overlap the sidewalks of many. A large limb growing out of one side at 130 feet above the ground—nearly halfway to the top—is more than six feet eight inches thick. There are taller trees (one of the coast redwoods is over 364 feet high) and thicker trees (the Boole Sequoia is 112 feet around), but none which combine the girth, height, and uniformity of taper to produce the pure bulk of the Sherman.

That is a single tree. A mile away on a sun-dappled path is the Congress Group, the Big Trees at their com-

*From a vantage point on Moro Rock in Sequoia National Park, tiers of mountains stretch
away to the foothills and a winter sunset, looking like a Chinese landscape on silk.*

The Kern River Canyon creates a dramatic trough through the southern Sierra, following closely along a natural fault line. This aerial view is taken looking south.

243

Another perspective on the Kern River Canyon, this time looking westward from Mount Russell.

bined best, where "great russet boles tower up with color and symmetry" amid less of the clutter of other species that is typical of most sequoia groves. Nearby is another great tree, the Chief Sequoyah, whose name, latinized, was applied to the species some time after it was first discovered. Although the trees grow naturally only in California, Sequoyah was a Cherokee, from Oklahoma, the inventor of a written language for his people; the name was bestowed by an Austrian botanist, Stephen Endlicher. At the time the Big Trees first came to public attention, there were no botanists in California to come up with a name of local significance.

Along the trail in the Giant Forest are individual sequoias of note: one with a room in it, one with a pine tree growing out of it, and another with fir trees sprout-

ing; there is another with a keyhole burned all the way through a still-living tree. There is the classically shaped McKinley tree (not all the Big Trees are symmetrical in the growth and survival of their branches) and the Cloister, where four fine redwoods enclose a growth of white fir. There are down trees with tunnels in them, but these individuals are curiosities and serve chiefly to point up the beauty and grandeur of the

others. Some of the trees in the Giant Forest are 3,500 to 4,500 years old.

AT THE SOUTH END of the Giant Forest, on a short side road, is Moro Rock—a 6,719-foot granite dome which rises out of the forest. Although not as perfectly shaped as many other domes in the Sierra, it is an example of the exfoliation process in which layers of rock unpeel themselves. The summit looks like a forbidding height from below, but it is reached by a short climb on a trail of steps from the back and gives the finest view in Sequoia Park: the Middle Fork of the Kaweah River 4,000 feet below, Castle Rocks to the south, the Great Western Divide to the east, Alta and Kaweah Peaks, and a host of other mountains—a view usually seen only from much less accessible vantage points.

Not far from Moro Rock is Crescent Meadow, an example of many such glades in the southern Sierra, where the Big Trees ring a spot of green on which abundant wild flowers grow and from which the mixture of tree species in the Sequoia grove can be seen— so much different from the groves of the coast redwoods where other trees do not penetrate. A pioneer here, Hale D. Tharp, made his home in a cabin in a down sequoia which had been hollowed out by fire after it fell—one of hundreds of such hollow trees, some large enough to ride a horse through.

On another short road, this one to the west of the Generals Highway, is Crystal Cave, where there are guided underground walks. Like most Sierra caves, this is in limestone, where water over centuries has dissolved the stone to make queer formations and has dripped from the ceiling to make glittering stalactites extending downward and cone-shaped stalagmites reaching upward. Although the dominant rock of the Sequoia-Kings country is granite, there are large patches of sedimentary rock, very old, like that around Crystal Cave.

The highway touches only the western part of Sequoia National Park and only a few of the Big Tree groves. To the east and southeast the park rises in tier upon tier of mountains to reach the main crest—not far in a direct line (about twenty-five miles) but reachable from this side by trail only, and the trails wind in and out so that the distance is doubled or

The Palisades: The crevasse between granite and glacier (Bergschrund) varies from dozens to hundreds of feet deep.

tripled. The first of the truly great peaks on the high-country trail is Alta Peak, 11,204 feet, only four air miles from the highway and only half of that from Tokopah Falls, but a substantial hike. Not in the park but reached on a low-standard road (low standard for the time being, anyway) is Mineral King, a secluded valley which is the jumping-off place for serious knapsackers and animal packers. The road provides access

to several small groves of Big Trees and also gives a cross-section of the other kinds of Sierra trees and shrubs.

Far to the east, making a great chasm between the region of the Great Western Divide and the main crest of the Sierra is the canyon of the Kern River, an almost straight gash in the range more than sixty miles long, almost as truly north and south as a natural feature could be. The main river itself wiggles along the bottom

The small lakes and network of creeks which form the upper end of the main river drain ridges which reach up well above 13,000 feet; by the time they have combined down around 10,000 feet, there is a respectable stream. At Junction Meadow, about six miles directly west of Mount Whitney and about six miles south of the Kern source, there is a marker that reads "8,036." Lake Isabella, sixty miles away, is at about 2,000 feet, so the main Kern drops only about one hundred feet to the mile and is not a roaring cataract.

But its canyon is impressive, for much of this gorge is a result of tilting, faulting, glacier action, and erosion by the flowng water; its depth of about 2,000 feet is still increasing through erosion. At the upper end is typical glacier country—clean-scoured granite, with lakes and tarns where the ice scooped out depressions, and avalanche chutes where snow and rock slid down from the ridges to the top of the moving ice. The rest of the canyon corresponds to the line of an earthquake fault, and it is probable that this made a good track for the glacier, and later for the stream.

On both sides of the gorge are rolling plateaus, the remnants of old erosion surfaces in what was a broad valley before the uplift. The Chagoopa Plateau lies west of the river, between the canyon and the Great Western Divide, and is almost matched on the east side of the canyon by the Boreal Plateau.

While the overall appearance of the country is typically granite, there are patches in the main Kern watershed of very old pre-Cretaceous metamorphic rocks (around Triple Divide Peak, for example), a little Triassic volcanic material (near Mount Kaweah), some lava along Golden Trout Creek, Mesozoic basic intrusive rock around Hockett Peak, and, as would be expected, glacial debris and moraines in many places.

The heights around the upper Kern are impressive: Kaweah at 13,802, Guyot at 12,300, Johnson at 11,371. Farther south, the mountains are lower but still substantial: Hockett at 8,551, Manzanita at 9,121, The Needles at 8,245, Sherman at 9,909, and Siretta at 9,977. But this is where the Sierra is running out, and where it merges into the subranges of the Greenhorn and Piute.

There is a South Fork of the Kern, totally different from the main stream. It starts at about 10,000 feet in the granite, then winds southward through a series of

of the canyon, but if a line is drawn along longitude 118 degrees 25 minutes, it will be close to the line of the canyon all the way from the little lakes up under the Kings-Kern divide on the north to where the river subsides into Lake Isabella on the south. A road parallels the twistier part of the river from the lake northward for about twenty miles; the rest, the most spectacular part, has only a foot-trail.

alluvial meadows, making a big bight around Templeton Mountain (a Tertiary volcanic peak) and later around Monache Mountain, almost a twin. From there, only a short distance from the main crest, the river winds through the Kern Plateau, an area until recently hardly known to recreationists but now, with a road leading into it, becoming popular for fishermen and campers.

Below Yucca Point, at about 3,200 feet above sea level, the North Fork of the Kings River meets the Middle Fork in a great foaming of waters, especially in the spring, for the Kings drains a large area of the Sierra, and the melting of snow releases torrents down the granite canyons. The road into the national park meets the river here, and parallels it for another fifteen or twenty miles to Cedar Grove and Zumwalt Meadows —where the pavement ends and the walking begins. The last seven miles is within the park, and its commercial area and refined campgrounds along the south fork of the Kings is the only incursion of civilization into a vast wilderness.

This is not yet high country, for the elevation is only about 5,000 feet, but there are heights enough nearby. Standing some 4,000 feet above the valley floor are North Dome, Buck Peak, Glacier Monument, and Grand Sentinel, somewhat resembling the sides of Yosemite Valley but not quite as perfectly arranged. While the views from Zumwalt Meadows are superb, the finest panorama requires a seven-mile hike up the south side to Lookout Peak; from the 8,531-foot top, most of the Kings Canyon is in view.

About ten airline miles northwest is the Tehipite Valley, another Yosemite-like canyon on the Middle Fork of the Kings. Above the valley rises Tehipite Dome, one of the Sierra's spectacular granite knobs rivaling Half Dome and El Capitan in impact, although seen by far fewer people. This is walk-in country, and from Tehipite a trail traverses gorge after gorge which open into high-country meadows, finally reaching, on a long arc, Muir Pass. On the way, at about 8,000 feet, Palisade Creek comes in from the east, and at the head of that side valley is what some term the most impressive mountain mass in the Sierra: the Palisades, all the peaks of which are over 14,000 feet.

The Kings country was grooved out by glaciers working in old stream valleys, and the canyons have the typical U-shape. Unlike Yosemite, though, the side canyons run down almost to the level of the main streams, so that the waterfalls are really cascades and lack the grand height of those farther north. Notable among the low falls is one on Roaring River, a large stream which pours down from two big glacial canyons, Cloud and Deadman, whose cirques are high up on the Great Western Divide. At the top of Cloud Canyon, Triple Divide Peak splits the drainage of three rivers so that within a mile of each other are the headwaters of the Kings, Kern, and Kaweah rivers, each, in the style of the Sierra, different from all the others and yet sharing the characteristics imposed by granite and glaciers. Part of the slope of Triple Divide Peak is pre-Cretaceous metamorphic rock, some of the ancestral Sierra which time and the forces that shape mountains have not succeeded in removing from this lofty domain.

Most of the Sequoia-Kings country is a powerful wilderness, not a barred-off and inaccessible place, but one where personal effort is required to penetrate, and like all wilderness, a place where man may go for a while but where neither he nor his possessions may remain.

The "front country" between the national parks and the Great Valley is mostly under the control of the U.S. Forest Service. Much of it is managed under the multiple-use concept, with lumbering, grazing, and mining permitted; but above the foothills and up toward the land of the peaks, there is a vast acreage held as wilderness. The Sierra National Forest reaches up to the LeConte Divide and Kettle Ridge, and includes some formidable country up around 10,000 to 12,000 feet, threaded with creeks running into the North Fork of the Kings. The Sequoia National Forest occupies a narrower belt west of Sequoia Park, and extends down around the southern end and up into the middle of it. This national forest has more groves of Big Trees than any other, some near roads and some reached only by trail. The lower Kern Plateau is in its territory and so is most of the land which drains into the Kaweah, Tule, and lower Kern rivers. The Inyo National Forest runs along the eastern sides of Kings and Sequoia Parks, holding the higher elevations as wilderness.

Two national parks and three national forests hold the southern third of the Sierra Nevada in trust for the future.

Those energetic enough to climb Mount Whitney are rewarded with this view from the top, looking past the east face of Keeler and Day needles toward Pinnacle Ridge.

Chapter 15

THE BEGINNING AND THE END

*Lassen Peak—born in volcanic fires only to be shattered
by them—the northern terminus of the Sierra Nevada*

AT FIVE O'CLOCK IN THE AFTERNOON on Memorial Day, 1914, lava and ashes, smoke and steam shot up from the top of Mount Lassen, opening a new crater smaller than a city lot. For months there were irregular explosions, and a year later came the big blowoff; then until 1917 there was minor activity. People kept climbing the peak during all that time, and no one got killed, although one man was injured so badly he was left for a time as dead. The 1914–15 series of eruptions changed the shape of the top of the peak, sent a huge mudflow down one slope, blasted flat a section of the forest, caused a flood which swept over small ranches, and was responsible for the establishment of the vicinity as a national park.

Lassen could blow again, and it certainly had blown before. In the Pliocene epoch, a million and a half to two millions years ago, lava poured out of a vent in the vicinity of Willow Lake, near the southern boundary of the park, leaving basalt rocks, and a short time later there was an eruption somewhere near Juniper Lake, much farther east, which left andesite over about four square miles. Meanwhile, in the central portion, black lava flooded out for about thirty square miles and then vents opened near White Mountain, pouring andesites four or five miles southeastward to the head of Warner Valley. By that time, most of the eastern part of the present park was a relatively flat lava plain, upon which later flows from still farther east piled up. The inevitable erosion year after year then produced the rugged hills along the eastern park boundary and formed the terrain of the Caribou Wild Area.

While this was going on, an enormous volcano (Tehama Volcano or Brokeoff Cone) had been rising in the southwest part of the park, forming a cone about fifteen miles across and two miles high, and there were other volcanoes busy building peaks now named Raker, Prospect, Harkness, and Red Mountain. On that enormous volcano a new vent opened up, pouring out lava fifteen hundred feet thick, which cooled to form the dark and glassy columns encircling the present Lassen Peak. Domes rose from other vents, some connected by shorter flows which made ridges from one to another. Finally, probably weakened from within, the big volcano fell in on itself and formed a caldera, or large basin, in which many hot springs and mudspots still simmer; Brokeoff Mountain and other sharp points jutting into the skyline mark the remainder of what once were the sides of the high cone. It is probable that the main vent of this ancient volcano was at Sulphur Works, where there is still thermal activity right beside the highway.

So Lassen Peak is part of the remains of a bigger volcano, now evident only by studying a relief map or looking at the terrain from a high airplane. It derived mainly from volcanic activity of the times when the seas were receding from the Sierra Nevada itself. Although not strictly in the Sierra, Lassen is underlain by the Sierra, and becomes a natural northern terminus for the range.

All around the mountain and on it, activity continued. A flow on the northwest built the Crescent Cliffs; around A.D. 500 violent explosions formed the Cinder

*Lassen Peak reflected in Manzanita Lake, looks deceptively tranquil, but it blew its top
less than half a century ago, confirming its status as an active volcano.*

Stage 1: Lassen Peak was formed as a plug of volcanic material that slowly rose in the crater of an earlier volcano, whose glassy black lava flows are still visible.

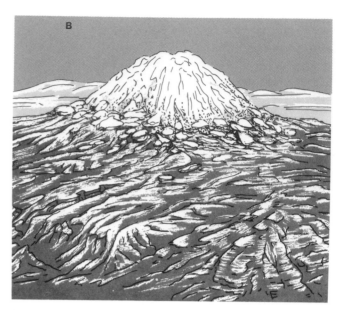

Stage 2: As the plug rose, its surface pressed against the walls of the crater and broke up into blocks, which rolled down the slopes to form huge heaps of talus.

Cone in the northeast part of the park, showering ash and other material over thirty square miles, and occasionally blowing off as late as 1851. About two hundred years ago hot viscous material squeezed out of the peak itself to form Chaos Crags, part of which later collapsed and piled up the two and a half square miles of broken rock known as Chaos Jumbles. The crags were still steaming in 1857. In the 1700s, too, a glowing avalanche swept down the valley of Manzanita Creek, all the way to the present park entrance.

These activities of lassen became part of the knowledge and lore of the Indian tribes who came and went on the slopes of the mountains, although there was no one there who could write it all down, and the dates and data had to be supplied later by geologists. But the 1914 eruption and subsequent activity were seen from all angles by thousands of persons who could write and many with cameras, so the record is quite clear even on some disputed points.

The first explosion was relatively small, with lava and ashes shooting out to cover an area about two hundred feet in diameter, with a huge cloud of smoke; then for a couple of days there was additional puffing of smoke and an outflowing of mud on the snow-covered flank of the peak. Within a few days sightseeing parties were climbing the mountain to peer into the new crater and breathe the sulphurous steam. The puffing and rumbling continued intermittently through June and July, and B. F. Loomis of nearby Viola was able to take numerous photos which are now on display in a museum in the park center at Manzanita Lake. Visits to the top continued despite the danger, and one group of sightseers escaped a shower of rocks by flinging themselves onto the steep snow slope and tobogganing to the bottom without benefit of sleds.

At no time did the entire top of the mountain blow off, and more than a year after the first eruption portions of a lookout house on the peak were still visible. The greatest alteration to the landscape started May 20, 1915, when water and mud flowed out of a vent on the north side and poured down the valleys of Hat Creek and Lost Creek, where ranchers at small outposts barely escaped. There was so much mud and water, traveling at such a speed, that it sloshed up and over small ridges. Large boulders were carried along for miles, scraping the bark off trees to a height of eighteen feet in

Stage 3: Chiseled to a sharp peak by erosion, Lassen has produced its own lava flows, as recently as this century, continuing the endless work of landscape building.

some places but not knocking the larger timber down; the boulders were so hot they sizzled for days, indicating they came from the crater four miles or more away.

Two days later came the largest eruption of all. Loomis, who had been taking pictures of Lassen in action for a year, was caught without glass plates for his camera and stood frustrated while, in his words, "the eruption came on gradually at first, getting larger and larger until it finally broke out into a roar like thunder; the smoke cloud was hurled with tremendous velocity many miles high, and the rocks thrown from the crater were seen to fly way below the timber line before they struck the ground. As the rocks emerged from the smoke cloud they were followed by a comet-like tail of smoke which enabled us to tell definitely the path of their flight. For a short time the smoke cloud ran down the mountainside, melting the snow very fast, and the water could be seen running down the mountain side in a rush twenty feet wide." What he did not see was a great blast of steam and gas which slammed down the path of the previous mud flow; all the trees which had been left standing by that flood were blown down, all in the same direction, in what is now called the "Devastated Area."

The amount of mud, ash, and ejecta from this year or more of activity on Lassen Peak, and the ash and lava from other vents around the park, were reported with many exclamation points in the press of the day— but the time and space involved were insignificant in comparison with the scale of the volcanic activity which in the Tertiary period poured out flows all over the northern Sierra and southern Cascades, 500 to 1,500 feet thick, over hundreds of square miles, filling deep canyons almost level and extending to the edges of the Great Valley, where they can be seen today as dark vertical cliffs with tablelands on top.

MILL CREEK AND DEER CREEK have cut their channels deeper and deeper through the volcanic rock and soil southwest of Lassen Peak, running now on the ancient bedrock a thousand feet or so below the flattish uplands. The streams are clear and busy, even in the rainless summer, with alternate cascades and pools, full of oxygen collected in the spray and turbulence, shaded by high canyon walls and by overhanging trees and brush. Small aquatic life is abundant, and so are fish. There are occasional wide spots in the canyon bottom where grass and oak trees grow in little parks, but for the most part the walls are close together and steep, and halfway up there are numerous caves—not tunnels, but protected spaces under overhanging ledges. This remains a wild land, although there are some trails and jeep roads into it now, but in the heat of the summer not even the verdure along the streams keep it from being one of the most inhospitable places in California.

Here and along similar streams a few miles to the north lived the Yana Indians in stone-age simplicity, self-sufficient and quietly proud, each family group or subtribe dependent upon itself. The Yana were tough when forced to fight, and neighborly at get-togethers during the harvest season, but each group occupied its own stream drainage and communicated only a little with those over the ridge in the next stream canyon. Over the several thousand years in which the tribe lived this way, the dialect of each group developed in its own direction, until only a few words were used in common. The Deer Creeks could talk to the Mill Creeks next door, and the Mill Creeks could talk to the Ante-

*Brokeoff Mountain (foreground) and Mount Diller are remnants of the crater of the ancient
Brokeoff volcano, which is estimated to have been 11,000 feet high and fifteen miles in diameter.
In time its fury was spent, and the cone collapsed, as explained in the diagrams below.*

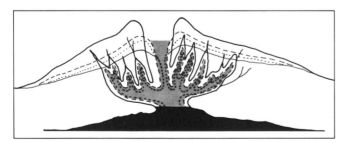

*Deep within a volcano are many chambers. With
the pressure of repeated explosions, these chambers are
expanded, and the "roof" becomes thinner. At the same
time each explosion leaves the level of magma in the
volcano a little lower (shaded areas) until it is empty.*

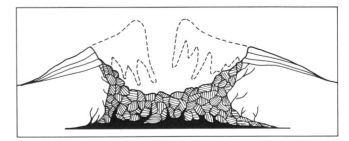

*With no molten magma to support it, the weakened
"roof" collapses into the empty crater. With no more
lava or volcanic debris to build them, the walls of the
crater gradually erode into separate peaks and valleys,
and lose their identity in the larger landscape.*

Bumpass Hell, a sulfurous area of steaming vents and boiling mud,
suggests the seething fury that underlies the surface calm of the Lassen area.
Visitors are warned to stay on marked trails to avoid accident.

lope Creeks, and so on—but the language changed so much, ridge by ridge, that a Deer Creek Yana would have trouble talking fluently with a Cow Creek Yana from twenty or thirty miles away.

Hardly any of the white arrivals in the Sacramento Valley coveted the land or goods of the Yana, and so they lived without much change in their habits well into the American occupation. Then there was friction, usually over the change of status of cattle, which the whites looked on as property and the Indians looked on as food. The settlers set out to eliminate the Mill Creeks and Deer Creeks as if they were wild animals. The odds, of course, were with the whites, and by the turn of the century the ranchers could congratulate each other that this threat to their interests was eliminated. The threat was gone, but they had missed a few Indians.

On August 29, 1911, Ishi, a Yahi from the south end of the Yana country, turned up in the corral of a slaughterhouse near Oroville, almost dead from starvation, exhaustion, and fear—drawn out of his home canyon along Deer Creek by some psychological impetus which overrode his Yahi instinct and training to stay hidden. He was the last of his people and probably the last of all primitive Indians in the United States. Fortunately, the county sheriff acted wisely; fortunately, there was no great feeling against Indians among the slaughterhouse crew; fortunately, the University of California acted promptly to send an anthropologist. The result was that Ishi lived for several years to tell about the life of the stone-age Indians who had adapted to the stringent requirements of the lava country—basically a gentle people in harsh surroundings, adaptive to circumstances yet following family and tribal traditions—California Indians as the settler with his abrasive ways never knew them. As for white men, Ishi craved no vengeance. He looked upon them as sophisticated children—smart but not wise, knowing many things including much that is false; Ishi knew nature, which is always true, and this was the source of his confidence and courage. The anthropologist who knew him best said, "He was kind; he had courage and self-restraint, and though all had been taken from him, there was no bitterness in his heart. His soul was that of a child, his mind that of a philosopher."

The paradox of gentleness against harshness is true throughout the Lassen region, and the beauty of the place belies the fact that somewhere down below lies molten magma, ready perhaps to break through. In protected places very near the top of the peak, around the crater, grow polemonium and buckwheat flowers with a fragile toehold in ash and a little soil from decomposed rock, existing on moisture from the air and from melting snow. Farther down are timberline phacelia and alpine pussytoes. Well down the sides are meadows with the great Sierran array of mountain wildflowers along with willows, grasses, and sedges; mule-ears, shooting stars, monkey flowers, and a special kind of paintbrush known only to Lassen. At higher elevations grow red firs, and a little lower are western yellow and Jeffrey pine, with some lodgepole pine around the lakes and wet meadows. Greenleaf manzanita covers the brushy slopes, and above 6,000 feet grows the pine-mat manzanita, making a carpet on the forest floor or sprawling with reddish stems over the basalt or dacite rocks.

WHERE THERE ARE PLANTS AND SEEDS, there are insects and birds—more of them in the forests around the foot of the volcano, but some on the upper slopes as the snow recedes in the summer. In the inhospitable heat and fumes of the hot springs and mudpots live green algae, somehow able to thrive where the temperature is 125 to 196 degrees and there is a minimum of oxygen. One-celled animals live a little farther from the center of heat, and there are water mites and midge larvae yet a little farther away in the trickles and ponds below the springs. Downstream are water beetles, caddis fly larvae, nymphs, and other tiny animals; the relatively small amounts of water from the volcanic activity areas are soon mingled with colder streams, where the usual life of flowing water goes on. Most of the springs and streams are cold, probably originating almost entirely from snow melt, although the surface and ground water which percolates deep into the earth also returns, pushing up through fissures as boiling water or sometimes superheated steam under pressure.

The steam vents, fumaroles, mudpots, boiling lakes, and volcanic ash show clearly that the typical Sierra Nevada is not to be found here—and there is one other clear sign: no granite.

As spring comes to Lassen Volcanic National Park, the heavy snow melts from exposed high ridges but remains thick on Kings Creek Meadow.

Lake Tahoe is unfurled in a grand panorama
from the ski slopes of Heavenly Valley. In addition
to the aerial tram, there are five double chair lifts; but
the popularity of skiing has boomed so rapidly that
here, as at other resorts, waiting lines are the rule.

259

Four-wheel-drive vehicles make wilderness areas much more accessible for the sportsman, but conservationists view them with concern. These wheel tracks in Lyell Fork Canyon may take a generation to heal.

The human foot is still the least destructive vehicle for taking man into the mountains, although so many people are discovering the satisfactions of backpacking that the once remote John Muir Trail is becoming a well-worn thoroughfare.

Thousands have enjoyed seeing the Sierra on horseback, but even hooves, when there are too many, can damage the fragile wilderness; recently the suggestion has been raised that pack animals be barred from the trails.

*For the serious angler, early spring fishing offers
solitude, beauty, and a good catch.*

*Even the vertical walls of the Sierra are experiencing a population boom.
Novices can learn the fine arts of belaying and rappelling in classes sponsored by the
Sierra Club. An iron-nerved few will go on to the ultimate challenge—El Capitan.*

THE CONSERVATIONISTS

The future will find abundant power outside the parks—parks for which there are no alternatives. So many of the parks are already overcrowded—certainly Yosemite is. And Hetch Hetchy could have given to millions, for ages, much of what Yosemite gives. Its waters could have remained an inspiration in their beautiful natural setting and then be put to practical use downstream—just as Yosemite's river is. The cliffs, the meadows, the groves, the streamside, the whole setting—what do they mean to man? Something that you can neither measure in dollars nor replace with dollars. Hetch Hetchy's setting is irretrievably lost to all of us and to all generations. It need not have been.

David Brower in *Wildlands in Our Civilization*, 1964.

The size and diversity of the Sierra Nevada, overlapping jurisdictions, conflicting interests, and the lack of any way to predict the future make it impossible to "conserve" the Sierra in the sense of keeping it entirely intact for future generations. The "good guys" and "bad guys" keep up a constant attrition on each other, and it depends on one's viewpoint what group wears each label.

The lower elevations are pretty well gone—both the grizzly and his country are extinct. There are predictions that in the growth of California a connected series of new cities will reach from the Yuba to the Stanislaus River, at 1,600 to 3,000 feet elevation, utilizing the poor agricultural land there instead of paving over the best growing lands in the Great Valley. There are already thousands upon thousands of subdivided lots within a few miles of the Mother Lode Highway, most of them not built on yet; but the predictions are for complete cities, not just country homes without economic support.

The natural streams in the foothills are almost extinct, too, their water switched out for domestic and industrial use and for irrigation, so that nearly dry riverbeds alternate with placid reservoirs. Where there are new roads, highways or freeways, what is left of creek or river is squeezed through a culvert or dribbles between concrete banks.

The masses of fouled air which used to hang just over the cities have spread outward and are now belts of brown haze all up and down the valley, with the edges touching the towns of the gold country foothills. And this spread is not confined to the foothills; it moves with improved transportation, and there are subdivisions, commercial facilities, and smog added each year

Presently accessible only by foot trail or unimproved road, the remote valley of Mineral King is planned for extensive recreational development, over the vigorous protests of conservation groups.

In 1903 President Theodore Roosevelt visited a number of the scenic areas of the West. Here he was photographed with John Muir (on his left) at the base of a giant sequoia. Between them is Southern Pacific president Edward H. Harriman.

Early-day hikers pause on Yosemite's Vernal Fall Bridge to rest and let the photographer record their outing. The man on the horse is none other than John Muir.

along every major highway into the uplands. When recreational facilities are installed, little metropolises spring up near them. On the other hand, developers complain that some counties are planning, zoning, and restricting them out of business, ruining the future tax base; livestock people complain that their range on the public domain is constantly being reduced or the cost is being increased; manufacturers and users of trail bikes, snowmobiles, and four-wheel vehicles cry dis-

crimination when motors are banned from large areas.

In the frontier tradition, verbal gunfights go on at the passes of county courthouses and in the Okay Saloons of state legislatures and the Congress; in each battle, it is a sure bet that someone is going to get hurt —participant or innocent onlooker. If there is a compromise, both sides may find they have been grievously wounded or at least are bleeding a little.

The issues are seldom as clear as either side would

imply. Here is a secluded valley at 8,000 feet at the end of a dirt road, just under one of the great divides of the Sierra. It is in a national forest and thus open to consideration for resort or other recreational use; it already is both an objective for campers and a jumping-off place for hikers and packers, especially those who want to go where few other people are. A resort developer wants to move in and make a great skiing center out of the isolated valley, serving thousands of persons instead of just a few, adding tremendously to the county's tax base, keeping vast numbers of people moving around, therefore spending money and providing employment for hundreds. The esthetic values will be preserved, perhaps by buildings designed as quaintly as those in Switzerland; while the skiing is a paramount consideration, there will be much summer use, too. Lots of people will have lots of fun, and lots of money will change hands.

That beautiful little valley, though, is tucked into a point of forest service land which thrusts up into the underbelly of a national park; the boundaries of the park are less than three miles from the little valley on three sides. National parks are more protected from development encroachment than national forests but may be more vulnerable, physically, to large numbers of people. In this case, will all those thousands of visitors be content to play games in the little valley when it is fully developed, or will they (and presumably their trash) spill over into the fragile wilderness around them?

But even that is not the main argument: the road to the valley is. For the only logical approach for a high-standard highway for all those thousands of people is through many miles of the national park, changing forever the environment there. Other parks have high-standard roads, though, opening up hitherto inaccessible wonders; why should the beauties and remoteness of this park be available only to the elite few who can afford to walk?

And what about the plight of the skier, who needs more facilities? The lines at the lifts in existing resorts are so long, it takes twenty minutes or half an hour to get a ride back up the slope; accommodations are crowded, and reservations on the good weekends are hard to get; the best building lots for private lodges and condominiums have all been taken. If skiing is to continue to grow, there must be more ski complexes, which

consist not only of snow on a few acres of slope but many additional acres of parking lots, lodges, bars, ski shops, souvenir counters, and service stations. One of these complexes can't be put just anywhere; it takes the right combination of terrain, accessibility, vision, and money. This particular valley has the terrain, the taxpayers will build the access, and the developer has both vision and money (and visions of money).

The valley's name is Mineral King; the developer is the Disney Corporation; the main voice protesting development has been the Sierra Club. The long impasse concerning its fate is typical of environmental questions in the Sierra Nevada—a condition that speaks volumes for the past (and future) of the mountain country.

Lands administered by the U.S. Forest Service are supposed to be managed and used for the greatest good for the greatest number in the long run, producing lumber, forage, water, recreation, and so on. Lands administered by the National Park Service are supposed to be kept as intact as possible to preserve places of special value. Logically enough, within the Forest Service boundaries are places which have special values worth preserving, and these get the special protection of a "Wilderness" designation or are set aside as primitive areas; in addition, there are small places in almost every national forest in the Sierra which are being protected under some formal or informal policy, or long range plan. Forest Service lands are vast, and the agency has many choices to make on the use of them. There may be significance in the fact the agency is in the Department of Agriculture.

The Park Service, however, has less land, fewer options, and a more limited mandate—but still not an easy one: to "conserve the scenery and the natural and historic objects, and the wildlife therein, and to provide for the enjoyment of the same in such a manner and by such means as will leave them unimpaired for the enjoyment of future generations." The key words may be "conserve" and "unimpaired," although there is pressure on "enjoyment," and the definition of joy may be different now than in 1916 when the National Park Service was established in the Department of the Interior. Other public agencies, such as the Bureau of Land Management and executive departments of

Before damming, Hetch Hetchy Valley was a dramatic product of glacial carving, only a little less grand than Yosemite itself.

Today a large reservoir fills Hetch Hetchy valley, providing most of San Francisco's water supply. The seasonal drop is visible in the water mark on the canyon wall, right.

two states, have land in the Sierra Nevada and make conservation decisions, but the Forest Service and the Park Service are the most concerned.

At one time, the Sierra Club was the only voice crying for the wilderness, and it remains the largest and most vocal; but other organizations, some with relatively limited objectives, are in the action continuously, and from time to time short-lived groups join the fray for or against specific projects. The effect of all these is measurable: much of the Sierra has been conserved almost intact, although it sometimes seems that the range is being nibbled away by "improvements" and "progress." What the Sierra would be like if these organizations had never sprung up to support the good intentions of the federal agencies or to oppose them in their errors is a depressing speculation.

John Muir was among the first to realize that preservation was necessary—that the taming of the frontier, the assault on forests, mountains, and other resources must be controlled. With some other outstanding individuals, he helped form the Sierra Club in 1892 to exert the necessary pressure. The Sierra Club won some and lost some—one notable loss being the devastation of Hetch Hetchy for a water reservoir, destroying scenic beauty second only to Yosemite Valley. Time tended to prove that the club's stand against Hetch Hetchy was more far-seeing than first realized, and the club gained membership and prestige through the fight. Much of the public came to realize that park boundaries were not an automatic insurance against inroads, and water projects were not automatically good. A notable win was the preservation of the boundaries of Yosemite Park against efforts by grazers and others to cut them down by half.

Another notable win was the establishment in 1940 of Kings Canyon National Park. Then, after much of the Sierra high country became accepted as more valuable as wilderness than for other uses, the club turned part of its attention to other places on the continent, again winning some and losing some, but always fighting for the preservation of wild places. There may have been some internal battles within the club on some of the issues, but once a course was chosen, the Sierra Club became a formidable protagonist in the news media, in legislative halls, and in the courts. Its influence has been based on careful and exhaustive marshal-

ing of facts combined with an emotional furor—beautifully presented pictures and words which somehow made opponents of the club's stand seem to be greedy, plundering, raping boors.

The club could vigorously oppose the Department of the Interior yet without blinking quote in its literature Interior Secretary Stewart Udall: "Beyond all plans and programs, true conservation is ultimately something of the mind—an ideal of men who cherish their past and believe in their future. Our civilization will be measured by its fidelity to this ideal as surely as by its art and poetry and system of justice. In our perpetual search for abundance, beauty, and order we manifest both our love for the land and our sense of responsibility toward future generations."

The Sierra Club knows the Sierra and uses it. Since 1901 there have been annual outings, drawing more and more people. Hiking and climbing guides are published, and the monthly Bulletin is filled with articles, scholarly and folksy—scientific information mixed with stories about interesting trips—and each of the many chapters puts out a newsletter or bulletin of its own. A constant emphasis is kept on the need for vigilance against encroachment—and on the responsibility of each individual to be careful in his own use of the mountains.

A biennial wilderness conference is held at which the scientific, historical, cultural, esthetic, and other reasons for preservation are exposed and discussed—a factual background for the almost inexpressible emotional and subjective case for preservation of the wild places. Not the least in the priorities of preservation, these conferences have pointed out, is the fact that wilderness preserves a genetic yardstick against which science can measure the effects of civilization. In the end, though, the strongest case rests in intangibles, expressed in one man's view by novelist-historian-conservationist Wallace Stegner in a statement to the Wildlands Research Center:

"Something will have gone out of us as a people if we ever let the remaining wilderness be destroyed . . . it was the challenge against which our character as a people was formed. The reminder and the reassurance that it is still there is good for our spiritual health even if we never once in ten years set foot in it. It is good for us when we are young, because of the incomparable sanity it can bring briefly, as vacation and rest, into our insane lives. It is important to us when we are old simply because it is there—important, that is, simply as idea. . . . While we were demonstrating ourselves the most efficient and ruthless environment busters in history, and slashing and burning and cutting our way through a wilderness continent, the wilderness was working on us . . . we were in ways subdued by what we conquered. . . . For all the usual recreational purposes, the alpine and forest wildernesses are obviously the most important, both as genetic banks and as beauty spots . . . for . . . spiritual renewal, recognition of identity, the birth of awe. . . . We need to put into effect, for its preservation, some other principles than the principles of exploitation or even recreation. We simply need that wild country available to us, even if we never do more than drive to the edge and look in."

Among the organizations paralleling the aims of the Sierra Club, although using different methods from a different base, are the National Parks Association, Izaak Walton League, Wilderness Society, National Audubon Society, and the Nature Conservancy, which have formed among themselves the National Resources Council of America.

The Nature Conservancy operates in a way all its own. It stays out of controversy, leaves public protest to other groups, and concentrates on grabbing threatened acres for posterity. It keeps some and turns most over to other agencies to manage. Unlike government agencies, the Conservancy can and does move fast when the occasion warrants. By early 1970, the organization had been instrumental in having nearly 150,000 acres set aside nationally as sanctuaries and preserves. It is a voluntary membership organization and uses this as a base to acquire funds and commitments from foundations, private business, and anywhere else it can find dollars. The Conservancy has been active in the Sierra, so far primarily in the Lake Tahoe area, and is open to suggestions on the acquisition of land which is vital to wilderness anywhere in the range. It is open, too, to individuals who want to help and does not depend on huge grants. "In the end," the organization says in its literature, "it is the private individual upon whom the chief burden of preservation falls."

In a culture in which the individual sometimes feels that he does not count, it may be significant that such a statement can be made: that it is wilderness which may save the individual, as stated by Wallace Stegner; and that it is the individual who must save the wilderness. Before the turn of the century, individual men and women started the work of conserving the Sierra Nevada, and the protected parks and wild areas are the result of their efforts—which have continued and increased over the years as the problems multiplied. For many persons the value in keeping much of the Sierra as intact as possible was simply in preserving its physical beauty and its spiritual impact, but there has been more and more emphasis on the need to keep unchanged large tracts of wilderness as a scientific tool. By having available a situation where the environment and the flora and fauna, even the weather, are relatively unaffected by man, it becomes possible to measure the effects of man where he is most active. The comparison, some say, might be so appalling that man might be better off just to slide into his doom without being tormented by a view of what his world might have been, and once was. But that apocalyptic stance is not shared by many, and there is hope that the artificial human environment may be improved, somehow, by a study of the natural environment in the wild part of these mountains.

The range is so big and so full of paradoxes, contrasts, and anomalies that to fully understand even a portion of it would require a lifetime of study; and it has been only a relatively few generations since the rudiments of study in the Sierra began. The accumulation of knowledge which started with the recording of "un gran sierra nevada" by a wandering priest, became more scientific with the maps of Preuss on the Frémont expedition, reached great descriptive heights through the writings of John Muir, and has become more exact and scientific in recent years, continues. Along with the official knowledge is a vast reservoir of private knowledge, the wisdom and lore gathered by unpublished persons in search of their own broadened horizons. In the end, it may be that the private knowledge is the more important, for in learning about the Sierra, people learn about themselves; and no person who has reached the heights of the mountains comes back to the lowlands unchanged.

A GUIDE TO THE SIERRA

One-day or weekend trips by car can give an interesting introduction to the Sierra Nevada, and may inspire one to become better acquainted through later trips into the back country. From Thanksgiving through Easter, it is advisable to wear warm clothing, carry snow chains, and be prepared for delays. Except on the one interstate highway (IS-80), it is not possible to maintain high speeds, but fast travel through the Sierra is not very rewarding anyway. In addition to the main routes mentioned here, there are side roads in profusion which provide access to interesting and scenic places.

LASSEN PEAK

This quiet volcano in Lassen Volcanic National Park is surrounded by places of great beauty. There are facilities for camping, picnicking, swimming, horseback riding and skiing. The through road is closed during winter.

HISTORY: Lassen Peak last erupted in 1915-1917; at one time a huge volcanic crater, it is now marked by separate mountains, of which Lassen Peak is only one. A museum at Manzanita Lake tells the story.

KEY FEATURES: Steam jets, boiling mud, old lava flows and other volcanic remnants, many lakes—all explained in Park Service pamphlets. There is resort-type skiing at Sulfur Works, near the south entrance, and cross-country skiing everywhere. A natural trout aquarium (protected) may be seen at Emerald Lake.

INFORMATION: Available from Lassen Volcanic National Park Headquarters, Mineral, Calif.

FEATHER RIVER COUNTRY

Much of this area is in the Plumas National Forest. Visitors will note more towns here than in the rest of the Sierra. For one thing, this is the most accessible part of the Sierra year 'round. Beckwourth Pass, at 5,218 feet, is the lowest in the Sierra, and State Highway 70 is open all year except for occasional short periods after heavy storms.

HISTORY: Maidu Indians once lived here year-round. In 1848, gold was discovered at Bidwell Bar, and placer, hydraulic, and quartz mining continued until World War II. Some other minerals are mined in the area as well. After the gold rush, the base of the economy shifted to lumbering, and there are still many mills and logging operations. Hydroelectric generation was begun in the early 1900s, evolving into a vast network of dams and power plants that now utilizes the same water over and over in its descent from the upper basin of the Feather River.

KEY FEATURES: The canyon of the North Fork, where the highway and railroad run along narrow shelves above the river and reservoirs; Oroville Reservoir, with the largest earthfill dam; old mining and lumbering towns above the South Fork, particularly LaPorte, accessible via paved county roads; Feather Falls with its 640-foot drop, accessible by dirt road and footpath; Bucks Lake, Lake Almanor, Lake Davis, Frenchman Lake—all popular for fishing and camping.

INFORMATION: Available from the Oroville Chamber of Commerce, Oroville, Calif.; Plumas County Chamber of Commerce, Quincy, Calif.; Plumas National Forest, Quincy; Pacific Gas & Electric Company, San Francisco.

YUBA RIVER COUNTRY

Most of the Yuba country is located in the Tahoe National Forest. There are some towns and year-round communities. Yuba Pass (State 49) is closed only occasionally in winter; Donner Pass (Interstate 80) is theoretically open all year but is subject to delays when there are high winds and blowing snow.

HISTORY: The major emigrant trails ran through here, including that of the Donner Party. Gold was discovered early in the gold rush days. Later mining included hydraulicking and deep quartz mines, and some old mines are still visible. Mining was major industry until World War II, but the economy is now based on lumber and tourists.

KEY FEATURES: Old but busy mining towns of Nevada City and Grass Valley in the foothills, Downieville and Sierra City in the mountains; Sierra Buttes and other spectacular canyon-and-peak scenery, with many lakes and streams. Historically-minded communities have museums.

INFORMATION: Available from the Nevada County Chamber of Commerce, Nevada City, Calif.; Tahoe National Forest, Nevada City; Grass Valley or Nevada City Chamber of Commerce; Golden Chain Council, Auburn, Calif.

ECHO SUMMIT AND LAKE TAHOE

Scenery in this area is renowned. Much of it lies in El Dorado National Forest, some in Tahoe National Forest. Recreation activities include all varieties of summer attractions and several fine skiing centers. There is a variety of fishing from small creeks to the largest lake in the Sierra. Most urban facilities are at the south end of the lake.

HISTORY: The present U.S. 50 follows the approximate route of the major stage and freight road to Virginia City and the Comstock Lode during the silver boom; prior to that this was an emigrant route. The Lake Tahoe basin was extensively logged for many years, then became an exclusive playground for the wealthy; now it is heavily populated with both permanent residents and seasonal visitors.

KEY FEATURES: Fine scenic drive from Placerville to Tahoe with a spectacular descent into the Tahoe Valley; short side trip to Echo Lake; 71-mile tour around Lake Tahoe; excellent Forest Service visitor center, nature walk, and underwater fish observation basin near South Tahoe; summer tram rides at ski centers; beaches, boating, water skiing, gambling, cold-water swimming.

INFORMATION: Available from the chambers of commerce at South Tahoe and Tahoe City; El Dorado National Forest, Placerville, Calif.; El Dorado County Chamber of Commerce, Placerville. Many communities, resorts, and real estate developments around the lake also give away descriptive leaflets.

CARSON PASS COUNTRY

From vantage points along the west slope, the Carson Pass route offers motorists some of the widest and loveliest views of the Sierra. Located in El Dorado National Forest, the country along this route provides typical mountain scenery and activities spring through fall. A pleasant summer loop trip is to drive east on State 88, turn north on State 89 to Lake Tahoe, then return west on U.S. 50. In winter there are ski resorts on the west slope.

Continuing improvements of the highway will eventually keep Carson Pass (8,573 feet) open year-round, but it is presently closed to auto traffic in winter months.

HISTORY: Carson Pass was used by Captain John C. Fremont and Kit Carson in 1844, then became an emigrant road presenting less formidable problems than Donner Pass in getting wagons up the escarpment; still later it was a seasonal freight and stage road.

KEY FEATURES: Interesting geological formations along the highway; many streams and lakes with summer resorts; mining artifacts in Jackson; Tragedy Springs, historical site where Mormon soldiers were mysteriously killed in 1848; ski areas easily reached from Sacramento and the San Francisco Bay Area; Faith, Hope, and Charity valleys on the east slope, with fine ski touring and snowmobiling at Hope Valley. Driving east on State 88, south through Markleeville, then west on State 4 provides a weekend tour with fine views of contrasting parts of the Sierra, away from the most-traveled highways.

INFORMATION: Available from the Amador County Chamber of Commerce, Jackson, Calif.:; Alpine County Chamber of Commerce, Markleeville, Calif.; El Dorado National Forest, Placerville, Calif.; Pacific Gas & Electric Company, San Francisco; Golden Chain Council, Auburn; Sacramento Municipal Utility District, Sacramento.

EBBETTS PASS COUNTRY

This beautiful country is not overrun with visitors, yet offers all the usual mountain recreation, with many camp and picnic sites. There are numerous small lakes, including scenic Lake Alpine. Calaveras Grove was one of the first sequoia groves to be opened to the public; adjacent South Grove requires some walking but is worth it. Angels Camp and Murphys are famous old mining towns in the foothills. Ebbetts Pass (8,730 feet) is closed in winter, but the highway is kept open to ski resorts on the west slope.

HISTORY: All except top portion was an emigrant and gold rush route; then a toll road to Nevada during the silver excitement; it opened as an auto route in 1910.

KEY FEATURES: Mining towns in the western foothills and on the east side of the pass; Calaveras Big Trees State Park; excellent high country for knapsacking; winter skiing; spectacular view of Mokelumne Wilderness from Bear Valley (Mount Reba) ski area; interesting mountain road for several miles on both sides of the pass (somewhat difficult trailering); hot springs at Markleeville.

INFORMATION: Available from the Ebbetts Pass Wonderland Association, Arnold, Calif.; Stanislaus National Forest, Sonora; State Department of Parks and Recreation, Sacramento; Alpine County Chamber of Commerce, Markleeville.

SONORA PASS COUNTRY

This is a rugged mountain pass (9,624 feet), closed in winter above the ski resorts. Reached by a steep, winding highway on both sides of the crest, it offers spectacular scenery and excellent camping and fishing. There are year-round resorts at lower elevations on the west slope but few settlements higher up because of severe winters; there is almost no development on the east slope. At Dardanelle is an interesting basalt formation, well marked and explained; other sites of geological interest are visible along the highway.

HISTORY: Like most other trans-Sierra roads, the present 108 was pioneered by miners and a few hardy emigrants. Another emigrant road crossed Sonora Pass, then swung off toward Yosemite.

KEY FEATURES: Old mining town of Sonora; state mining park at Columbia, just north of Sonora on Highway 49; skiing at Dodge Ridge; Dardanelle Visitors' Center; near-wilderness on both sides of highway at upper elevations.

INFORMATION: Write to Tuolumne County Chamber of Commerce, Sonora; Stanislaus National Forest, Sonora.

YOSEMITE AND TIOGA PASS

Yosemite information is available in dozens of books; Tioga Pass (9,941 feet), though less well known, is one of the Sierra's most interesting trips. This is the last auto pass for almost 170 miles.

HISTORY: The story of the Yosemite area has been told oftener and in more detail than that of any other part of the Sierra. First seen by the Walker party, it was later the site of Indian battles. Commercial development has been forestalled (at least in part) by national park status; however, the Yosemite Valley is so popular with tourists that it is in danger of destruction.

KEY FEATURES: Yosemite Valley; Glacier Point; Sequoias near Wawona; Tenaya Lake; Tuolumne Meadows. Almost every mile of the road above the 4,000-foot elevation has something of interest.

INFORMATION: Available in any library, or from Yosemite Park & Curry Company, Yosemite; National Park Service, Yosemite; Chamber of Commerce, Merced; Toiyabe National Forest, Reno; Inyo National Forest, Bishop.

KINGS CANYON AND SEQUOIA PARK

Some of the most spectacular scenery in the Sierra, as well as grove after grove of Big Trees, lies in these two parks. It is also unexcelled hiking country.

HISTORY: This area was probed by a few early explorers and later used by cattle- and sheepmen; some of the Big Trees were logged for fenceposts and low-grade lumber in the early days before the groves were incorporated into two national parks.

KEY FEATURES: The Generals Highway, connecting the groves of Big Trees; Mineral King, a secluded valley being considered for ambitious recreational development; Moro Rock, a great vantage point that is fairly easy to get to; Cedar Grove in Kings Canyon; remote high country reachable only on foot or horseback.

INFORMATION: Available from the National Park Service, Three Rivers, Calif.; Sierra National Forest, Fresno; Inyo National Forest (east side), Bishop; Sequoia National Forest, Porterville, Calif.

THE EAST SIDE

A drive to the Owens Valley through Walker Pass (5,248 feet) or Tehachapi Pass (3,793 feet) and along U.S. 395 gives an unexcelled view of the tremendous western escarpment of the southern Sierra. The Mammoth Lakes area and Devil's Postpile are also a worthwhile objective.

HISTORY: The Owens Valley and Walker Pass were traversed by numerous early explorers and later by wagon trains. The Owens Valley was the scene of a conflict between local ranchers and the City of Los Angeles over possession of water. In recent years there has been considerable military activity in the vicinity, particularly testing of aircraft and gunnery.

KEY FEATURES: The view of Mount Whitney and the eastern escarpment from Lone Pine and other points; desert experience, especially in Red Rock Canyon; side roads to trailheads leading up to the top of the Sierran peaks; summer and winter resorts at Mammoth and June lakes; summer tram up Mammoth Mountain; Mono Craters; desert lakes.

INFORMATION: Write to Inyo County, Bishop; Inyo National Forest, Bishop; Mammoth Lakes Chamber of Commerce, Mammoth Lakes; Mono County Chamber of Commerce, Bridgeport, Calif.

GLOSSARY

ablation area: the part of a glacier or snowfield, usually at the toe, where evaporation and melting reduce the volume of glacial ice faster than it can be supplied from above.

achene (*a-keen*): a small, dry, one-seeded fruit that ripens without bursting its thin outer sheath. Buttercups have achenes, and so do the sedges of the Sierra.

accumulation area: the place on a glacier, usually at the head, where new snow collects; also known as the "surplus area."

algae: simple plants commonly seen in the Sierra as pond or stream scum, but very important in the food chain.

alluvial: pertaining to material deposited by a flowing stream of comparatively recent times.

alpine belt: the highest mountain zone, above timberline. It occurs from 8,000 to 10,000 feet in the northern Sierra and above 10,000 or 11,000 feet in the Yosemite and Kings-Kern country. Conditions are similar to the "Arctic-Alpine Zone" in the Merriam system.

andesite: a volcanic rock, usually dark gray, which in an earlier molten state often filled vertical cracks in other kinds of Sierran rock, so that *dikes* were formed below the surface. With erosion, the softer rocks on each side were worn away, leaving the andesite dikes as low walls.

aqueduct: any conduit for water; usually used to refer to combinations of pipes, ditches, siphons, trestles, etc., which move large quantities of water long distances.

arete (*"arrettie"*): a sharp and rugged crest of a mountain or mountain range, often used to mean the carved ridges which form the sides of a cirque or bowl at the head of a glacier.

basal leaves: leaves which grow near or at ground level; an example is buckwheat (*Eriogonum nudum*), which grows throughout the Sierra at most elevations in dry and rocky places.

basalt: a fine-grained, dark-colored igneous rock.

basic intrusive: rocks, containing less than 50 percent silica, which were once hot enough to flow as a liquid and which penetrated into or between other rocks while molten, cooling before reaching the surface.

basin: in the Sierra Nevada, usually the drainage or catchment area of one or more streams or lakes. (In the Rockies, a cirque; and in the desert, a depression which water can flow into but not out of.)

batholith: a gigantic chamber containing molten material when within the earth's crust; if uplifted, the material cools to igneous rock, usually granite.

bedrock: any solid rock, either exposed at the surface or overlaid by soil, gravel, etc.; in mining, the solid rock under gold-bearing gravel, sand, or clay.

bole: the trunk or stem of a tree.

bract: a leaf from the base of which a flower or the stem of a flower arises; a leaf growing on a flower stem.

browse: as a noun, tender leaves, twigs, and shoots; as a verb, to eat those things. Often used to indicate feeding on shrubs and trees, in contrast to grazing (eating grass).

calcareous orthoquartzite: clean sandstone containing more than 80 percent quartz grains; the grains are well-rounded and uniform in size, indicating they have been highly re-worked by current action. Cement between grains is not abundant, but contains silica and calcium carbonate.

caldera: a very large, basin-shaped depression resulting from a volcano, much larger than the present vents. There are three major types, caused by explosion, collapse, or erosion.

cascade: a series of small, closely-spaced waterfalls; sometimes, a single small waterfall.

cataract: a large waterfall; sometimes, a cascade in which the vertical fall has been concentrated into a sheer drop or overflow.

catkins: a hanging, spike-like arrangement of flowers—as on "pussy willow" trees, aspens, cottonwoods, and others.

chaparral: a dense growth of low to medium-height plants, with many stiff branches, deep root systems, and small leaves. In the Sierra Nevada, common chaparral plants are manzanita, huckleberry oak, chinquapin, service berry, bitter cherry, and ceanothus.

chutes: in the Sierra, most often applied to parallel or converging gullies, often quite deep, which have been furrowed into steep mountainsides by avalanches of snow mixed with rock; also used to describe a narrow, sloping passage in a stream. In mining, an elongated body of ore extending downward within a vein.

cinder cone: a symmetrical, cone-shaped hill formed by the accumulation of loose volcanic cinders (sometimes ash) around a vent.

cirque: a recess in a mountain, shaped like half a bowl, where the upper end of a glacier or series of glaciers eroded the rock heavily, usually leaving a small lake, or tarn.

clear-cutting: a logging method by which all the trees in a tract are removed (usually when they are of nearly the same age), as opposed to *selective* cutting, where only trees of a certain diameter or age are cut, leaving the others.

conifers: trees which bear cones—for example, pines, firs, sequoia, incense cedar, hemlock.

cradle: a device by which one or two miners could separate unwanted material from placer gold. Much like a baby's cradle, it could be rocked from side to side while water was poured in, usually by hand; sand, clay, and pebbles washed away, and gold, it was hoped, remained. It was more efficient than panning, the first method used in California, but not as efficient as the sluice box, which succeeded it in most places.

crest: the highest natural projection of a hill or mountain from which the surface slopes downward in opposite directions. In the Sierra, usually used to mean the highest ridges connecting the highest peaks, from which rivers flow on one side westerly to the ocean and on the other side easterly to the desert. The *Pacific Crest* usually refers to a continuous line connecting all the highest peaks of all the highest mountain ranges from which water flows to the Pacific Ocean.

crown fire: fire in the branches of a forest; most wildfires run along the surface of the ground, consuming duff, litter, herbs, and shrubs, but in the hottest fires flames may break out in the upper branches and foliage, jumping from tree to tree. Among fire-fighters the standard answer to the question, "What do you do if a forest fire crowns?" is "Throw down your tools and run!"

deposition: the laying down of potential rock-forming materials; sedimentation.

divide: the line along a mountain summit or series of summits from which water flows in different directions; the division between two or more watersheds. Often used by hikers to mean the highest point of a mountain pass.

dome: a smoothly rounded, rock-capped mountain summit, usually quite symmetrical; in the Sierra usually formed of granite which has been stripped of overlying rock and soil by glacial action or other erosion.

duff: the partly decayed vegetable material

on a forest floor, made up of fallen leaves and needles and decomposing material from down logs and branches. Duff burns, in contrast to the underlying mineral earth, which does not.

ejecta: any of the material thrown out by a volcano, including *ash* (dust and particles less than 4 millimeters in diameter), *lapilli* (particles from 4 to 32 millimeters), and *bombs* (larger particles up to several feet in diameter, which were liquid or plastic at time of ejection and which show forms, marks, or internal structure acquired while flying through the air or hitting the ground).

erosion: the wearing away of land by water, ice, or wind, often aided in the early stages by chemical disintegration or such mechanical forces as the expansion of water into ice or the scuffing of animal or human feet.

escarpment: a steep face of a mountain or mountain range which gives the appearance of having been sheared off; usually used to indicate a feature larger in scope and appearance than a cliff or steep hill. Commonly interchangeable with *scarp*.

exfoliation: the peeling off of sheets of rock by mechanical or chemical action; in the Sierra, the onion-like peeling of granite domes, probably started by weaknesses caused during cooling of the molten rock and aggravated by the prying effect of freezing water as successive layers become exposed to the weather.

fault: a line along which an earthquake operates; a fracture or fracture zone along which there has been a displacement of the sides relative to each other, either horizontally or vertically. A *fault zone* may be hundreds or thousands of feet wide, with many interlacing small faults. *Faulting* is the movement of rock masses along a fracture. A *fault scarp* is the cliff formed when such movement is vertical.

firn: a name given to ice granules that result when snow melts and refreezes, but has not yet become glacier ice.

flumes: artificial ditches for conveying water, often over many miles. In the early days, these were made of wood and often were hung precariously on the sides of cliffs or arched over canyons on flimsy-looking trestles, but they worked and were the basis first of the mining industry and then of the hydroelectric system and agricultural irrigation.

gorge: a narrow river-cut passage through mountains, having a V-shaped cross-section and steep rock walls.

granite: a plutonic rock consisting essentially of alkalic feldspar and quartz, with some darker minerals included, formed from molten material which cooled below the surface; loosely used in the Sierra Nevada for any light-colored, coarse-grained igneous rock.

granodiorite: one of the specialized rocks which most visitors to the Sierra Nevada mistake for granite. To the geologist, however, it consists of quartz, calcic oligoclase or andesine, and orthoclase, with biotite, hornblende, or pyroxene as mafic constituents.

hardrock mining: mining, usually underground, which requires drilling and blasting for removal of rock, which is then transported to the surface for crushing and extraction of minerals. (In *placer* mining, minerals, especially gold, are extracted from surface sand, gravel, or clay by washing with water.)

headwaters: the sources of a stream, often used to mean all the smaller flows, named or unnamed, which finally come together to form a named river.

hornfels: a fine-grained rock which was changed in composition, texture, or internal structure when magma welled up near the original rock.

humus: the organic component of soil, formed by partial decomposition of animal or vegetable matter.

hydraulicking: a mining process in which water pressure was used to wash down hillsides in order to loosen gold-bearing sand, clay, and gravel, which the flowing water then separated from the gold in a long corrugated channel. While this was economically effective in getting gold, it played havoc not only in the mountains but in the agricultural valleys, to which huge amounts of debris were swept down by spring floods.

igneous rocks: rocks which have been formed by solidification from a molten or partly molten state; sometimes called *plutonic* or *volcanic* rocks.

intrusions: bodies of rock which once were molten and invaded older rock, but solidified before reaching the surface. Intrusions usually followed an upward course, but could move horizontally where there were weaknesses or fissures.

lichens: plants which grow on rocks, bark, etc., composed of an alga and a fungus, each of which provides essential life support for the other. Minute amounts of chemicals secreted by lichens play a part in decomposition of rocks in the Sierra.

magma: molten material contained within the earth's crust, derived from the melting of deep-lying and crustal rock.

metacherts: *chert* is a compact rock of organic or precipitated origin, often very hard (e.g., flint); *metachert* is a chert which has been modified by pronounced changes of temperature, pressure, and/or chemical environment.

metamorphic rock: rock which has been altered in composition, texture, or internal structure by pressure, heat, or the introduction of chemical substances.

metasediment: rock which was formed from small particles deposited by water (or sometimes by air), usually compressed into layers or *strata*, and which later was partly changed in composition, texture, or internal structure by pressure, heat, or chemicals.

metavolcanic: rock which came to the surface in a molten form or by volcanic action and later was partly changed in composition, texture, or internal structure by pressure, heat, or chemicals.

monitor: a large metal nozzle through which great amounts of water under high pressure were directed against old stream beds in order to wash the soil, clay, and gravel through sluice boxes in which riffles caught most of the gold; by an ingenious device which used the pressure of the water for power, even the largest monitor could be aimed by one man.

monolith: a large single piece or block of stone.

moraine: rock material such as boulders, till, gravel, sand, or clay which has been accumulated in a glacier and deposited where a glacier slowed or stopped. *Lateral* moraines are levee-like ridges along each side, paralleling the direction of flow; *medial* moraines are ridges paralleling the flow but within the glacial bed, caused by one or more glaciers which came in from the side, each carrying its own rim of debris into the main stream; *terminal* moraines are ridges which mark the farthest advance of a glacier and lie across the end, sometimes forming dams.

mulch: material, usually organic, on the ground which protects roots and young stems from heat, cold, or drought.

obsidian: an ancient name for volcanic glass; may be red, green, or brown, although black is most common. The crystal structure, too small to be seen by the unaided eye, permits it to be chipped by pressure; it was widely used by Indians for arrow points and tools.

outcropping or outcrop: bedrock or strata exposed through the overlying soil or rock, usually by erosion.

pater noster lakes: a series of water-filled hollows or lakes connected by a stream and resulting from glacier-gouging of a valley surface.

penstock: a pipe on a steep incline which conducts water from a higher elevation to a lower one in order to utilize the energy for hydraulic mining or for generating electric power.

plankton: a general term for the small animal and plant life in a body of water, an important part of the food chain.

plateau: a tableland, or elevated area, comparatively flat, usually with an abrupt descent on one or more sides.

plucking: the process by which a glacier lifts large blocks away from a mass of rock at fractures and weak places, and carries them along as part of the moving stream of ice.

plutonic rocks: rocks which have been formed by solidification from a molten or partly molten state; igneous rocks.

pyroclastic material: fragments of material that have been thrown out through the air from a volcanic vent, including various sizes from ash to large rocks; *lava*, by contrast, is material which *flows* from a volcanic vent.

quadrant: an arc of 90 degrees, or the area enclosed within a quarter of a circle.

rain-shadow: the region of diminished rainfall on the lee side of a mountain or mountain range, where the rainfall is noticeably less than on the windward side.

riffle: a place in a stream where shallow water flows rapidly down a mildly sloping bed, often over boulders and rocks. In mining, a groove or low projection on the bottom of an inclined trough, intended to catch gold carried by a flow of water.

roof pendant: older rocks projecting downward into granite. Much of the Sierra is based on granite which welled up as molten rock under the older rocks; often this magma flowed around more resistant parts of the older rock, which remained in place as the magma cooled and hardened.

saddle: a low point on a ridge or crest; often a divide between the heads of streams flowing in opposite directions.

saprophyte: a plant which lives on dead or decaying material, the beautiful snow plant being the best known in the Sierra.

scarp: see *escarpment*.

sedges: grass-like or rush-like plants which grow at most elevations and in either wet or dry soils, in the Sierra most commonly in wet places. Their small, dry, one-seeded fruit is a valuable source of food for small animals and birds.

sedimentary rocks: rocks formed by the accumulation of rock fragments, sand, remains of plants or animals, or products of chemical action or evaporation; usually deposited in layers or strata which are sometimes tilted from their original horizontal position.

shorthair meadows: the somewhat sparsely vegetated meadows of the high country, with thin soil and difficult growing conditions.

silt: very small fragments of rock or organic material (between $\frac{1}{16}$ and $\frac{1}{256}$ millimeter) usually carried or deposited by water. Loosely used to mean any small and relatively light material, such as clay particles, in the water or bed of a stream or lake.

sink: a depression in the land, usually in an arid area, into which water flows but from which it cannot escape except by evaporation, leaving concentrations of salts and alkalis. Some of the eastside Sierra rivers run into sinks rather than to the sea.

slash: the abandoned or rejected treetops, branches, and debris left after salable logs have been taken from a lumbering operation. In some places, this material is run through a chipping machine and spread as humus on the forest floor, but in most logging operations it is either partially burned or simply left where it fell.

sluice box: a long, narrow box, usually of wood, open at the top and ends, and with crossbars ("riffles") on the bottom to catch gold. When ore was washed through the sluice box, lighter sand, clay, and pebbles passed over the riffles while the heavier gold sank to the bottom and was trapped. Occasionally, carpeting or other devices were used to catch the fine gold.

snowline: the elevation at which precipitation from a storm appears as snow instead of rain; the average elevation at which this occurs in a season; the elevation at which snow can be expected to fall often during a winter—as shown in winter by snow which remains between storms, and in other seasons by the type and appearance of vegetation.

spur: a lesser ridge which extends from a main ridge or crest, much like a rib from a backbone.

stalactites and **stalagmites:** cylindrical or conical deposits of minerals, usually calcite. A *stalactite* hangs from the roof of a cavern; a *stalagmite* rises from the floor. When the two finally meet, they become a *column*.

subalpine belt: sparsely forested area near the summit of the range—above 7,000 or 8,000 feet in the northern Sierra, and 8,000 to 11,000 feet in the southern. Conditions are similar to the "Hudsonian Zone" in the Merriam system.

switchbacks: a series of sharp, zigzag turns on a trail or road by which a higher (or lower) elevation can be reached without going directly up or down a steep slope.

tailings: discarded mining ore which was considered too poor in mineral content to process any further. Old tailings were sometimes reworked and large amounts of metal recovered.

talus: *("taylus"):* a sloping pile of broken rock at the foot of a cliff.

tarn: a small lake or pool, usually in a glacial basin.

tilting: a change of position toward one of higher or lower inclination, done without rotation. The general shape of the Sierra Nevada is due to the tilting of a huge block, which slopes gently on the west and steeply on the east.

timberline: the elevation beyond which trees do not grow. Level can vary with soil type, climate, and other factors. At timberline the trees are smaller and farther apart, usually twisted or stunted, with the growing branches longer on the side away from the wind.

tributary: any stream which contributes water to another, larger stream or to a lake; a smaller glacier which contributes to a larger one.

turbulence: the churning and confused mixing of the flow of water or air so that it does not move smoothly but rapidly changes direction both horizontally and vertically.

volcanic fissure: an extensive crack in rock, from which molten material pours or has poured; contrasts to a *volcanic vent* from which molten material is ejected in an eruption.

vulcanism: volcanic activity; sometimes used to describe less violent manifestations than actual volcanic eruption. Often spelled *volcanism*.

watershed: the entire area in which water for a particular stream or lake collects, including all the springs, trickles, creeks, and other tributaries—usually set off by a rim of hills, ridges, or mountains. Although the word is sometimes used to mean an actual ridge from which water flows in two or more directions to widely separated rivers or lakes, this is more properly called a *divide*.

ACKNOWLEDGMENTS

So many people have helped with this book that it would be impossible to thank them by name. There were casual interviews beside trails, at highway overlooks, on remote ridges—and in city canyons; there were question-and-answer interviews on strict time schedules — and delightful informal brain-picking sessions that lasted many leisurely miles. Each individual will know I mean him or her, even though I list only these:

California state agencies including the Department of Fish and Game, Department of Parks and Recreation, Division of Highways, and Division of Mines and Geology; various chambers of commerce; libraries at the state capital, state resources building, Sierra Club, and various county seats, especially Nevada City; museum people at Sutter's Fort, the Oakland Museum, and local museums in various towns; newspaper people in many places; Placer County Planning Department; Pollock Pines elementary school children and their teacher; the U.S. Geological Survey, the Forest Service, the National Park Service, the Bureau of Outdoor Recreation, the Soil Conservation Service, the Weather Bureau... and my family.

—P. W.

PICTURE CREDITS

FRONT—Pages 2–3: David Muench. Pages 4–5: Gerhard Bakker. Pages 6–7: Ed Cooper. Page 8: Lloyd Ingles. Page 13: John Trimble, courtesy of the Sierra Club.

PART ONE—Pages 18–19: United States Geological Survey (USGS). Pages 20, 29, 30, 32: Ed Cooper. Pages 34–35: Christian Hansen. Page 36: Ernest Carter. Page 37: Ed Cooper. Pages 38, 39: Tom Myers. Page 41: Gerhard Bakker. Page 42: Paul Webster. Page 43: Tom Tracy. Page 44: *top,* Gerhard Bakker; *bottom,* Don Greame Kelley. Page 45: Ed Cooper. Page 46: *top,* Gerhard Bakker; *bottom,* Tom Myers. Page 47: Nancy Fouquet. Page 48: Paul Webster. Pages 51, 55: Christian Hansen. Pages 56–57: Paul Webster. Page 62: Lowie Museum of Anthropology, University of California, Berkeley. Page 64: Oakland Museum. Page 66: Tom Myers.

PART TWO—Pages 70–71, 72, 74: Ed Cooper. Pages 76, 77: Lloyd Ingles. Pages 78, 80, 82, 84, 85: Ed Cooper. Page 86: David Muench. Page 89: Ed Cooper. Pages 90 91: David Muench. Page 92: Don Greame Kelley. Page 93: David Muench. Page 94: Tom Tracy. Page 95: Christian Hansen. Page 96: Sally Myers. Page 97: David Muench. Pages 98-99: Gerhard Bakker. Page 100: *top left, top right, center left,* Lloyd Ingles; *center right,* Gerhard Bakker; *bottom left, bottom right,* Lloyd Ingles. Page 101: *top left,* Lloyd Ingles; *center left, bottom left, top right, center right,* Gerhard Bakker; *bottom right,* Don Greame Kelley. Page 102: *top left, bottom left, center top,* Gerhard Bakker; *bottom center,* Don Greame Kelley; *top right, bottom right,* Gerhard Bakker. Page 103: Gerhard Bakker. Pages 104, 108, 109: David Muench. Page 110: Paul Webster. Page 112: David Muench. Page 114: Wells Fargo Bank History Room. Page 117: Bancroft Library. Pages 118, 119, 121: Wells Fargo Bank History Room. Pages 122, 123: Bancroft Library. Page 124: California Department of Parks and Recreation.

PART THREE—Pages 126-7: USGS. Pages 128, 130: Southern Pacific Railroad. Pages 132, 133: California Division of Highways. Pages 134–5: Tom Myers. Pages 136, 138: Southern Pacific Railroad. Page 140: Paul Webster. Pages 142–3: Tom Myers. Pages 144–5: Paul Webster. Pages 146–7, 148–9: Tom Myers. Page 150: Gerald L. French. Pages 153, 154–5: Paul Webster. Page 156: Henry Miller. Page 157: Don Greame Kelley. Pages 158–9: Paul Webster. Page 160: Tom Tracy. Pages 162, 164–5, 166: Pacific Gas & Electric Company. Page 168: Sally Myers. Pages 170–1: David Muench. Pages 172–3: USGS. Pages 174–5: Sally Myers. Page 176: Tom Myers. Pages 178, 180, 182, 184, 186–7, 188, 190–1: Ed Cooper. Page 193: Tom Tracy. Pages 194–5: David Muench. Pages 196–7: Ed Cooper. Page 198: Christian Hansen. Page 199: David Muench. Page 200: Nevada Historical Society, Reno. Page 202: Gerald L. French. Page 203: Bancroft Library. Pages 204, 205: Wells Fargo Bank History Room. Pages 206–7, 208: Gerald L. French.

PART FOUR—Pages 210–1: USGS. Pages 212, 214: Gerald L. French. Pages 216, 218: Tom Myers. Page 220: Ed Cooper. Page 222: Arnold Thallheimer. Page 226: USGS. Page 233: Gerhard Bakker. Pages 234–5: David Muench. Pages 236, 237: Ed Cooper. Pages 238, 239: Don Greame Kelley. Page 240: David Muench Pages 242–3: USGS. Page 244: Christian Hansen. Pages 246, 248: Ed Cooper. Page 250: David Muench. Page 255: Tom Myers. Page 257: David Muench. Pages 258–9: Ray Atkeson. Page 260: Wayne Howell. Page 261: Studios Kaminski. Page 262: John Butler. Page 263: Studios Kaminski. Page 264: Don Greame Kelley. Pages 266–7, 268: Bancroft Library. Pages 270–1: J. N. LeConte, courtesy of the Sierra Club. Pages 272–3: John Duryea.

Maps: C. E. Erickson.

Diagrams: Gail Feazell.

SOURCES AND SUGGESTED READING

There are many books on the Sierra Nevada, either general works or specific discussions of certain places or certain aspects. Only a few are listed here, but most of them have an additional bibliography so that the student of this great range may explore in his easy chair when he cannot actually go to the mountains.

General

Bulletins of the Sierra Club; 220 Bush St., San Francisco (sent to members; many libraries have back copies, and the club has its own library at its headquarters, available free to interested persons).

California Information Almanac; P.O. Box 400, Lakewood, Calif. 97014.

High Sierra Country by Oscar Lewis; Duell, Sloan & Pearce, 1955 (available through Meredith Press, Des Moines).

Historic Spots in California by Hoover, Rensch, and Rensch; Stanford University Press, 1966.

1,000 California Place Names by Edwin G. Gudde; University of California Press, 1965 (condensed from *California Place Names,* same publisher, 1962).

The Sierra by W. Storrs Lee; G. P. Putnam's Sons, 1962.

Sierra Nevada, Range of Light by Roderick Peattie; Vanguard Press, 1947.

Geology

California's Changing Landscapes by G. B. Oakeshott; McGraw-Hill, 1971.

Dictionary of Geological Terms; Doubleday, 1957 (paperback).

Discovering Rocks and Minerals by Roy Gallant and Christopher Schuberth; Natural History Press, 1967.

Earth Song by Charles L. Camp; American West Publishing Co., Palo Alto, Calif., 1970.

Evolution of the California Landscape; California Division of Mines and Geology, Sacramento.

Field Guide to Rocks and Minerals by F. H. Pough; Houghton Mifflin, 1955.

Geologic Studies in the Lake Tahoe Area; Geological Society of Sacramento, 1968.

Geology of Northern California; Bulletin 190, California Division of Mines and Geology, 1966.

Mountaineering in the Sierra Nevada by Clarence King; W. W. Norton, 1935.

Tales Told by Fossils by Carol Lane Fenton; Doubleday, 1966.

Up and Down California: The Brewer Journal; Yale University, 1966.

Nature

Birds and Mammals of the Sierra Nevada by Lowell Summer and Joseph S. Dixon; University of California Press, 1953.

California Mountain Wildflowers by Philip A. Munz; University of California Press, 1963 (paperback).

The California Wildlife Region by Vinson Brown; Naturegraph Publishers, Healdsburg, Calif., 1957.

Field Guide to Western Birds by Roger Tory Peterson; Houghton Mifflin, 1941.

Forest Trees of the Pacific Slope (1908) by George B. Sudworth; Dover, 1967 (paperback).

Lake Tahoe Wildflowers by Kenneth Legg; Naturegraph Publishers, Healdsburg, Calif., 1970.

Manual of the Flowering Plants of California by W. L. Jepson; University of California Press, 1925.

Pacific Coast Trees by Howard E. McMinn and Evelyn Maino; University of California Press, 1937.

Sierra Nevada Natural History by Tracy L. Storer and Robert L. Usinger; University of California Press, 1963 (paperback).

The Sierra Nevadan Wildlife Region by Vinson Brown and Robert Livesey; Naturegraph Publishers, Healdsburg, Calif., 1962.

Trees of California by W. L. Jepson; S-H Service Agency, Inc., New York, 1909.

Wild Flowers of California by Mary Elizabeth Parsons; Dover, 1966 (paperback).

Ecology

An Island Called California by Elna Bakker; University of California Press, 1971.

The Balance of Nature by L. J. and M. Milne; Knopf, 1960.

The Life of Rivers and Streams by Robert L. Usinger; McGraw-Hill, 1967.

The Life of the Mountains by Maurice Brooks; McGraw-Hill, 1967.

The Mountains of California by John Muir; Century Co., 1917.

One Day on Beetle Rock by Sally Carrighar; Knopf, 1956.

Patterns of Survival by L. J. and M. Milne; Prentice Hall, 1967.

The Web of Life by John H. Storer; New American Library, 1953 (paperback).

History

Alpine Heritage; Alpine County Historical Society, Markleeville, Calif., 1964.

California's Historical Monuments; Pacific Gas and Electric Co., San Francisco, 1965.

The California Trail by George R. Stewart; Houghton Mifflin, 1960.

Donner Pass by George R. Stewart; Lane Book Company, 1964 (paperback).

The Elephant As They Saw It by Elisabeth L. Egenhoff; California Division of Mines and Geology, Sacramento, 1949.

The Emigrant's Guide to California by Joseph E. Ware; Princeton Press, 1932.

Exploring with Fremont by Charles Preuss; University of Oklahoma, 1958.

Fremont, Pathfinder of the West by Allen Nevins, 1939.

History of the Sierra Nevada by Francis P. Farquhar; University of California Press, 1969 (available in paperback).

In the Heart of the Sierra by James M. Hutchings, 1886.

Jedediah Smith and the Opening of the West by Dale L. Morgan; University of Nebraska Press, 1953.

Kit Carson's Own Story by Blanche C. Grant, Taos, N.M., 1926.

Narrative of the Adventures of Zenas Leonard by Zenas Leonard; originally published by D. W. Moore, Clearfield, Pa., 1839; available from University Microfilms, Ann Arbor, Mich.

The Opening of the California Trail by George R. Stewart; University of California Press, 1935.

Ordeal by Hunger by George R. Stewart; Houghton Mifflin, 1963.

Pictorial History of the Lassen Volcano by B. F. Loomis; Anderson News Press, Anderson, Calif., 1926.

Pioneer Skiing in California by Robert H. Power; Nut Tree, Vacaville, Calif., 1960.

The Year of Decision: 1846 by Bernard DeVoto; Little, Brown, 1942.

Hiking and Mountaineering

Sierra Nevada Place Names Guide; an index to the topographic maps; Wilderness Press, Berkeley, 1969.

Guide to John Muir Trail and the High Sierra by Walter A. Starr; Sierra Club, 1953.

The Mammoth Lakes Sierra (Third Edition) by Genny Schumacher et al; Wilderness Press, 1969.

Sierra Club: many books and bulletins; list available from 1050 Mills Tower, San Francisco, 94104.

Sierra North and *Sierra South* by Karl Schwenke and Thomas Winnett; Wilderness Press, Berkeley, 1967 (two books, each with 100 back-country trail trips).

Pathway in the Sky: The Story of the John Muir Trail by Hal Roth; Howell-North, Berkeley, 1966.

Indians

The Ahwahneechees: A Story of the Yosemite Indians by John W. Bingaman; End-Kian Publishing Co., Lodi, Calif., 1966.

The California Indians by R. F. Heizer and M. A. Whipple; University of California Press, 1951.

Handbook of the Indians of California by A. L. Kroeber; California Book Company, Berkeley, 1953.

Indians of the United States by Clark Wissler; Doubleday, 1966.

Ishi in Two Worlds: A Biography of the Last Wild Indian in North America by Theodora Kroeber; University of California Press, 1961.

Miwok Indian Culture: Indian Life of the Yosemite Region by S. A. Barrett and E. W. Gifford; Milwaukee Public Museum and Yosemite National History Association, 1933.

Prehistoric Rock Art of Nevada and Eastern California by Robert P. Heizer and Martin A. Baumhoff; University of California Press, 1962.

Yosemite Indians, Yesterday and Today; Yosemite Natural History Association, 1946.

Weather

Compendium of Meteorology; American Meteorological Society, 1951 (excellent chapter on snowflake forms).

The Lightning Book by Peter E. Viemeister; Doubleday, 1961.

Snow by Thelma Harrington Bell; Viking Press, 1954.

Snow Cover and Climate in Sierra Nevada by David H. Miller; University of California Press, 1955.

The Storm by George R. Stewart; Modern Library (Div. of Random House), 1941.

Maps

The basic map for the hiker (and very useful for the day visitor) is the 15-minute topographical quadrangle which shows features and elevations of from 197 to 282 square miles at one inch to the mile—a relatively small area so that two or three maps are required for most trips. An index showing all of these that are available for the Sierra may be obtained free by writing the U.S. Geological Survey, Denver, Colorado 80225 or Washington, D.C. 20242, or in person at regional map offices, one of which is at 630 Sansome Street in San Francisco.

The same agency sells another useful type of topographical map in which an inch represents four miles (referred to as the 1:250,000). Six of these (labeled Chico, Sacramento, Walker Lake, Mariposa, Fresno, and Bakersfield) cover most of the Sierra, the equivalent of perhaps a hundred of the 15-minute quadrangles, although not as detailed. Some of these maps are available some of the time at sporting goods stores, survey-equipment or blue-printing companies, and stationery stores.

The California Division of Mines and Geology, Sacramento, sells geologic maps, six of which cover the same areas of the Sierra under the same names as the USGS 1:250,000 maps, with the emphasis on the rocks rather than the contours. Supplemented by a dictionary of geological terms and a chart of geologic time, these make any Sierra visit more enjoyable, and they are of a handy size to carry in pack or car. A separate explanatory sheet with each provides additional source material and indicates which 15-minute maps are involved in the area.

If all the appropriate quadrangles, plus the 1:250,000 map and the geological sheets, are filed and used together, a great deal of information about a specific area is quickly and easily available.

All national forests have visitor maps and recreational information. An excellent example is the Mammoth–High Sierra Recreation Area, Inyo and Sierra national forests (1967), covering the high country from Mono Lake and Tioga Pass on the north to the Palisades and Shaver Lake on the south. National forests on which there are back-country pack train operators will also supply the names of these. The regional office of the U.S. Forest Service is at 630 Sansome Street, San Francisco 94111. Information about a specific area is best requested from the forest involved, however: El Dorado National Forest, Placerville; Inyo, Bishop; Lassen, Susanville; Plumas, Quincy; Sequoia, Porterville; Sierra, Fresno; Stanislaus, Sonora; Tahoe, Nevada City. Part of the east side is in the Toiyabe National Forest with headquarters in Reno.

District ranger stations are scattered through the Sierra near or below snow line, and during the summer many provide naturalist service, operate visitor centers, and in many ways serve recreationists; often more information is available at the appropriate ranger station than at the forest headquarters or the regional office.

The U.S. Geological Survey (Denver 80225) has a fine map of Sequoia and Kings Canyon national parks and vicinity on a scale of one-half inch to the mile or 1:125,000, and a similar one for Yosemite National Park. These are more convenient than matching several 15-minute maps to get the overall picture of the parks.

Major power companies have maps and descriptive material available for the areas in which they have power plants and reservoirs, as part of their increasing effort to serve recreationists using their lands; and most counties and towns, even some of the smallest, have chambers of commerce which provide maps or folders telling of interesting things to see and do in their vicinity.

The California Department of Fish and Game publishes a series of "angler guides" which include many of the Sierra basins, as well as pamphlets on almost all the fish and animals found in the Sierra.

* * *

FOR ADDITIONAL BOOKS, consult "Yosemite, the Big Trees, and the High Sierra" by Francis Farquhar; University of California, 1948. This is a selected bibliography. Most of the books referred to in this chapter also have lists for further reading.

INDEX